CW01371340

'Touching, thoughtful and frank – Jenn is a wonderful writer'
David Nicholls, author of *You Are Here*

'Reading *The Parallel Path* feels like going on a long walk with an old friend: Jenn Ashworth is exceptionally good company. I loved it'
Mark Haddon, author of *The Curious Incident of the Dog in the Night-Time*

'As Jenn Ashworth walks across the country, she learns the strength and precarity of inhabiting a body, and the measures we sometimes take to resist softness. She considers what it means to be from the North, a place which predicates itself on toughness, and how to make space for vulnerability within that'
Jessica Andrews, author of *Milk Teeth*

'Whether it's strange and haunted novels that linger long after the last page has been turned, utterly unnerving short stories or brave memoir excursions in which her own life is laid bare, whatever Jenn Ashworth turns her hand to, I'm there to read it'
Benjamin Myers, author of *The Offing*

'A life exquisitely examined over a long walk across the North of England, from one of our finest human nature writers'
Richard Beard, author of *The Day That Went Missing*

'From the moment I picked up this book, I knew I was in the hands of a master storyteller'
Lily Dunn, author of *Sins of My Father*

'The Parallel Path is a pilgrimage through one woman's life of loss and love, and a powerful friendship . . . a masterclass in memoir and place writing'
Louise Kenward, editor of *Moving Mountains*

Jenn Ashworth is the author of the novels *A Kind of Intimacy*, which won a Betty Trask Award, *Cold Light*, *The Friday Gospels*, *Fell* and *Ghosted: A Love Story*, which was shortlisted for the Portico Prize. In 2011, she was featured on BBC Two's *The Culture Show* as one of the twelve Best New British Novelists. She has also written a memoir-in-essays, *Notes Made While Falling*, which was shortlisted for the Gordon Burn Prize. She lives in Lancashire and is a Professor of Writing at Lancaster University.

Also by Jenn Ashworth

FICTION
A Kind of Intimacy
Cold Light
The Friday Gospels
Fell
Ghosted

NON-FICTION
Notes Made While Falling

The Parallel Path

Love, Grit and Walking the North

Jenn Ashworth

Sceptre

First published in Great Britain in 2025 by Sceptre
An imprint of Hodder & Stoughton Limited
An Hachette UK company

The authorised representative in the EEA is Hachette Ireland, 8 Castlecourt Centre, Dublin 15, D15 XTP3, Ireland (email: info@hbgi.ie)

1

Copyright © Jenn Ashworth 2025

The right of Jenn Ashworth to be identified as the Author of the Work has been asserted by her in accordance with the Copyright, Designs and Patents Act 1988.

Maps designed by Barking Dog Art

All rights reserved. No part of this publication may be reproduced, stored in a retrieval system, or transmitted, in any form or by any means without the prior written permission of the publisher, nor be otherwise circulated in any form of binding or cover other than that in which it is published and without a similar condition being imposed on the subsequent purchaser.

A CIP catalogue record for this title is available from the British Library

Hardback ISBN 9781399725057
ebook ISBN 9781399725064

Typeset in Sabon MT by Hewer Text UK Ltd, Edinburgh
Printed and bound in Great Britain by Clays Ltd, Elcograf S.p.A.

Hodder & Stoughton policy is to use papers that are natural, renewable and recyclable products and made from wood grown in sustainable forests. The logging and manufacturing processes are expected to conform to the environmental regulations of the country of origin.

Hodder & Stoughton Limited
Carmelite House
50 Victoria Embankment
London EC4Y 0DZ

www.sceptrebooks.co.uk

For my friend Clive, and his family

Contents

Part One: *Circling Home*

Preambles	3
Crossing Bowland with Clive	15

Part Two: *Two Weeks on Wainwright's Coast to Coast Path*

DAYS ONE and TWO: *Purpose and Pilgrimage*	23
DAY THREE: *Alone at Last*	36
DAY FOUR: *Friends in High Places*	55
DAY FIVE: *Walking and Mourning*	72
DAY SIX: *A Spare Macaroon*	91
DAY SEVEN: *A Girl from the North Country*	109
DAY EIGHT: *Brown, Blue, Black*	124
DAY NINE: *On Walking Well*	140
DAY TEN: *To Accompany a River*	155
DAY ELEVEN: *The Green and the Grey: A Difficulty in Staying Upright*	170
DAY TWELVE: *A Marathon with the Almost-Dead*	188
DAY THIRTEEN: *Every Home a Hospital*	209
DAYS FOURTEEN and FIFTEEN: *The World's Greatest Moaner*	237

Contents

Part Three: *An Autumn Weekend on the North York Moors*

The Return	263
Muscling Through	272

Part Four: *Salford Neuro Ward via the Preston Guild Wheel*

Walking Widdershins	281
Tethered, Again	302
Acknowledgements	317
Notes and References	319

The North Country

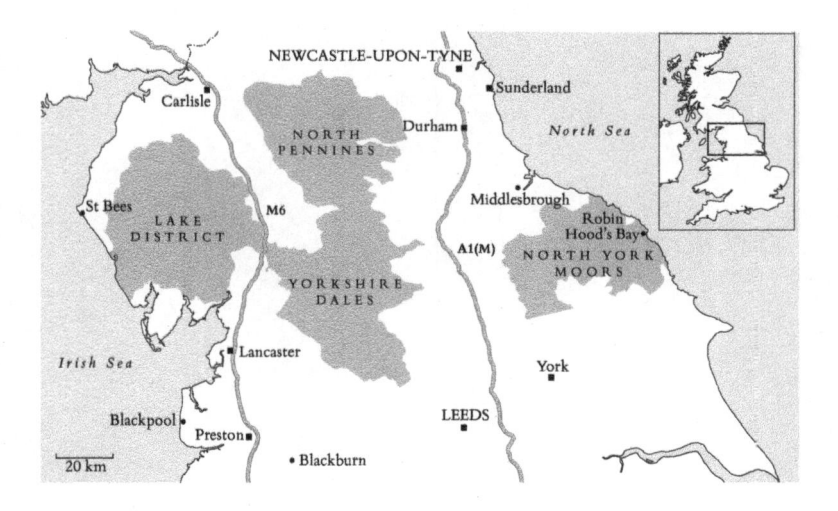

PART ONE

Circling Home

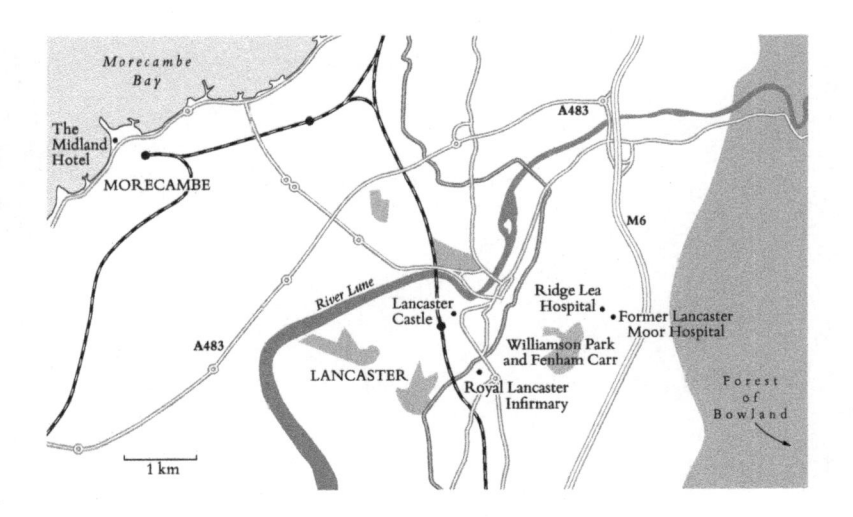

Preambles

Round and Round Lancaster

I bought my boots on the first day of a late-arriving spring.

The man in the shop had measured my feet and ankles in eight different places and got me walking on a machine that recorded how much weight I was putting on each foot. He had me try on six different pairs and pace about the shop until he identified exactly the right brand for my narrow feet and rickety knees. There was a room upstairs to try them on and, nearby, a machine he took them to that fired steam through the leather at the heel and toe to soften and stretch and make tiny adjustments. He knelt in front of me to lace them as I sat up high on a raised chair. There was a right and wrong way to lace up these boots and he asked for my phone and filmed himself as he did it so I'd have it to refer back to later. On a shelf by my elbow were larger than life-sized bony anatomical models of feet and ankles that you were allowed to touch if you wanted to.

'What kind of walking will you be doing?' he asked, as he pulled the laces tight. I felt like a child being fitted for school shoes.

'I'm going to walk across the country,' I said. 'All the way. Roads, fells, fields, moors. Bogs. All kinds of walking.'

The man looked at me, his expression unreadable. Did I look like someone capable of walking across the entire country? That's what I wanted to know. He saved the video and handed my phone back to me.

'You'll want good socks,' was all he said, and brought me a few pairs to look at.

When we went down to the counter and I got out my purse to pay he said I should get an extra pair of laces 'for emergencies', and though I suspected he was only trying to extract more money from me, I chose some anyway. He threw them in for free and wished me luck.

Back home, Duncan and our son were out in the garden making the most of the first sunny day in a long time. They were mowing the lawn, sorting out the plants, playing with the dog. I'd been out for ages; choosing boots had turned out to be a task that required more effort and precision than I'd anticipated.

'Are you pleased with them?' Duncan asked.

I pulled the new boots out of the box and handed them to him. He turned them over in his hands and made admiring noises as he examined them. I *was* pleased. But all I said was: 'They were really expensive,' though I knew he wouldn't care.

Get the good ones, he'd said that morning, as I set out in the car. *Don't cheap out on yourself.*

It was me: I have always struggled with buying a good version of what I need. Now he tried to persuade me to enjoy what I'd bought. 'They're nice. They're really good. Aren't they?'

He waited as I put them on and humoured me by watching the film that demonstrated the correct way to tie their laces. I walked up and down the half-mown garden, kicking the grass clippings around and repeating what the man in the boot shop had promised me: these boots were so well fitted they wouldn't even need breaking in.

'They're great,' I said, finally allowing myself to have that little pleasure. Such a small thing, though it wasn't about the boots, not really. Buying them had turned a wish into a plan. I paced another little circle around the garden, feeling the thrill of a pipe dream becoming real.

I'd been talking to Duncan about the idea of a really long walk for months. The desire came from nowhere: it was out of character. During the spring lockdown I'd walked my government-mandated hour like everyone else: traipsing around the park near where I lived, or up and down the canal. The spring of 2020 was tough, but at least the weather was good and walking in circles around the park felt more like leisure than punishment. When the country shut down again that December, I was already in the habit of getting outside to rest my eyes on the distant view of the sea and the western Lakeland fells at the end of each day. So all through the winter of 2020 and early 2021 I carried on walking.

A friend dubbed this dark time 'the winter of fractions' as we both tried to work and teach our sons primary school maths. My daughter stayed in her bedroom, toiling through her GCSEs and becoming more despondent by the day. Duncan is a radiographer: he went to the hospital, he worked, he slept. When he was in the house, I locked myself away to talk to my students on Microsoft Teams. Other mothers seemed to handle this time better than I did: they arranged Zoom quizzes and online drinks parties and enjoyed socially distanced carol concerts in the street with their neighbours. I managed none of this. In the evenings, I went out into the city and paced but the darkness came earlier and earlier and the fells on the horizon disappeared into the streetlight-stained dusk. In the dark early mornings, I took the dog out in our morning circle, down the canal towards the hospital and back through the emptied town centre. The streets grew icy, and I looped around the city, looking at unlit Christmas trees in the shop windows. My new walking habit was compulsive, metronomic, habitual: I imagined wearing a groove in the pavements I walked on but the pavements wore their groove into me.

Kinhin is the Zen practice of slow, deliberate walking in circles. I have spent some time practising kinhin in Lancaster cemetery, following a black-robed priest between the stones with my head bowed and ignoring the flashy view out towards Morecambe Bay's shining sandflats. When you slow walking down like that, balance becomes difficult: what was easy and thoughtless becomes awkward, ungainly and difficult. Like all good spirituality, kinhin is also practical; it provides a break from extended periods of sitting zazen, which tends to give you pins and needles in your feet. At the time, I thought this practice – to walk slowly and to pay attention to motion without destination – was about trying to learn self-control and balance. I thought walking like this was supposed to be a reminder of the human's two-footed state of rational uprightness – something that separates us from the other animals. I was never very good at it, and would lurch and wobble, sometimes bumping into the walker in front of me as the urge to get it done surfaced in my body.

I tried to bring a patient curiosity about the experience of getting nowhere to the circular lockdown walks I traced around Lancaster that winter. But the walking seemed to cause and not ease a steadily increasing sense of constriction. There's a scene in *The Wicker Man* when Sergeant Howie, who has been sent to the remote Scottish island of Summerisle to investigate the disappearance of Rowan Morrison, visits the local school where she is supposed to be. He's enraged by what he finds there: the children have lessons in elementary witchcraft rather than reading, writing and arithmetic. One pupil lifts the lid of her desk to reveal not books, but a beetle tied to a nail by a thread. Howie watches the beetle in horror as it circles the nail. It scuttles slowly but determinedly, as if walking this way is work, as if it chooses its own route, as if there is a point to this. The girl whose desk it is laughs at his reaction: 'The little old beetle goes round and round. Always the same way, y'see, until it ends up right up tight to the nail. Poor old thing!' she explains. That's what it felt like: my lockdown walking made that invisible thread tethering me to home, to the desk, to the kitchen gradually grow shorter. It was as if I was both inscribing and reducing the edge of my own world, hemming myself in, building a prison by pacing out the perimeter of it.

Even in less dramatic times, most of the walks I went on were circular ones. My dog and I would start and end from home or the car. The walk itself was sometimes a break, sometimes a duty, sometimes a treat, but it was always an interruption to the real substance of my life: one spent inside and in company; at home, at work and at the shops. The idea of reversing this and making walking the real thing, and my life indoors a mere interruption to it, started to intrigue me. How long and how far would I need to walk before walking would turn my life upside down and inside out? There was no chance of testing this. I would stretch that government-mandated hour to its absolute limit but home and the computer always lay in wait. Sometimes I set an alarm on my phone and at the half-hour point it would vibrate in my pocket and that string attaching me to the house like an umbilical cord would tighten and twitch and haul me back.

Plenty has been said about the benefits of slow strolling through the city. Walter Benjamin's *Arcades Project* and Virginia Woolf's 'Street Haunting' both give the reader the 'flaneur', the urban idler, the people watcher. Woolf insists that to walk through London is 'the greatest rest', because her imaginative contact with others freed her from the lonely prison of self. Benjamin understands his strolling through Paris as a means of subversion. The urban walker's purposeless meandering resists the oppressions of designed spaces, loitering refuses the busy ritual of the commute and idling enacts a creative 'no' to the city's ceaseless imperative to buy things. Both writers consider city walking a way to shatter ego: there's something truthful, necessary and humbling about being just one of a crowd. Walking could change the walker and the world. And though I couldn't take the kind of long walk that would let me turn the way I lived on its head, maybe circling around my home city could create its own kind of change.

Preambles

But as the French philosopher Frédéric Gros says, 'This form of strolling presupposes three elements, or the presence of three conditions: city, crowd and capitalism.' That winter I still had a city to walk through, but lockdown had cleared out the crowds and stilled the shopfront manifestations of its capitalism. I walked through Lancaster town centre in the middle of a Saturday afternoon, and it was quieter than at two in the morning. Ghost town. Crossing a footbridge over the M6 during rush hour presented me with an uncanny view of an emptied motorway: I could have sauntered across it safely. Though I did see more Amazon and supermarket delivery vans than usual, the shut-up shops kept their Christmas decorations in the windows until March and there were no commuters, only empty buses advertising films that had never been released and police cars circling the pedestrianised areas. Woolf may have found her refuge by disappearing into London's crowded streets, but I found you cannot flaneur properly if they've closed the cafés and put police tape over all the benches.

Winter passed. Spring returned, as it always does, and I carried on my walking in circles even as I began to know I needed a different way to stretch my legs and ease my mind. A couple of Google searches later and I found it. Alfred Wainwright's Coast to Coast Walk; not a loop and not an amble through a city but a determined beeline slicing its way through the entire North of England. Wainwright, the Lancashire-born author of the intricately illustrated series of books known collectively as *A Pictorial Guide to the Lakeland Fells*, devised this walk in the early 1970s. I lay in

The Parallel Path

bed and studied it obsessively, the laptop screen glowing in the dark.

Wainwright's walk begins at St Bees headland and crosses three national parks – the Lake District, the Yorkshire Dales and the North York Moors – on its way to its final destination, the tiny fishing village of Robin Hood's Bay in Northeast Yorkshire. The successful coast-to-coaster crosses seven rivers (the Ehen, Derwent, Rothay, Lowther, Eden, Swale and Esk) and completes a range of ascents and descents equivalent to getting up and down Everest. Could I do that? And if I did, would it make me different? The desire started to bloom. Wainwright's books are small, his cramped handwriting not always easy to read. His tone is superior and sometimes bossy: he always assumes a male reader, someone who needs to convince his wife to let him out into the countryside, who needs advice about how to avoid barbed wire snagging the testicles on an awkward clamber over a fenced-off right of way. I read and reread a book that was not for me, giggling at the thought of doing this. Even imagining the walk felt both silly and joyful – mainly because it was not the sort of thing someone like me (bookish, poor with directions, fond of warmth and home comforts) would do. The possibility of stepping out of character for a time and of being someone other than myself became as tempting as truancy.

Wainwright's walk has always attracted the competitive. Fell runners and army cadets get it done in relay shifts with support teams carrying their kit. In 2021 Damian Hall did it in 39 hours and 18 minutes, beating a record held by ultra-fell runner Mike Hartley since 1991. He'd done it in 39 hours and 36 minutes. While Wainwright himself intended his book more as a set of suggestions than a strict guide, he also endorses this effortful, self-propelled style of walking. No strolling for him: the way a person walks is also a reflection on the way a person lives: 'One should always have a definite objective. In a walk as in life – it is so much more satisfying to reach a target by personal effort than to wander aimlessly. An objective is an ambition, and life without ambition is ... well, aimless wandering.' Reading that, the wild giddiness I felt at the prosect of setting out ebbed away and I closed the book. The mid-life aimless wander my life had become had been seen and disapproved of.

The end of the pandemic and the return to normal life had brought rapid changes to the lives of every member of my family but me. My son moved from primary school to high school and my daughter from high school into sixth form. Duncan changed his job and moved from radiography into CT, involving an adjustment to his working hours and a long period of training. The three of them were leaving the pandemic behind them, finding their new 'objectives' and 'ambitions' – to take Wainwright's words – and emerging – not unscathed – into the next part of their lives. It wasn't like that for me. I stayed where I was to welcome in the next influx of students who were also alive with their own hopeful ambitions; and when I wasn't working, carried on wandering with my dog around the park, a part of me still locked down inside my own head. Some anxiety had gathered in my body and when I sat in front of a computer I started to fidget, wanted the windows open, wanted to rest my eyes on some point in the distance, some fell or sea view. When I was in a meeting on campus, I wanted everyone to hurry up and stop talking so I could get out, so I could breathe, so I could rest myself in silence.

I had become difficult, I think, to live with. Impatient, irritable, impossible to please. It was hard to work out what the problem was. I was healthy. I enjoyed my work and was lucky to have it. It wasn't quite depression and not quite anxiety. The fact that I had nothing to complain about but the routine ordinariness of being needed by people who were important to me made it worse. I only knew I had felt like this before, a long time ago, and back then, walking was an instinctive thing my body did when it tried to soothe itself.

When my daughter was a few months old and not sleeping, I remember calling her father and asking him to come. He lived nearby and turned up within the half hour. By the time he arrived I had packed a bag and left a credit card with the pin number for it carefully written on a Post-it note on the kitchen table. I told him he'd need to buy formula milk and bottles, and I left. I didn't have any plan other than to feel the joy of walking away from the house and to find a place to sleep. I was not walking *away* from the beloved baby but *towards* a place where I would not be caring for someone else. Most of all I wanted walking's promises; I think I knew even then that a walker is always between here and there, in the process of leaving and arriving, and so never quite herself. There is freedom in this betweenness, especially for someone learning to become someone else's solid ground for the first time.

It was early evening: the streetlights were glowing yellow and the possibilities – a hotel, a night-coach, the train station, even an airport – fizzed around in my blood like a hit of some euphoria-causing drug. There was a moment of vertigo as the door closed behind me. But by the time I'd walked to the end of the street a distinct and intense sensation overtook me: a pulling, as if there was some kind of string between my sternum and my child. It didn't hurt. It was gentle: I was pulled into the place that held me and reminded that I belonged to a street, to a house, to my daughter. That was the first time I felt it: that physical sensation of being tethered to home and to the work of love. I went back, and my daughter's father made me a cup of tea and told me to go upstairs and sleep while he looked after things.

Now, that baby girl was on the brink of leaving home and there were no children crying in the night; no nappies to change. But the old feeling had returned: a desperate, skin-deep itching to be out and away that, when indulged, brought on the pulling at my head and chest that reminded me of how tethered I was. The competing sensations paralysed me. I became resentful. Taciturn. What had brought all this on now? Life had gone back to normal. Everything I'd wanted during those long months of lockdown – a noisy creative writing workshop, coffee with my friends, browsing in bookshops and being able to pick up and feel the yarn in bricks-and-mortar knitting shops – I now had. Why wasn't I happy? It would be months before I read about burnout and understood how so many of us had emotionally locked down as a response to the overwhelming demands the pandemic had placed upon us.

A very long walk was a lot to ask for. A lot to want. There were lots of reasons not to go. But all the same, I was going to do it: some wild part of me had already made its decision, and everything that followed was only about the practicalities. In the evenings I looked at wet-weather gear online, eyeing the Lakeland fells from my bedroom window and reading about what a hiker was supposed to do if a fog came down when she was up high, if cows chased her, if she lost her compass or her blisters got infected. I booked a string of nights in B&Bs from one seashore to the other and a train ticket to St Bees. Duncan arranged some annual leave, looked at the tattered trainers I walked the dog in and suggested I stop being so tight-fisted and go and spend some money on some proper walking boots. *Don't cheap out on yourself*, he'd said.

Crossing Bowland with Clive

Around this time, I started talking to Clive. Though we were neighbours, we met online first, both of us chatty on social media about art, about writing, about what these things had to do with the places where we live and how we live in them. To carry on the conversation in person we went walking together in Silverdale and hiked through a wood where we just missed the bluebells and could smell the tail end of the wild garlic, the leaves bruised and limp. I was wearing my brand-new boots with the bright blue laces. He admired them and I was pleased about it.

On a bench overlooking Morecambe Bay on a day that reminded me of how ostentatiously vivid that crazy lockeddown spring was, Clive told me about a project he was developing which involved working with artists and filmmakers who had something to say about dying. He had read my other books and wondered if I might like to participate. I didn't answer, but asked about what had inspired his work and we talked about the screenwriter Dennis Potter's last interview, given just a few months before his death from pancreatic cancer in the summer of 1994. In it he's both theatrical and mystical, talking about the 'nowness of everything' – some sense of presence he'd discovered long before mindfulness became trendy, and which had quelled any fear he might have faced and left him with peace and a determination to finish the script he was working on. Clive told me he had recently left his academic job and would be working on his own art full time now. The reason he'd left, he said, was because he was dying too.

The trees around us were wearing their brand-new leaves, the colours so vivid they looked synthetic. The news was easier to absorb in this place, the two of us held by the cup of Morecambe Bay in its blue and silver Sunday best, the spring in full bloom around us. Death is one of the things that happens in the world, and lots of other things were happening too. I stared at Clive, trying not to make it obvious I was checking him for signs of dying. He seemed pretty hale to me. Clive looked back, clocking what a nosy woman trying to discreetly inspect the state of his mortality looked like.

Clive told me about the type of cancer he had and a little bit about the way it was unfurling through his blood and bones. I thought about his partner and his children. I did already know what it was like to watch someone die: not to care for them, that wasn't my work, but to be a bystander to the suffering, the anticipatory grief, the shock (and it is still shocking) afterwards. My daughter's father, who'd once made me a cup of tea and told me to go to sleep when what I really wanted to do was run away, had been slowly devoured by bowel cancer and in dying had left his wife, their two daughters and the daughter we had together. The aftershock of the loss was still being felt across our family. Earlier that month a friend of my daughter's had ended his own life. I didn't know this boy, but I'd been thinking about him often. I worried about my own students, had told them what had happened, had asked them to look after each other, to talk to each other, to come and talk to me, if it came to that. Her friend's death had reminded my daughter (*remind* is the wrong word: as if any of us ever forgot) about the death of her father: fresh grief triggering older losses. The news wasn't reporting the daily numbers of people who had died from Covid anymore, but to me, death still felt like it was everywhere.

Clive carried on speaking. He was having treatment that would hold the inevitable at bay, for now. But though he would carry on eating well and letting the doctors look after him, he wasn't going to get better.

Over the following few weeks Clive and I went out walking again. On one of our walks, we hiked thirteen miles right across the Forest of Bowland. It's not a forest (that's a legal term indicating that the monarch owns it), it's old royal hunting ground, and instead of trees, we crossed a large expanse of moorland and peat bog covered in gorse and heather. I brought a big flappy Ordnance Survey map to practise map reading in advance of my 'big walk', and though we didn't get lost (Clive had been walking there for years) I did lose my compass, and this did not feel like a good omen. I fell in a bog and complained about being hungry and Clive told me a little about his experience of diagnosis and treatment: the stem-cell transplant, the stays in hospital, the visits to clinics to get his 'numbers'; the test results that measure how well his chemotherapy is working.

Sometimes we spoke about what else is incurable but must be lived with: addictive illness, broken hearts, difficulties in childhood – all the things that gathered in my mind during the lockdowns and brought me to the place I was when I met Clive. Conversation was never a problem but even though we always had plenty to say, how I might respond to that initial invitation to be one of Clive's artists and someone who had something to say about dying and death evaded me. If there was a story to be told about the nowness of 'being-towards' death then our walking and talking did not help me figure out what it might be. Instead, I came away with muddy boots, sunburn and the feeling that it was my job to hear that story and not to tell it.

I think Clive came to that conclusion too.

'I'm going to write you letters, if that's all right?' he said, some other time.

We were sitting in his little garden, the spring almost over. Soon I'd be setting off. He'd remembered that I liked sweet things and bought chocolate biscuits from Marks and Spencer's. He remembered my love of the ghost story and showed me a Ouija board a man in an antiques shop had given him, throwing it in with another purchase because they are too unlucky to sell. He let me play with a real crystal ball he had knocking around in his home office. I said writing to me while I was walking would be all right and I'd brought the list of B&Bs with me so he could send the letters in time to arrive just ahead of me each day.

'You're walking away from home,' Clive said, as he looked through the list, making notes of dates and postcodes. I was, but it wasn't just that. For me, Wainwright's walk would be a nearly two-hundred-mile trek both *from* home (I'd start on the Cumbrian west coast, close to where I live) and at the same time an exploration *of* home, as I'd slowly cross every terrain the North of England had to offer. The ambivalence of that appealed to me and felt almost like an alibi: I wasn't running away, not really – I'd be at home in the North the entire time.

Clive was a bit nervous about the letters. There was a risk they wouldn't arrive early enough for me to pick them up before I moved on each morning. Maybe the owners of the B&Bs would find passing them on to me an imposition. He wondered if I would find them a burden. And maybe his nerves were about something more than that. It is scary, writing into the dark and sending off your words into the world.

'Write what you like,' I said, wondering what the distance might allow him to get off his chest. I was vague about what he might expect to get back from me. My taciturnity and inability to be pleased had spread into my writing. I too often found myself too cynical or jaded to say much of anything.

Postcards, I thought. *I could send postcards.*

I suddenly felt sad, so I made a joke.

'I've decided this is my mid-life crisis. Shirley Valentine in a North Face jacket,' I said.

Clive was polite enough to laugh. But there was truth hiding in the joke I was trying for. The summer I'd walk across the country I would turn forty and my daughter, eighteen. I was emerging from my children's childhoods as if from a darkened tunnel, or perhaps into one. My sense of humour, my excitement, my creativity had been almost obliterated by trying to make the lockdowns better for the people I felt responsible for. That task – as huge and impossible as walking across the country – I had failed in utterly and the parts of me that had tried to help were frozen now.

Clive took photographs of the addresses, a list of eastward-tracking postcodes: sixteen of them. What kind of friend, what kind of listener, what kind of pen-pal I would be capable of being for him remained to be seen.

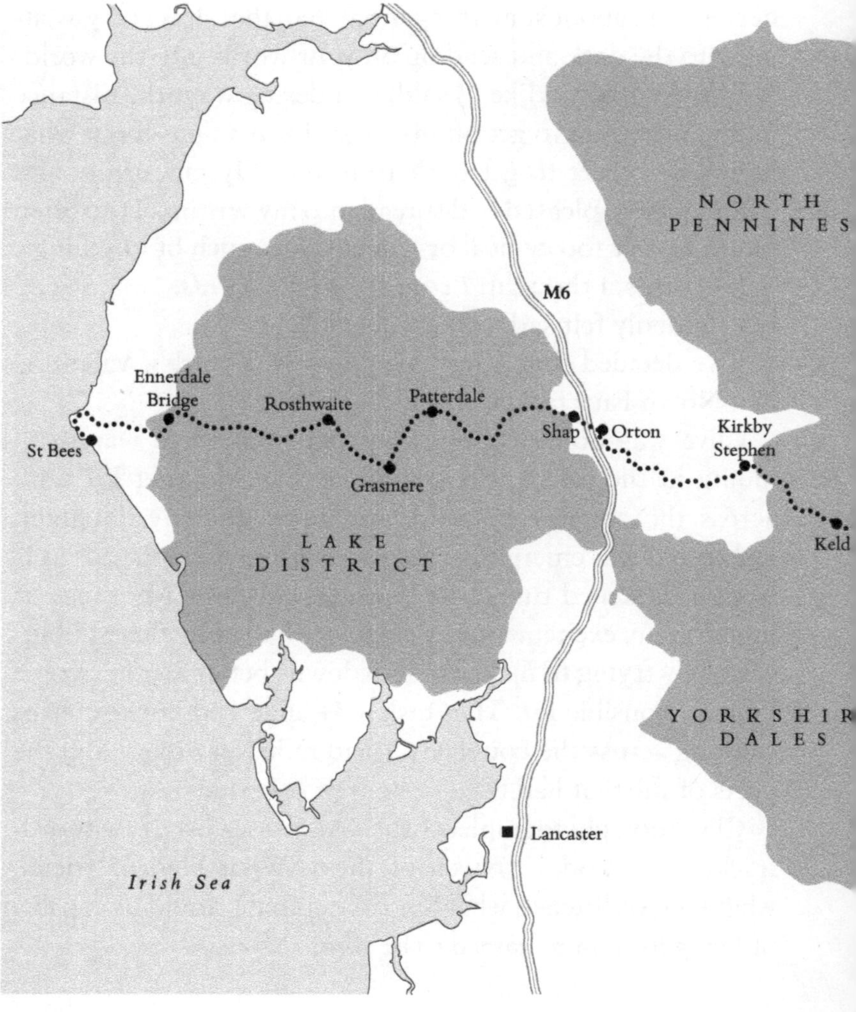
NORTH PENNINES
M6
Ennerdale Bridge
Rosthwaite
Patterdale
Shap
Orton
Kirkby Stephen
St Bees
Grasmere
Keld
LAKE DISTRICT
YORKSHIR
DALES
Lancaster
Irish Sea

PART TWO

Two Weeks on Wainwright's Coast to Coast Path

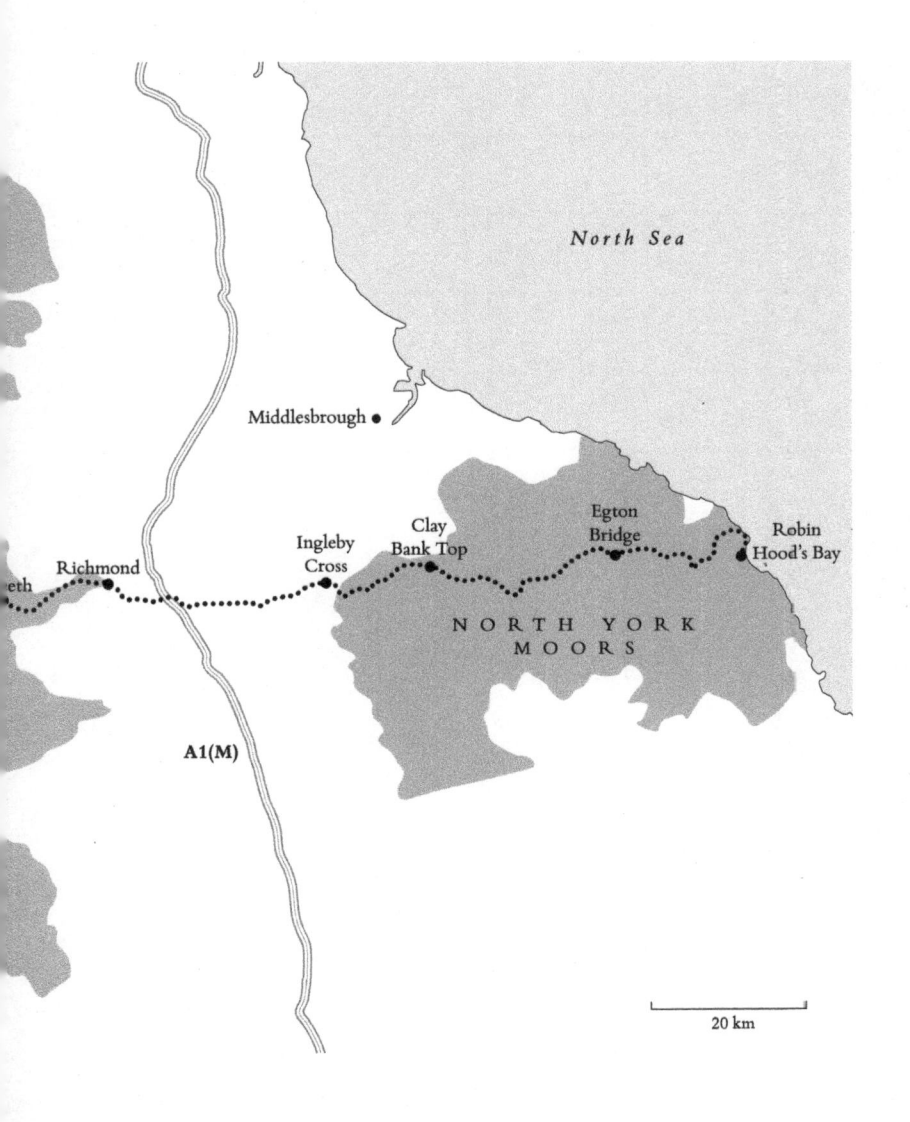

DAYS ONE and TWO

Purpose and Pilgrimage
St Bees Head to Ennerdale Bridge (16 miles)

The trainline hugs the west coast through Lancashire and into Cumbria and I let it take me northwards, enjoying familiar glimpses of Silverdale and Grange-over-Sands' genteel seaside charms. I was excited and impatient as the track curled around the Barrow peninsula. This is when the place names started to get old-fashioned and portentous: Ravenglass, Drigg, Seascale, Sellafield. The sea glittered through the train windows as I left Morecambe Bay and home behind. In the seats opposite, two cyclists returning home to St Bees from a trip to the Isle of Man told me how to find my way to my B&B from the station. Later, when I shouldered my bag to leave the train, they laughed at how much stuff I was carrying.

'What's in there?' they asked.

'Books.'

'You won't want to lug them the whole way across.'

They knew what I was doing without asking: the only reason anyone turns up to St Bees with a rucksack and walking poles is to start the Wainwright walk.

'I will,' I said.

I hoped I sounded rude. A bookworm, yes, but a toughened and heroic one. I'd actually arranged for my bag to be shipped between stopping places by a packhorse company, but these guys didn't need to know that.

* * *

The Parallel Path

I went straight to the beach to watch the sea and choose my pebbles because tradition – if a ritual invented by Wainwright in the early 1970s can be called tradition – dictates that the coast-to-coaster gets her boots wet in the Irish Sea at St Bees and picks up a pebble or two to carry across the country with her. Once the walker makes her triumphant arrival at Robin Hood's Bay, she wets her boots again and drops the pebbles into the North Sea. I lingered, choosing four of the shiniest pebbles I could find: stones that would feel good in the palm of my hand. One for Duncan and each of my kids, generously content to be left behind, and one more for Clive, who'd be coming along with me in some strange way we hadn't quite worked out yet. The beach was empty, and I sat there for a while, feeling sick with excitement and dizzy with pleasure. I didn't imagine putting the pebbles back in the water on the other side: the joy I felt at setting out was enough and I let the sun dry my boots as I savoured it. Then I went to find St Bees Priory.

St Bees is named for Bega, a British saint who lived at the same time as the better-known St Hilda of Whitby. Her priory is a late nineteenth-century reconstruction of the twelfth-century Benedictine church that itself occupied the site of St Bega's even earlier building. It was pretty and empty and smelled like dust and hoovered carpets and I wandered the aisles for a while, rattling my pebbles in my pocket and drinking pineapple juice out of a carton. On a table at the back were a number of books and leaflets on display for the visitor, including *St Bega: Cult, Fact and Legend* by the historian and theologian John Todd.

Bega was an Irish princess who arrived on the west coast of Cumbria in a curricle having run away from her father, who'd decided she was going to marry a Viking. According to one old hymn, Bega escaped through a set of locked doors – a miracle worthy of Houdini. An angel had protected her during her flit, guided her across the water and given her a bracelet, the ownership of which can be traced through church and parish records through the centuries. Just outside the train station on the road down to the beach there's a sculpture depicting her standing next to her curricle, her arms held aloft as she either prayed for a sea wind or offered thanks for the one she got.

St Bees felt like an auspicious place to begin because this was a village that had a proven track record in both offering hospitality to the stranger and knowing when to leave a woman alone. And best of all, Bega's most well-known miracle featured a walk. Once ensconced in the village as an anchoress Bega set up the priory, which was endowed with lands by a local baron. It became the tradition for this priory – as was common for many villages and parishes during the medieval period – to perform an annual 'perambulation' known as the 'beating of the bounds'. This involved the monks ceremonially walking around the perimeter of the priory's land. The ritual was religious and solemn, dedicating the land for the use of the religious community that lived and worked it, but, like kinhin, it also had a practical element: these walks reminded everyone about who owned what and an annual check of the priory's boundaries prevented rural neighbours making sneaky encroachments. At the time of one of these perambulations the monks of St Bega's were embroiled in a land dispute and feared a miscarriage of justice. The dispute was solved by an act of God: after one of the walks a sudden snowfall marked out the route their walk had traced, secured them the use of the land and became the runaway Irish princess's first miracle.

I set off early the next morning, a grey windy day, the sea so whipped up that the soft and sparkling turquoise of the evening before was now the colour of cardboard. The route is one long trek east so to start by following the edge of St Bees Head north feels like a waste of miles. You go for a few miles past an old lighthouse and along a path that hugs the crumbling edge of the red sandstone cliff and hardly anyone skips this part because usually the views out to sea are worth it. On my first day the Isle of Man hid out there somewhere behind a fuzz of grey and blue and the wind forced overgrown brambles against my legs. The black and white seabirds nesting on the cliff edges either side of Fleswick Bay – a deep gash between the north and south heads – were tossed around in the air like they were bits of newspaper.

Before too long, Whitehaven came into view. From where I stood on the headland, the grand buildings – reminders of the money made from the coal-pits around St Bees and Cumbria's involvement in the trade of enslaved people – were reduced to pale outlines, the business of the old port town still silent and far away. The sheer glee I felt at the fact I was actually doing this sent me quickly away and eastwards along the edge of a disused quarry. I took a good look at the faded navy mistiness of the sea, wishing it goodbye, and from there I hiked towards some unlovely parts of West Cumbria.

This is the part of the county excluded from the money that accrues in the Lake District National Park and it shows.

Purpose and Pilgrimage

The dull weather that day didn't help but even Wainwright remarks that the residents here are too busy earning their own livings to worry about making a special welcome for the walking tourist. I'd get to the expensive, flashier Cumbria of William and Dorothy Wordsworth later in the week, but for now there was the distant view of the Whitehaven Chemical Works and, after a while, the tiny, terraced houses of Moor Row on the way to Cleator. I tramped down cracked pavements in a bit of drizzle, my walking poles dangling from my rucksack as I passed the peeling front doors and grubby net curtains in the cheek-by-jowl terraced houses that were exactly like the type of house I grew up in in Preston. The path took me down the side of a cricket pitch and a sewage treatment plant.

St Leonard's church in Cleator promises a welcome to walkers and, this being the last settlement before the climb up Dent Hill, I decided to inspect it. I'd see plenty of churches along the way over the next two-and-a-bit weeks, and, deciding that my walk would at least acknowledge the idea of pilgrimage, if not exactly being one, stopped to take a look at what St Leonard's had to offer. It was raining a little. I discovered that the church doors were bolted shut and there was nothing to see but a pair of plastic crates and a dry metal dog bowl in the porch.

Cleator was once a thriving mining village that fell on hard times with the closure of the mines and has never recovered from them. Wainwright calls this bit of Cumbria 'a sad area already badly scarred by the rubbish dumps of abandoned iron ore mines and smelting works, spoil heaps and derelict railways'. A path down the side of a children's playground has been named 'Wainwright's Passage'. The ignominy and mild inuendo of it made me laugh and I imagined the Cleator powers-that-be indulging in a bit of petty revenge by naming this specifically unlovely track after him after all he said about the state of the West Cumbrian industrial belt. Nobody invited him, after all. I said hello to a couple of women out walking their dogs and felt conspicuous and ridiculous in my walking kit. It was painfully obvious what I was up to; a walking cliché, to the extent that as I got on to the main road a man unloading his supermarket shop from the back of his car nodded at me and cried out, 'Only a hundred and ninety miles to go, love, have a can of pop!' and I nodded back, pretending I saw the funny side.

No pilgrimage is an aimless wander, even if they're done as slowly as shuffling along stony ground on hands and knees would suggest. Historically that purpose was often – though not always – to do with the recovery from illness. Along the way, the pilgrim would be relying on a network of monastic 'hospitals', demonstrating the deep connection between healing and hospitality: our holiest places are those that offer refuge for those ailing in body and spirit.

These days, the pilgrimage's old association with healing – both spiritual and physical – has evolved. Now these walks are more often money-raising ventures for cash-strapped charities. Cancer Research UK runs Lake District Challenge hikes around Windermere, and Macmillan Cancer Support urges its supporters to sign up for the sponsored Mighty Hike on the Ullswater Way. The local hospice in Lancaster runs regular Moonlight Walks where you can walk all night from the hospice gardens to the sea's edge at

Morecambe and finish by watching the sun come up from the old stone jetty. The last time I did the famous Cross Bay Walk, crossing the flats of Morecambe Bay safely conveyed by Cedric, the Queen's Guide, I didn't just do it, I put a post on my Facebook page and asked people to donate money to the local theatre's schools' programme. When I started planning my Coast to Coast, lots of people asked me not *what* I was doing it for, but *who*, expecting to be presented with a sponsorship form, as if every moment of solitude needed an alibi to justify it. No, I was not walking for bowel nor breast nor testicle nor blood: I walked only to please myself, or for no good cause at all.

In the years between his diagnosis and his death, my daughter's father, Ben, started running marathons wearing shorts with a pair of plastic arse cheeks stuck to the back of them. His aim was to combat some of the stigma around bowel cancer's early symptoms, a stigma that prevents early diagnosis in thousands of patients every year, and also to raise money for cancer research charities. I think he wanted to get better too and I wondered if he hoped the running would help with that: there were special diets and muscle-building regimes and he'd sometimes talk to me about red blood cells and sugar and muscle mass.

Round the outskirts of our hometown, Preston in central Lancashire, there's a twenty-one-mile path and cycle track called the Guild Wheel. It's called a wheel because its various 'spokes' connect the route to the National Cycle Network, but it's hard not to see the traces of another one of those circular walks. Ben used it to train for his marathons and ran in the early mornings alone or with friends from his running club. He'd post pictures of sunrises over Preston marina or the tram bridge over the River Ribble on his Facebook page. This was his perambulation; right around his hometown on a circle that took in the suburbs and green spaces and always returned him home. Ben spoke carefully about all of this to his children: this attention to his health was about extending his life, not curing his illness. But the possibility of outrunning his cancer if only he tried hard enough was always there. Someone had to win the lottery, after all.

As he was dying Ben ran dozens of marathons and half marathons and raised hundreds of thousands of pounds. This generated so many opportunities to talk about his experience of diagnosis and illness, perhaps sending people with troubling symptoms to their GPs early enough to make a difference. His running saved lives and improved his own. But if these trips around the Guild Wheel were also a way of making a wish, the universe said no: he got sicker and sicker, then he died. The day after his death one of his friends set up an online petition asking for a section of the Guild Wheel to be named after him, and a year after that the mayor unveiled a red plaque: the Ben Ashworth Way. His children all had their photographs taken in front of it during the official unveiling, the little kids squinting at the camera in their summer clothes, my girl a bit bigger, torn between her pre-teen shyness and urge not to be left out, hiding behind shades and a big hat. This all came with me as I brought my own ailing heart out on my walk: the parts of grief that make you cynical, that make you hard, that make you doubt that anything can help.

* * *

Purpose and Pilgrimage

Inside St Bees Priory there'd been a space to the left of the main arch and altar and in that space a table with a prayer tree on it. Alongside was a tray full of little pens (like the type you used to get in Argos, before they went digital) and scraps of paper. The idea was to write up your prayer and push it on to one of the branches. Had other walkers used the start of their walk to ask for miracles or offered to dedicate their efforts to the memory of Bega or for the benefit of someone else? Most people had asked for peace in Ukraine. I thought about Clive. We'd met the morning I caught the train and had coffee in Lancaster Castle. We'd taken some going-away pictures and he'd brought me a present: the compass I thought I'd lost when we went out walking in the Forest of Bowland together. He'd gone back out, retraced our steps and found it lying in the long grass where I'd dropped it. The generosity of this was startling and I'd worn the compass around my neck on the train and as I wandered through the priory too; a regular little Girl Guide; Clive's scout.

I eyed the prayer tree again. The medieval pilgrim might be walking for the good of his master's soul as well as his own: it was possible to pay someone to go on pilgrimage for you, and these proxy pilgrims would take the journey and dedicate the merit of their efforts to their sponsor. Clive is too sane to want me to ask for a miracle for him and if prayer worked like that nobody would ever die of anything, would they? Clive is well loved: decades with a partner, children, a lifetime full of friends and colleagues. He is not a man who is short of people who'd want to pray for him, if that was his thing. All the same, the proxiness of the walk started to feel important to me. I'd taken photographs of the sculptures of sleeping children that Josefina de Vasconcellos had donated to the priory to create a garden of remembrance for babies because I imagined it was the kind of thing he might have wanted to see if he'd been hanging about in St Bees instead of me. I'd tried to film the patterns the wild wind blew through the long grass, making it look like a green ocean during a storm, and texted the pictures and film to him. He was going to write to me, and I was going to be eyes and ears for him. And that felt important.

So, feeling embarrassed and silly but doing it anyway, I'd written Clive's name on a scrap of paper and pushed it on to one of the tree's branches. I had refused to ask for a miracle cure or a remission of his suffering or for anything else because I already knew that asking for these things – asking in the most nakedly extravagant, generous, hopeful way that you could, like Ben had – did not work. I could not ask for anything. The only thing I could write was my friend's name.

The shop on the main road in Cleator is famous for its baked goods. According to some, the meat and potato pies create early-morning queues and have inspired fist fights in the street but all I wanted was a can of Coke.

'You're making good time, love,' the woman behind the counter said.

I nodded, and she smiled warmly – managing to show some genuine interest in one of hundreds of strangers she'd meet that summer, most of them hurrying their way through her much-derided hometown to get to the grander spectacle of the national park. She thought I'd walked very quickly up the headland: I didn't tell her I'd set off two hours before

I really needed to because I was dreading falling into step with another hiker who'd want to make small talk with me for the full sixteen miles.

Hikers on the walking forums often commented on how *friendly* everyone on this walk was: even those who opted to do it alone would be reassured they were certain to find companions as they went along. This expectation of friendliness was sometimes couched in more generalised discussions about what a walker from elsewhere could expect from the North – when we weren't being sulky and dour we were all so *chatty* up here. The men who'd spoken to me the day before at St Bees might have been surprised by my surliness: I was out of step with my friendly fellow walkers, prickling at even the prospect of being greeted by others. It wasn't shyness, not exactly. And it wasn't misanthropy either: I know most people are friendly enough most of the time. Instead, my reluctance had something to do with my burnout. Sooner or later, I thought, someone would want me to help them read the map or listen to their problems or laugh at their jokes or be impressed by their wayfinding skills. If they wanted to help me – whether I needed it or not – I'd have to be grateful and that felt like work too. Contact with others had reduced itself to a series of transactions that left me feeling out of pocket and I had no idea what to do about it other than avoid it.

Still, I liked this woman. She didn't tell me to enjoy every moment or to embrace the view or to stay safe. She didn't ask me who or what I was doing the walk for. She just sold me my can of Coke.

'Are you off up Dent now?' she asked. Dent – the hill she was referring to – was the first proper ascent of the walk and marked the gateway to the Lake District National Park. I nodded, and she handed me my change and said, with what I hoped was not the characteristic understatement of the North, 'It's not *that* bad.'

But before the possible badness of Dent, there was Black How Farm, the last farmhouse before the fells. The fell road runs around the back of the sixteenth-century farmhouse, all low roofs and little windows, and took me past some ornate iron gates (rusted shut) and a skip filled with rolls of barbed wire and the skeletons of a few old motorbikes. From there, it was a steady and fairly boring trek up a gravelly plantation path through the woods. It was still early afternoon, but the densely planted pine trees cut out most of the light and the ground beneath them was dark with dropped needles and huge shiny black slugs. This was not a beautiful place but I was happy. The signage was patchy and unofficial: arrows were spray painted on trees or on the plastic lids of feed buckets nailed to fences, but still, I didn't get lost because the uphill route was obvious and the woman in the Cleator shop was right: it wasn't *that* bad. When I got tired I stopped and lay on my back in the wet grass eating my sandwiches, drinking my Coke and letting the rain hit my face.

Up top (*summit* is too strong a word for the top of Dent Fell, a mere 352 metres above sea level) the ground was boggy and, because the weather had come in, the promised view back to the sea I'd just left and eastwards to the Lakeland fells I'd be crossing over the next days was indistinct. Sellafield's chimneys were just about visible. This was disappointing: I'd had my phone in the pocket of my leggings all day wanting to capture that last proper sighting of the Irish Sea. I didn't wait long, and managed to avoid the worst of the bogs, though the descent was steep, and once the ground hardened up I made parts of it on my backside, sliding and bumping down rough and muddy grass and arriving, eventually, at Nannycatch Beck. This tiny chattering brook is famous only because it marks the coast-to-coaster's entry into the Lake District National Park. The word 'nannycatch' means – among other things – a mischievous sprite or fairy but I saw nothing but a few chewing sheep and a profusion of wildflowers as I strolled on tired legs through a pretty valley on the final easy stretch into Ennerdale Bridge.

I arrived in the late afternoon, just as the rain started to fall more heavily, easily finding that night's lodgings, which was the Fox and Hounds pub. My room was a goth's dream, with lots of shiny dark wood and heavy purple curtains (through which was a view of the graveyard in the church opposite). There was a letter from Clive waiting for me too: a big cardboard envelope with his sprawly handwriting urging the carrier to handle 'with care, please' on the back. I propped it up on the desk. *I'll just rest my eyes for a few minutes*, I thought. Then it was morning.

DAY THREE

Alone at Last
Ennerdale Bridge to Rosthwaite (16 miles)

I woke early and took Clive's letter down to the dining room with me but before I could read it, the man serving breakfast came over to chat to me about my walk. He suggested, seeing as I was on my own, that I should take the easy route along the north shore of Ennerdale Water. He must have caught me looking doubtful because he popped into the back and brought out a calendar with a glossy photograph showing the rockiness of the southern edge and pointed out the awkward scramble up and over a crag known as Robin Hood's Chair. I put Clive's letter away, told the chatty man I'd take the easier route – just to make him happy – then left the Fox and Hounds and headed for the south side.

By mid-morning it was bright and hot, the surface of the glacial lake blue and glossy. The silence was startling, the stillness complete. As I picked my way over rocks and tree roots, there was a flash of something to the right of me, something four legged and gingerish. Whatever it was broke cover with a snap and a rustle, then darted away before I could turn my head. Had I seen a deer? A big fox? Something else? In the 1810s there were rumours of a wild dog of some kind that roamed around the Ennerdale Valley. It was sometimes spotted harmlessly urinating on a thistle; the reporting is weirdly specific – as if the creature had one preferred

Alone at Last

thistle for its pissing. At other times, it spent the pitch-black nights killing and drinking the blood of sheep. 'No one ever knew how or whence he came,' one chronicler remarked, though the creature's ending was more certain: a brindled dog was hunted by hounds, killed and its skin displayed at a museum in Keswick for a time. Whatever I'd seen, the creature was my only company for my entire walk beside the lake (including a very easy scramble up and over Robin Hood's Chair), save for a few definitely unimaginary cows breaking the silence with their soft chewing at the eastern end.

Here, I was presented with a choice of routes. The high path up to Red Pike and Haystacks is more difficult, with some tricky scree and a tough ascent to the highest peak on the walk: High Stile, at over 800 metres. The low route follows a shepherd's track turned into a forest road and follows the softly gurgling River Liza down in the valley. Wainwright calls the high route 'for supermen' and, not feeling particularly super, I took the low, and still regret it. The cheat's path was a long, slow, hot trek though the Forestry Commission plantations that are still as Wainwright described them, the trees 'deformed, crowded in a battery, denied light and air and natural growth'. I took photographs of their dry, broken branches, wondered about the views I was missing, plodded for two hours, got bored, thirsty and sunburned, and eventually stopped for water at the Black Sail Youth Hostel, nestled at the tight end of the valley at the foot of Loft Beck.

You can stay in the hostel if you book it in advance, but I had miles and miles to go. The kitchen and toilet facilities are open to all, so I let myself in and refilled my bottle and

The Parallel Path

ate the packed lunch I'd been issued with that morning. It was dim and cool inside; some unseen hand had stocked a basket with snacks, left a first aid box out on the kitchen counter and had cleaned the toilets. I noticed this work: the way the welcome remained, even though the person who provided it was probably miles away. I felt like Goldilocks, sitting in someone else's chair and drinking tea made with someone else's milk.

I got Clive's letter out. He'd sent a copy of a photograph he had up over his writing desk at home. The copy was an *exact* reproduction – right down to the smudged Blu Tack on the back. The picture showed Clive's seaside hometown of Morecambe in its heyday, the view looking northwards along the main drag, the fells I was moving through visible behind the hotels and cafés and picture houses. The street was crowded with old-fashioned cars and men in dark coats and hats. The letter was brief, and Clive was clearly in a reflective mood, lining up his own life and memories against the photograph.

'It is so strange I was born just a decade after it was taken. Everyone loves to hate this little seaside town, but for me, I'm so wrapped up in its history, its people, and streets, I can't help but have a love for the place.' This was the coast I was steadily walking away from, the sea at my back, the sense of home and nostalgia – of being 'wrapped up' in a history, a people and a place – that I felt myself wanting to peel away from entirely. I had been anxious to open this letter, wondering what Clive might want or need from me. Instead, my friend showed me where he came from, and let me see his thoughts turn towards home and his childhood. For the first time in a long while being company for someone else did not feel like work. Before I'd set off, Clive said I should burn his letters as I went along. Instead, I tucked this first one carefully inside the pages of a book. Before long, a trio of young men on bikes arrived and started to take their shoes off on the grass outside. They were loud and happy, shouting at each other and emptying water bottles over their heads. I said hello quickly then moved on.

In the early spring, I had devoured books about walking as I tried to understand my post-Covid cabin fever. During the pandemic all the newspapers were carrying articles about the crisis of loneliness and the secondary epidemic of 'touch hunger'. One morning, Radio 4 interviewed a doctor who suggested that being alone too much was as bad for you as smoking. There were campaigns and initiatives to get people together: the local library staff were keeping in contact with their housebound borrowers over the phone and my street had a WhatsApp group buzzing with messages as everyone on the street checked themselves in and made arrangements for shared music on Sunday afternoons. I bounced between what my children and my students needed from me, constantly engaged in the work of domestic and professional care. I cooked. I checked in with people. My phone rattled with so many notifications from the newly formed virtual communities I belonged to that I turned it off and put it in a drawer.

Whatever this out-of-step urge to be outside and alone meant, I wasn't the only one who'd ever experienced it. William Hazlitt, in his 1822 essay 'On Going a Journey', declared that 'One of the pleasantest things in the world is going on a journey; but I like to go by myself. I can enjoy society in a room; but out of doors, nature is company enough for me.' For him, one of the primary pleasures of walking alone is freedom from social etiquette and the expectations of others. While walking alone he is free to indulge a bad mood or get lost in a daydream. He harms or bores no one. His relief is palpable: even his enjoyment of the landscapes he moves through seems to depend on the fact he's under no burden to point out the view or explain it to someone else. 'Is not this wild rose sweet without a comment?' he asks. It didn't seem to me that Hazlitt was a misanthrope, only that he was sensitive to what being in a good relationship with someone else required and keenly felt the work involved in making sure he was good company.

His essay helped me to understand what I had been feeling. I had tried to be there for my children and my students in ways that were helpful, nurturing – or at the very least not out-and-out irritating. This involved trying to forget about myself. Sometimes that happened naturally but more often I achieved it with brute force and a paradoxical, obsessive maintenance and pruning of who I was in the attempt to turn myself into a thing that was both useful and appealing to others. Anyone who has sat up and helped with GCSE Chemistry when they wanted to go to bed, who has answered the Teams call when they needed to eat, who has tried hard to be interested in someone else's news when they wanted to watch the telly, knows what this work is, but Hazlitt really understood just how utterly exhausting that intricate tending of self that is part of the labour of care could be. And he said walking freed him from that in a way that nothing else did. The essay felt like a promise: maybe the walking would work that way for me too.

Alone at Last

Hazlitt isn't the only writer who has associated writing's comforts with aloneness. In May 1862, just a month after his death from tuberculosis, *The Atlantic Monthly* published what would become Henry David Thoreau's most famous essay, 'Walking'. Thoreau shared my new distaste for circular walks ('half the walk is but retracing our steps') and – with some humour in the telling – suggests that the *real* walker should set forth in such a spirit of adventure that they expect 'never to return – prepared to send back our embalmed hearts only as relics'. The world he walks through is defined primarily by what is not there, 'Man and his affairs, church and state and school, trade and commerce, and manufactures and agriculture, even politics, the most alarming of them all – I am pleased to see how little space they occupy in the landscape.'

Thoreau also suggests that readiness for a proper walk requires a complete detachment from past and future: home and family left as if you'd never see them again, debts settled, will made, and no expectation you'll be back to tread the path a second time allowed to form. This attentiveness to the present is synonymous with being alone. Even a relationship of care to another person (he remarks on 'good works') becomes a kind of distraction from the woods and is apt to drag the mind away from where the body is.

That determined, cold-blooded shedding of anything other than *now* reminded me of Clive's fascination with Dennis Potter and the way Potter's sense of impending death unencumbered him from past and future and somehow made him more available to the world. Clive and I were both envious of that, I think, and for different reasons found the state elusive. The difficulty for me was that most spaces and places contained 'man and his affairs' and that being fully available to the world also involved being in connection with other people and their needs. Caring involves a type of attentiveness that sends parts of me forwards and backwards through time (*was the school uniform put in the washing machine last night? Have the next set of dentist's appointments been made?*) or, in Thoreau's parlance, takes me 'out of the woods'. So many parts of myself had been off on their errands it felt as if the present was scooped out and empty. There was an extremity to the solution Thoreau proposed that had appealed to me: certainty can obscure nuance, but I'd been seduced by his witty confidence. What could be more drastic than setting off to walk across the country?

From the Black Sail Youth Hostel, the path runs steeply upwards beside Loft Beck to join the high route; it is nearly a climb in places. The trickle of the falling water was so lively after the wide silence of the lakeside path that I sat down on a rock and got my boots wet leaning in to record the sound of it: something to send to Clive instead of a postcard. As I remember this, I notice now what I didn't then: the trouble I took to hold my breath as I recorded the sound of the beck – the urge I had to show Clive what I was listening to, but to absent myself from the scene. At the very top of Loft Beck where the high and low routes converged, I looked back to see how far I'd come. The ancient tracks a glacier had made through the landscape were clearly apparent; the stranded boulders, huge rocks gouged by the passing ice, the soft round swells of the grass-covered drumlins.

This remote and relatively less visited part of the Ennerdale Valley had been earmarked as a disposal site for nuclear waste, although over the years various pressure groups had delayed the proposal until alternative plans were made to create an underground chamber offshore near Workington. Clive is curious about shadows and traces, the echoes of ourselves – afterlives, for good and bad – that we leave behind. He's a collector of beautiful artworks and personal ephemera. I scrub footprints off the kitchen floor, wipe fingerprints off the shower door and try to make my house look like nobody lives in it. For Clive, there's some comfort in the thought that nothing ever goes away, not really. At the top of Loft Beck, I tried to photograph the view for him without catching my own shadow, and imagined how the disposal site might have worked: the excavation and burial of depleted uranium in double-lined lead coffins sunk into concrete chambers, the hot, softly glowing poison tucked in beneath the drumlins, seeping death with a half-life of centuries through the rock. After some deliberation (the doubling back would add an hour or so on to my day's walk) I nipped back a little way along the tail end of the high path to Innominate Tarn.

The detour was another kind of pilgrimage, another opportunity to think about what these so-called empty places might hold. Wainwright's ashes had been scattered here in the early 1990s and the edge of the tarn was as high as I'd get that day – just southeast of Haystacks and a full 800 metres above the Black Sail Youth Hostel. 'Innominate' means 'without a name', which isn't quite true – it was called Loaf Tarn for a while, though everyone but the cartographers forgot. In the late 1990s someone hatched a plan to rename it Wainwright Tarn, which fell at the last hurdle due to an administrative issue with boundary lines.

> All I ask for, at the end, is a last long resting place by the side of Innominate Tarn, on Haystacks, where the water gently laps the gravelly shore and the heather blooms and Pillar and Gable keep unfailing watch. A quiet place, a lonely place. I shall go to it, for the last time, and be carried: someone who knew me in life will take me and empty me out of a little box and leave me there alone. And if you, dear reader, should get a bit of grit in your boot as you are crossing Haystacks in the years to come, please treat it with respect. It might be me.

There's something haunting and self-indulgent and sad and human and silly about this passage – published in Wainwright's memoirs and often quoted in guidebooks. Did Wainwright ever actually ask his wife Betty and his son Peter directly to make sure he'd end up here, or did he just hope that the message tucked into his memoir would do the trick? His sad surrender to the inevitable fact that the last time he'd take his 'superman' route he'd be carried, rather than arriving under his own steam, is tempered by the fantasy that he'd hang around somehow, both entirely alone, and cropping up persistently in the boots of all the walkers following the paths he'd laid out for them. Would Thoreau have considered even Wainwright not a 'real' walker, given how carefully he'd planned and imagined his own relic's final return?

Alone at Last

It is possible to swim here but the edges of the tarn were boggy and rocky and I only dipped my hands. The absolute euphoria I felt in that moment – alone in a high place with the wind throwing my hair about and soothing my sunburn, my feet solid and hot inside my boots, my hands in the cold water – brought tears to my eyes. It was partly the view – the awesome grandeur of Gable and Pillar, just as Wainwright had promised. This was the sort of thing I'd usually only see via a screen; a dose of sublimity to which the internet had left me immune. But here, alone, I was met by the world. I forgot to be ashamed at how easily I was affected by it because there was no audience to displease or satisfy, nobody to tend to, nobody to remember. I took my time, picked my way around the edge of the tarn, and because there was nobody there to see me, laughed out loud with the joy of it.

Wainwright, despite two marriages, was a man who felt he was the best version of himself when he was alone. Even once the publication of his books had made him famous he refused most publicity and interviews until very near the end of his life, and when he started getting recognised on his walks, would nip behind walls and pretend to be taking a pee until the person who wanted to speak to him had passed by. Late on in his career he agreed to be a guest on the Radio 4 programme *Desert Island Discs*. This was out of character, but maybe it was the conceit of the programme – alone on a remote island – that appealed to him.

I don't think the privations of island life, solitary and minimalist, would cause Wainwright any particular suffering. He'd often brag about spending entire weekends up in the Lakes with nothing on him but a map in one pocket and a spare pair of socks in the other. He didn't own a proper waterproof jacket until the 1970s and though his books sold well and could have funded any number of luxuries, he gave away most of the money he made to animal charities. But when presenter Sue Lawley asked what luxury item Wainwright would like to take with him to make his time on the island more pleasurable, he didn't ask for drawing supplies or a pair of hiking boots or an unlimited supply of Kendal Mint Cake. Instead, he asked for a mirror.

I thought about that mirror a lot and about the addictive comforts of becoming your own adoring audience as I crouched on the rocks that afternoon, peering into the glassy surface of Innominate Tarn like a little Narcissus. Could the joy I was experiencing alone that day actually be the stickier, more addictive pleasure that results when a person gets exactly what they want? What is the difference between a *carefree* shedding of responsibility and a *careless* denying of the inevitable fact of relationship? Even at the time my pleasure didn't feel entirely healthy; like the difference between intoxication and nourishment, there was something ungenerous about it. All the same, in the months to come, this is the part of the walk that I'll do over and over again in my head, just for the pleasure of feeling again that slowly building joy as I climbed upwards, eastwards and away from home. Before I left the tarn, I flipped my phone's screen and took the first in a long line of sweaty, bedraggled, but still artfully posed selfies.

I returned to the point where the two paths converged and found the path towards Grey Knotts and Honister Pass. It

Alone at Last

became busier and I spotted the brightly coloured waterproofs and rucksacks of other walkers some miles off. The place started to feel a little more like what it was: a tourist destination in midsummer, though the sudden company was comforting: the path is less distinct and needs a bit of concentration here. Once I spotted a walker ahead, I was able to take my eyes off the map and ignore my compass for a while and use that person as a kind of mobile cairn.

The landmark to look out for here is Drum House: a heap of stones and slate that I needed Wainwright to tell me was the remains of a building that housed the cable that operated an old tramway. The path resolves itself and becomes arrow straight as it traces the tramway, then there's no map reading at all, but just a steady plod with other walkers, the remoteness of the Ennerdale Valley long behind me. After a couple of miles, I caught up with a woman I'd seen back in St Bees. She was sitting near a cairn drinking water from a bottle and using her phone to take photographs of the view. She was from Australia, was still jet-lagged and had set off at four that morning to take the high route at first light, with a plan to see the sun rise at Innominate Tarn. So far, I hadn't seen another woman doing this walk alone and at both B&Bs had been treated as something of a novelty. I asked her if she'd like me to use her phone to take a photograph of her.

'Oh no,' she said, smiling slightly, as if she was too polite to point out how daft my suggestion was. 'I already know I've been, right here.' She tapped at her chest. She seemed as reluctant to fall into step with me as I was with her, so I went on quickly, taking a long time to pick my way down to where the path joins the B-road between Buttermere and

Seatoller. On this road is the old Honister slate mine, and what this mine has become is a noisy demonstration of the kind of adaptability and diversification common to the Lake District, which is not quite the unspoiled wilderness that Thoreau described – if such a place ever existed outside of a tired person's wishful thinking.

Nobody's making money from the 450-million-year-old Westmorland green slate anymore, though you can buy engraved bits of it to take home for your garden or order a handsome-looking headstone for later. The dormitories that used to house the miners are now another youth hostel and a big café. The old mine shafts have been converted to a mini-museum and the mine runs tours of an exhibition about the area's industrial heritage. The landscape bears the marks of industry: there are huge scoops and steep troughs in the fellsides. But the old slate quarries have been repurposed for the thrill seekers now; you can buy a ticket to cross them on high wires, rent ropes and a helmet to scramble up and down the sides of them, and (I am so afraid of heights I couldn't look at this part of the leaflet for very long) even pay for a permit to do something horrific in a dangling tent called 'cliff camping'. I bought a coffee and two flapjacks and spent a half hour with my boots off watching people arrive and leave in their cars before heading slowly (knees and feet really feeling it) down the hill along a path through grass nibbled short and neat by sheep towards Seatoller and the Borrowdale Valley.

Considering how you are seen or will be thought about by others in some imagined future after the walk (or even after death) seems a strange thing to spend your hard-won solitude on, but it's a very persistent feature of the literature, especially for the solitary walkers I'd turned to in the spring to help me understand my own desires. They may have been carefree and released from the burdens of society, but this experience was shaped by their care for what others might think or say about it.

Early on in his walking essay Hazlitt quotes from a poem by William Cowper. Cowper praises solitude by conjuring 'a friend in my retreat' – the sole purpose of that friend, according to the poem, is to be the one who listens to the speaker of the poem whisper 'solitude is sweet'. For what is time alone with nobody there to listen to you brag about how amazing it is to be free of their company? Similarly, Thoreau's impassioned instruction to the *real* walker to leave all social connections behind him is undercut almost as soon as he has issued it: 'my companion and I, for sometimes I have a companion', he says, and much of the rest of the essay narrates the experiences of that 'we'.

Wainwright, famously taciturn at home and abroad (his wife, Betty, when away with friends, had to set up an elaborate appointment system so he would answer the telephone to her), conjures an imaginary female presence to comfort and soothe him after a day's walk. In his account of walking the Pennine Way, Wainwright describes 'the girl of my dreams' who comes to him each night. 'We have been companions on many a delightful journey and known the quiet joy of comradeship.' In his many letters to friends – and he was a committed and frequent letter writer – he would often describe his solitude through metaphors of companionship: 'Nobody here knows me, yet I am surrounded by friends; the tall trees by the river, the enchanting path over by the castle'. In another letter, he imagines himself as 'Patriarch of the fells' and, yes, he's making fun of himself to make his friend laugh, but still, the man he finds himself to be while out walking is a genial host with 'a smile and a warm greeting and helpful advice for those he meets on his wanderings'. This version of the man – the hospitable *paterfamilias* – is the one he offers his reader throughout the Pictorial Guides, addressing him directly and as intimately as any other of his pen-pals. Even for solitary walkers 'alone' is more often – or most often – 'alone with'.

It didn't escape me that most of what I read during this time as I was being seduced by the promises of what walking alone in nature would offer me were stories about *men* walking, and men walking alone, drunk on the ecstasy of their own company. Walking is as historically determined as anything else: its cultural identity first started to develop in the eighteenth and nineteenth centuries when walking began to become a choice rather than a necessity. A choice for some, that is, and the perspectives of that 'some' – those with the social freedoms to stroll without worrying about safety or propriety and who didn't have to be at the business of earning money – persist in walking's associations with the joy and freedom of solitude. Even though I found myself with no particular problem in empathising with the risky, complicated and indeed, often self-indulgent joy of these solitary male walkers, walking, Geoff Nicholson insists, 'is different for women'.

There are actually very few walking women in a book whose title, *The Lost Art of Walking: The History, Science,*

Philosophy, Literature, Theory and Practice of Pedestrianism, suggests the author was aiming for some kind of Grand Unified Theory. The two species of walking women he does imagine – the catwalk model 'scissoring' before her audience and the sex worker or 'street walker' 'strutting' for her punter – don't quite allow him to elaborate on what he thinks this difference might be. He mentions Mrs Dalloway but only in the context of questioning whether this fictional character is really a walker at all. She is, he notes, far too excited about a mere trip to the florist and the novelty suggests she doesn't do it often enough to have earned her stripes. *What a lark! What a plunge!* she says, and her joy irritates him. 'You'd slap her, wouldn't you?' he says.

A woman knows the ways she might be held in the mind of someone else: those images of strutting and scissoring, her vulnerability to the slap – or worse. And if walking really is different for us, this is why. It might be easier for a man to be nourished by a carefree solitude that includes imagining or anticipating a willing reader, a grateful recipient of a letter, an interested companion, some kind of friend eager to hear news of the day. Lots of women find it more difficult to imagine the friendly encouragement that nourishes a free and lonely day. But I had Clive, imagining me from back home in our patch of Lancaster, writing me letters as I made my way eastwards. It felt comforting to know my friend had my list of destinations on his desk and was following my progress across the country day by day. To be held in the mind of someone else is a kindness too.

I remembered again that conversation we'd had at Silverdale where Clive had tried to explain to me what

The Parallel Path

interested him about the way Dennis Potter was thinking about his own death. I'd come home from our walk and found the interview that Clive had told me about online and rewatched it, more fascinated by Melvyn Bragg than I was with Potter. Bragg is every inch the LWT interviewer in his dark suit and tie, coming into the studio holding a folder of papers and research notes he doesn't refer to once. Their conversation starts with some solicitous fussing about where the chairs should be, what the best position of the ashtray is, where Potter's hipflask will be stashed and who is going to be in charge of passing it to him. Bragg does not interrupt Potter once, even as – feeling the effects of the glass of champagne he's asked for and whatever is in the hipflask – Potter gets a little lost for words and repeats himself.

This spaciousness was striking; I was more familiar with Bragg's intrusive, chivvying interview style on Radio 4's *In Our Time*. This is a different sort of Bragg entirely. He is well prepared and professional and asks Potter what we want to know – about his work, his childhood, the way his politics have shown up in his writing. He builds rapport by alluding gently to what the two of them have in common: Potter was a working-class boy who'd gone to Oxford, Bragg the Cumbrian son of a mechanic who'd navigated the grammar-school system to read History there too. About halfway through this much gentler conversation, there's a lovely exchange when Potter asks Bragg if he minds him smoking. Bragg is almost embarrassed at this moment of care ('Why should I mind?'), makes a little joke about passive smoking and threatens to join in with Potter if he carries on going on about how much he loves his fags.

Alone at Last

Professionalism falls away. Bragg is tentative and a little cowardly at times. 'When you knew you were, you were, er, when you knew you had cancer . . .' Like so many of us, he won't say 'dying' but his dithering gives us the opportunity to see Potter smile and the space he leaves around the word invites Potter to use it boldly. He mercilessly counts the weeks he imagines he might have left and expresses how determined he is to finish his work. The interview ends prematurely and painfully; Potter is suddenly too unwell to continue, the strain shows, and he is almost apologetic. 'That will have to do. I'm done . . . At certain points I felt like I was flying with it.' It's tempting to overread this. All endings feel like interruptions to a conversation that should have gone on for longer, but Bragg's answer to Potter is intriguing: he has become a fan, not an interviewer and maybe even a friend. He has the last word, but it is a word that only confirms what Potter has already expressed. 'You were,' he says simply. They sip their champagne and leave the studio together. Was this where Clive had learned to hold his own friend in mind so gently, and with so little sense of imposition? My friend back home in Lancaster had shown me the way without knowing it.

Down in the Borrowdale Valley, I found the Scafell Hotel after some hopeless zigzagging along the lanes that link the villages. Another letter from Clive awaited me, and the carefully taped-up cardboard package with his now-familiar handwriting on the front appeared as a comfort, turning the unfamiliar bedroom into a temporary home. Something had changed for me that day. The bad temper of my first day had given way to a sudden kind of

The Parallel Path

euphoria, yes – and that had been just what all those books about walking had promised me. Shedding home and responsibility and getting outside *had* made me happy, or something like it. But just as the landscape holds the traces of everything that it once was and 'natural' unspoiled emptiness is only a fantasy, it had become clear to me that whatever the walking literature said, I would always be inhabited and contained by others, aloneness was a fantasy too and the temporary glee I'd enjoyed at getting my own way contained other risks. Could walking offer me nothing more substantial than that? I picked up Clive's letter from where it had been left on my bed and turned it over. 'With care, please,' he'd written on the back. An instruction for me as much as the postie.

DAY FOUR

Friends in High Places
Rosthwaite to Grasmere (9 ½ miles)

'The best form of walking is fell walking and the best part of fell walking is ridge walking and the best part of ridge walking is the traverse of high connecting skylines between neighbouring summits,' Wainwright had decreed, when describing the route between Rosthwaite and Grasmere. The word 'ridge' made me think of the spine of an animal or a book. On aerial photographs it looks like that too: a winding track along the fine narrow edge of the fell, a precarious thread between high points, the ground falling away steeply each side of the path. Wainwright's pompousness nearly inspired enough rebellion in me to book an Uber but I was determined to make up for taking the lower path the day before and ignored the pages where he described a gentler alternative way along the valley bottom.

The day began softly, and I traced an easy route through fields alongside Stonethwaite Beck, Eagle Crag looming overhead. There were sheep and long grass, yellow flowers and white butterflies and low, lichen-spotted stone walls. As the path started to lead upwards the way became stonier and narrower. I got out of puff, and wondered why Wainwright thought ridge walking was the best. He was a man who loved solitude and you'd think there'd be nowhere as lonely as the threadlike route on the slopes and summits. But as every guidebook praising a high place invites others

The Parallel Path

to go up and inspect the view from it, in the summer months a walker is as likely to be alone in the valleys as she is to be in company on the ridges and peaks. A couple of times that morning I had to pause and step off the thin path to let groups of teenagers carrying enormous rucksacks pass me and stride their way effortlessly upwards.

If not solitude, then the view? The higher I got, the more impressive the view back down to the Borrowdale Valley became: the ideal vantage point for Wainwright to take the photographs he'd use for his carefully framed, intensely detailed illustrations. I imagined him up high, looking down, as satisfied with his own heroic efforts as he was with what he saw. Maybe this is why he'd described yesterday's high route as one for 'supermen': there was something about the slog upwards that made it very easy to be pleased with yourself. I felt like that too: impressed I was walking even though my feet hurt. Impressed I found the way without too much trouble and impressed I had got really good at folding the map back up even when a wind was blowing. I relaxed into this new way of striding about the world, being a coast-to-coaster, having the gear, knowing the lingo.

Up high, I stopped to read the letter from Clive that had arrived in Rosthwaite the day before. It was a curious thing: an artefact with a blue cardboard outer layer surrounding several finer sheets of yellow paper, covered with densely packed typewriting. The blue cardboard was embossed with the phrase *Feats of Strength* and I flipped it open to see a picture of a man wearing not much, showing off his muscles. This was Charles Atlas, an Italian-American body builder who, during the 1920s, developed the most famous advertising campaign in the world.

Atlas's strong-man origin story has become a bio-mythography told in comic strips. 'Before' he is always a pale weedy weakling who has sand kicked in his face and loses his girl to a bigger, stronger specimen. 'After', the drip has become a muscle-bound being, more god than man. What happens between 'before' and 'after' is a transformation fuelled by a level of self-hatred known only to incels and a series of secret muscle-building techniques using 'dynamic tension' that apparently Atlas gleaned from watching caged lions at the local zoo. And it worked too. Writers at *Physical Culture* magazine described Atlas as the nation's 'most perfectly developed man', as if Atlas's body really was a thing that he'd made all on his own by skill and brute force.

I know about this because when I was a prison librarian, the modern versions of Charles Atlas's courses were often requested by the men who used the library. They promised muscle-building exercises that could be done in a small space, without any particular gym equipment. The men would also request books by Charles Bronson, a career criminal who had been incarcerated for most of his life, his sentence ever-lengthening due to violent crimes committed while he was in prison. Influenced by Atlas's 'dynamic tension' exercises, Bronson had developed a training programme that could be done from inside a cell and no matter how many copies of his *Solitary Fitness* I bought for the library I could never keep it on the shelves. The self-mythologising of Bronson was an obvious antidote to the routinely petty humiliations of the prison's regime. Among the claims he makes in his autobiography, *Loonyology: In*

The Parallel Path

My Own Words, is the strength to do press-ups with three men sitting on his back and, for an encore, to lift a full-sized pool table. I had imagined the Charles Atlas and Bronson books to be a niche interest for confined men. But when the gyms closed in spring 2020, Bronson's book gained a surge in popularity with people looking for ways to keep up their own strength and fitness while they were locked down at home. In moments of fear and enforced helplessness, we all need a way to feel a bit like supermen.

What Clive had sent me, maybe thinking about all the training walks and heart rate counting I'd been doing before setting off, was the first lesson of the Charles Atlas correspondence course. Lesson one is about sleep, and receiving it felt like kindness; Clive had remembered my troubles with insomnia. The lesson itself makes strange claims about sleep's effect on various magnetic energies in the body. Health and long life are within everyone's grasp. Sleep itself is something that can be achieved by willpower alone. As a lifelong insomniac I was amused by Atlas's insistence (in block capitals) that sleep will surely follow if a person could just 'LET GO AND AVOID ALL TENSED STIFFNESS'. Sleep achieved, the reader can expect a 'rapid increase of power'.

Clive had doctored the document to include the story of how this object came into his possession. His handwriting was uneven and sometimes difficult to read. He'd warned me about this: as a side effect of the drugs he is taking, his hands shake. At the start of the pandemic, which was also about the time he started chemotherapy, he was out walking when he spied three suitcases lined up neatly but clearly abandoned in the undergrowth. The letter includes a photograph he took of them. The first two suitcases contained some ordinary, neatly folded though dated clothing. The last suitcase was locked, and Clive tore into it to discover, tucked inside a folder, the entire Charles Atlas 'health, strength and physique building system'. (There was also, Clive wrote bashfully, a couple of dirty magazines ('from another era') called *Spick & Span*.) Clive had gathered up the lessons from Atlas that promised 'the perfect body and mind' and, as he carried his spoils home, ran into two friends on their way back from a long lockdown cycle to Glasson Dock. They had a bit of socially distanced chit chat, and the pair asked carefully about Clive's health and the progress of his treatment, all the while looking at the folder he was clutching to his chest. The image Clive conjured for me here is funny and painful. I imagined Clive's healthy friends looking between the sick man and his good luck charm: the image of a man both shirtless and oiled peeping out from the first lesson like a page-three model.

If I had learned to become suspicious of the sickly pleasures of my own company, then perhaps striving, Atlas-like, towards the view would offer the change in perspective I was seeking. The path curved around the edge of Eagle Crag and rose higher alongside one of Stonethwaite Beck's tributaries, Greenup Gill. The walking here became more like climbing and there were times where I tucked my map away and used my hands to heave myself upwards, scrambling inelegantly up Lining Crag. There was a path, though it wasn't obvious to me until I was at the top and looking back at what I'd missed, the route now visible between the unevenly exposed rocky outcrops.

The Parallel Path

I'd come as close as I'd get on this walk to Scafell Pike. The exact measurement of the pike's highest point shifts from season to season because the top is buried under metres of shattered rock and gravel but is generally agreed to be around 978 metres, which makes it the highest mountain in England. It was donated to the National Trust in 1919 by its then owner, Lord Leconfield. When he gave it away, he said the donation was in memory of the Cumbrian men who had died in the Great War, and the sheer scale of his sacrifice – divesting himself of an entire mountain – was meant in some way to echo theirs. The day was warm and bright but there was something shadowy about the pike: I looked upwards and knew it would be cold up there, the stones on the summit slack and shifting, the wind a chilly sparring partner. The pike carried its own quietness; heavy and observant, a suitable payment for countless deaths. This was one of the views I was climbing for, but it felt more accurate to say that I had slowly exposed myself by moving into *its* view, rather than, on hauling myself up Lining Crag, managed to achieve a better view of Scafell. Though of course that's wrong too: the most affecting thing about the mountain is that it gazes indifferently at nothing.

Dorothy Wordsworth lived in Grasmere for a long period of her life and was no stranger to a high place. In October 1818, with her friend Mary Barker and a guide, she climbed Scafell Pike. This is an early recreational climb – mountaineering was still in its infancy – and she and Mary might have been the first women to undertake it. Her written account of the journey was published as part of a larger collection of sketches about walking by her brother William, the implication being that it was his work – though this may have been at her request. The way she writes about both the climb and the view privileges not the might of the mountain or the awesome view from the top of it, but the small detail glimpsed near-at-hand. At the top she remarks not on the amazing sights below, but about the colour of the moss and lichen growing on the exposed rocks. But why should the steep drop down to the Easedale Valley, the lake at Grasmere reduced to a glittering blue puddle, be a more spectacular sight than the skipping insects I observed skating around on the surface tension of water caught between clumps of grass in a fellside bog?

Critics suggest this perceptual angle is supposed to be a specifically feminine way of engaging with the world, and distinct from the more masculine accounts of rock climbers listing the names of everything distant they could now see, turning seeing into naming, which is a kind of owning. This careful way of seeing is also related to an anxiety about safety and comfort and a sensitive awareness of vulnerability. Those who already know that the world has not been specifically designed for their comfort train themselves to notice the loose stone in the path and to imagine what might be crouching behind that low wall. Those whose work involves designing and maintaining places of care and comfort for others also see the world in this way, and some of Dorothy's work involved making a home for her brother, and later for his wife and their children. She knew about detail, about the unglamorous precision and persistence of hospitality. Her work prefigures the writing of Nan Shepherd, who in her own account of walking in the Cairngorms, expressed this type of bodily small-scale noticing and linked it specifically with walking: 'my eyes are in my feet'.

The way care teaches you to see was something I'd already learned, and in this place too. When I was seventeen, I'd walked along the screefalls of Wast Water's southern edge with Ben. Wast Water is the deepest of not only the Lake District's lakes, but the entire country, and tucked into Scafell Pike's southwestern slopes. Unprepared and daft, Ben and I had embarked on the hike not really understanding what it would be like to navigate the screes. The footpath runs along a steeply sloping edge that drops straight into the water and is made of countless pieces of shattered stone: the result of centuries of ice, water and wind eroding the ancient volcanic rock the fells are made of. We walked high above the water but were able to see a few metres into it – as far as vision failed – and understand a little about how deep it was.

'Maybe we should undo the straps on our rucksacks?' I had suggested, about halfway along. I'd been picturing one or both of us skidding on the rock debris in our cheap shoes, falling into the water and being pulled helplessly to the bottom of the glacial lake by the waterlogged tent and sleeping bag tied to our overloaded rucksacks. My head is like this: a constantly running public information video goes on inside, reminding me that the world is dangerous, that a precise effort of care needs to be taken at all times. Ben found it easier to imagine us tiptoeing along the screes and getting to the campsite in one piece with a good story to tell; it was instinctive to him to trust in the innate friendliness of the world. Though the path is only around three miles long, it took us all afternoon: we were unfit city kids who didn't know what we were doing.

Later on, we'd sometimes bring up this walk and use it as evidence that each of our ways of doing things was right. It had been such an ordeal that I became determined that in future I'd look at the map more carefully, plan for the unexpected and always take a first aid kit. But Ben remembered that it had, after all, turned out fine in the end. We'd got to Wasdale Head eventually and it had been a great day. He drew the conclusion that worrying about anything that lay ahead was pointless. It felt to me as if there was a finite amount of worrying to be done and if we didn't share it out equally, he was leaving me to do more than my fair share. It was like carrying the camping kit: somebody had to do it. We never resolved it, and this was an argument I've carried on having with various other people in my life over the years: I'd tired myself out with it during the pandemic, constantly trying to prepare for the very worst thing to happen and trying to go toe-to-toe with the fragile, shattering thing the world had suddenly become.

There are other ways to look at the view. That spring, I'd tried to plan weekend training walks that took me up hills and fells in preparation for the high routes of Wainwright's walk and tried to find a less careworn way of seeing. Most of the guidebooks I consulted for these training walks promised a worthwhile view as some kind of reward for an uphill slog, and after one sweaty weekend ascent during which I grumpily wondered if the promised sight of the Lune Estuary was really worth the trouble, I read about Frank White, the 'space philosopher' who interviewed astronauts about what it was like to look down on the earth from space.

Many of these men had described a near mystical experience of connectedness and a tenderness for the fragility of the earth that White called 'the overview effect'. White said that this experience could be triggered not only by 'perceptual' stimulus like the sight of the earth from space, but 'conceptual' too, like the dizzy, small feeling you can get when considering an idea like infinity. I get a sense of it when trying to imagine both owning, then giving away, the highest mountain in the country. Was a search for a tender reckoning with fragility and connectedness and a reminder of the call to care the thing that led Wainwright so relentlessly upwards? Far from that sense of tenderness, the feeling I get from Wainwright and his love of the high places is one of mastery: the comfort that comes from looking down at things, of a Charles Atlas-style squaring up to the vastness of what lies before you.

At the top of Lining Crag, the way back had become obvious, the way forward, less so. There were no trees or bushes here but everything was green, covered in long and short grasses, moss on the rocks, flatter areas covered in grass so dense and neat it looked like lawns and turned out to be bogs. Grasmere and its lake were visible from here, the soft shapes of drumlins in the valley far below. But there was also a more immediate problem. I was lost. I shambled about a bit. My feet got wet. I stopped, changed my socks. My feet got wet again. I fumbled with the compass Clive had retrieved for me and tried to spot the fence posts and cairns that would show me the way, struggling to remember what I'd been taught about 'setting the map' and 'taking a bearing' at the mountain navigation course I'd attended in the spring.

Eventually, a little pile of stones snagged my attention and I was flooded with a foolish relief. I could have waited and asked another walker for help but doing the walk unaided still felt important. I crossed the boggy ground towards the next high place: Greenup Edge. You can get lost here too; head the wrong way and you'll end up in Wythburn Valley, which can add miles and hours on to the day, but I carried on heading east, avoiding the wrong path downwards and contouring around the edge until I reached the unmistakable fence posts where the low and high routes to Grasmere converged.

There was no pride here at making it all this way, or navigating a tricky part of the path, or getting only a little bit muddy when I could have gone knee deep if I hadn't remembered the trick I'd seen from a hiker on YouTube. (Watch out for places where the grass changes colour, and *never* walk on a patch of ground where the little yellow flowers of bog asphodel grow.) Instead of the noisy euphoria of self-satisfaction I felt on the big climb up Loft Beck the day before, there was only gratitude, because what might have been obvious all along suddenly became very clear to me: I was following a map I did not draw, along a route I didn't plan, using a compass someone else had taught me how to use.

As soon as I'd got my 'eye in', the ways in which I saw I was dependent on others proliferated. I was heading slowly towards another set of clean sheets I wouldn't have to launder and a hot dinner I wouldn't have to cook. My rucksack had been lent to me by a friend, who had dropped it off at my house a month earlier and told me about his own long walk along Offa's Dyke. He'd warned me about the way my feet would hurt for the first couple of hours of each day, and remembering that had helped me that morning, where it hurt just to get out of bed and take a few steps across the room to the shower. And of course – and this was probably the deciding factor that triggered my change in attitude – I was relying not only on Duncan, but also his mother, who would do some of our childcare over the next couple of weeks while I was – and there's no way of polishing this up – off on a jolly. The phrase 'to get your eye in' was a gift to be grateful for too: I'd first heard it from a birdwatcher who had described the moment in the hide where, with a patience and a willingness to notice the unobtrusive detail, a barren field will suddenly resolve itself into one clogged and writhing with life. My birdwatching friend had reminded me that seeing isn't passive but is something like walking; the eye is a muscle that can be trained and developed too.

I thought about the man who fitted my new boots. How he advised me to get some spare laces, and I thought that was probably a good idea – mainly for him, as it meant I would be spending a bit more money in the shop. I was awake enough to be ashamed of the thought when he threw them in for free, and I said thank you politely because I am always polite and have taught my children the rules of good manners too. But good manners aren't gratitude: one is an action, the other a feeling. Was I pleased enough and happy enough that Clive went out and retrieved my compass? Thirteen miles to retrace our steps, his eyes to the ground the whole way? This isn't quite about dependency – I would have been okay without the compass and in fact had already ordered another – but it is about how being given things, and I have been given such a lot, makes me feel. What is it about this that makes me afraid? Gratitude suggests a power dynamic: we're never only grateful, but grateful *to* and grateful *for*: it is a word that implies a relatedness, and a relatedness of a particular type – one that foregrounds vulnerability, which I understand as a need for care.

Gratitude requires something of us too. Clive has reminded me of how so much of a patient's 'treatment journey' involves that patient complying, making themselves available at a place and time of the GP's or hospital's choosing, being polite in the face of confusing or badly explained treatments, being grateful for medicine that tastes bad and makes you vomit, for procedures that humiliate and hurt, for treatments that make things worse before they're better. Chemotherapy, when viewed from the outside, seems to be all of these things. Clive knows that gratitude, in these circumstances, can be dangerously self-eliding and can grease the wheels of the machine that is torturing you. He'd taught me that when we require someone else to be grateful and expect their vulnerability and compliance as a reward for our work, what we're offering is not care, but control.

Clive has enjoyed telling me about the times he has insisted on knowing and remembering the first names of the nurses and doctors treating him. About his policy of wearing his day clothes when he is in the hospital and making sure, when he can, he is out of bed and about his business as soon as breakfast has been served. His business is making films, taking photographs, 'curating' his hospital room and properly, meaningfully *encountering* those around him. Clive will make himself inconvenient if he needs to; these little resistances also perform the work of care: in refusing to be merely a patient he returns the staff around him to something other than the roles that they perform. He asks the nurses about their health, about their families, about their burdens.

One night, a nurse lingered in his room, sharing what troubled her in a conversation so profound I will not repeat it here. This conversation delayed the nurse's work, or the conversation was her proper work, or it was Clive's proper work, done during a time that looked like medical retirement from his profession. The fluidity of this murky labour that happened in the small hours is care. Perhaps in the midst of a long shift where time and exhaustion turn people into tasks, the medical staff are a little grateful for the careful inconveniences Clive causes for them too.

The ridge route towards Helm Crag started at the fence posts and the alternative route, along the gently green Easedale Valley, was clearly visible to be looked down upon, other walkers softly picking their way along the banks of Easedale Beck. Up high, the walk isn't difficult; the track is wide enough for several to walk abreast in most places, and though there are a few boggy spots between the peaks that I was unfailingly accurate in finding, there are also plenty of places to sit down, take a drink of water and top up on the suncream. It took a couple of hours but I stumbled and picked my way towards Calf Crag and took the ridge walk along the Pike of Carrs, Moment Crag and Gibson Knott with my heart in my mouth. The view down to Grasmere's houses and shops was – as the book says it would be – breathtaking.

The last of the day's high places is Helm Crag, also known as the Lion and the Lamb. It is a low fell, nowhere near the highest Wainwright has ever been, and not even the highest point on the walk itself – but it is narrow, reached after a winding steep path turns into a short scramble, and the sense of standing on the edge left me precarious and vulnerable. The view is spectacular; the temptation is to spin slowly around and enjoy the bird's eye 360-degree vantage point on the fells – Blencathra and Helvellyn to the north, Great Rigg to the east, Silver How and Loughrigg to the south and High Raise back towards the west. I succumbed to this temptation not in spite of my fear (this wasn't bravery) but because of it – still hoping that effort would make me strong. At the top, I turned slowly, my fear of heights and low blood sugar causing my legs to shake violently. No matter how solid the ground beneath me was, waves of nausea told me I was moving and the ground became a rickety ladder, swaying in a strong breeze. It is not clear to me if I was having vertigo or a sublime experience, though I doubt even Grasmere issues them so predictably.

Clive's letter changed my thinking. I realised I was always more comfortable when, Charles Atlas-like, I swaggered through the world pleased by the fruits of my own labours, surveying the view before me as if I was solely responsible for it. This type of pleasure happens a lot when I am walking, especially if walking involves following a difficult trail or getting to the top of a big hill or getting in a certain number of miles by lunchtime. It is easy for me to focus on the effort, and though walking is hardly ultra-running or weightlifting, there is always a certain amount of effort involved. When I put the focus on my own work, enjoying something becomes a way of praising myself; my foresight for wanting it, my struggle in getting it, my good taste for appreciating it. The position here is of a looking down – there's some superiority, some sense of mastery, some sense of surveying the landscape below. But on the top of Helm Crag, I realised there's something deadening about viewing the world in that way: I'm not sure we get to awe without some gratitude, and I am not sure we can be nourished or changed by experiences we persist in believing we have solely authored for ourselves. And if Charles Atlas is to be believed, all power comes from sleep, and sleep is achieved by a letting go – a relaxation of effort, not an increase of it. On that day, walking shifts and becomes a way to balance these two truths: the steady micro-effort of putting one foot in front of the other and the persistent appreciation of my own dependence.

I clambered down a steep and crumbling path and tried to bring myself and my shaky legs back down to earth. I skidded and stumbled downwards, my hands and knees still trembling. The last part of the walk would be a gentle little traipse through the woods where Dorothy sat and waited while William paced, composing his poems. Just got to get there first, and my ankle really, really hurt. A saying came to me, one not specifically Northern but capturing something precise about Northern sensibility: I should be careful not to *get above myself*. All I'd done is walk up a hill. I was still only an hour's drive from home. This wasn't adventuring. There's more fine poetry and nature writing and tales of people going out to find themselves in a green corner of Cumbria than you can shake a stick at. No need to perpetrate more of it. My brain ran on like that and gratitude, which asked me to look outward and upward and placed me not in the mud, exactly, but reminded me of my earthbound and connected nature, brought a relief from it. I felt the tender pleasures of dependence and, as I eyed the bog insects by my boots and the bowl of the valley, marvelled, childlike, at the loveliness of all that I didn't create and would never master. Imagine being able to own then to give away a mountain? The thought became ridiculous again, though because I'd met my own hubris, my laughter became softer, more affectionate. The path zigzagged downwards through banks of ferns. I fell a few times, grazing the heel of one hand and disturbing white and brown birds I didn't have a name for, their wings clapping the air, the noise a relic of childhood: blown-up crisp packets, popping.

DAY FIVE

Walking and Mourning

Grasmere to Patterdale (8 ½ miles)

I was still limping on the bad ankle when I left Grasmere early the next morning. Wainwright is nice enough about the little town in his book, but in interviews and later publications he made no secret of the fact he thought the place was spoiled, referring to it as 'Lakeland Babylon' and moaning about it being too busy, clogged with cars and become a high-end tourist trap ready for visitors who have money to spend on the Wordsworth Experience. I'd watched him grumble about it on the documentary Eric Robson had made about the Coast to Coast Walk in the 1980s, seemingly oblivious to the fact that some of the tourists that irritated him so much had been brought to the area by his own books.

Wainwright is taking his place as part of a fine literary tradition of opinionated guides, possessive about the places they describe. William Wordsworth himself published a Lakeland guidebook anonymously in 1810 that was reissued in the mid-1830s. *A Guide Through the District of the Lakes* includes a description of the route up 'Scawfell pike' that was cribbed from Dorothy's letter about her own ascent, and another about a journey from Grasmere to Ullswater taken from her diary entry about their trip. Though the book is aimed at tourists wanting to visit the Lakeland fells (and sold well to them: the book went through several impressions and reprints over the next twenty-five years), Wordsworth also complains about the way humans have ruined the landscape by painting their cottages the wrong colour or planting trees in unnaturally neat rows.

It isn't only Grasmere that Wainwright grumbles about. Most of the places Eric and 'A.W.' pass through in the documentary don't pass muster. Wainwright is perpetually, consistently disappointed. The Mardale Valley was better before the Manchester Water Board got to it. Crackpot Hall at Keld had a roof on the last time he saw it and the building has disintegrated far too quickly for his liking. The loss of the lead industry that had sent the inhabitants of Swaledale off across the North of England towards Durham's mines or Lancashire's textile mills in a kind of Yorkshire diaspora was another tragedy. For a man who liked solitude, even the abandoned emptiness of the Honister slate mine (the Robson documentary was filmed long before the skylines, mine tours and slate shop moved in) were remarked on as a special point of sadness: we see Wainwright imagining the miners, long gone now, and it looks as if he is in pain.

It's easy to dismiss Wainwright as nothing more than a reactionary. He provides plenty of evidence for that in his final book, *Ex-Fellwanderer* where, distracted from the task of writing about his walks, he opines about the deficiencies of modern culture and suggests capital punishment as a solution to society's ills. In the documentary, his gruff complaining becomes funny: Robson has to work hard to get conversation out of Wainwright, his only enthusiasm being for his pet topic: *things aren't what they used to be.*

The Parallel Path

The man can only bring himself to crack a smile when ushered into the Coast to Coast chippy at Kirkby Stephen and served a plate of cod and chips. Hunter Davies, Wainwright's biographer, suggests the only reason Wainwright decided to participate in the documentary was that the BBC had promised to hire quad bikes to get him up to the isolated spots he could no longer reach by walking.

What I see in this documentary is a man engaged in the work of mourning. He mourns the roof on Crackpot Hall, succumbing gradually to the elements. He mourns the working slate mine, the lead mining industry in general and the close-knit life in the villages it supported. He mourns a quieter, more 'unspoilt' Grasmere and, most of all, I see him mourning a body capable of taking him to those places without the assistance of the noisy and humiliating quad bike, the supervision of a film crew anxious about his health, the oversight of a production company.

On leaving Grasmere I limped the wrong way down the A591 for a mile because I'd failed to 'set the map' – which is the first and most basic instruction I'd been taught on the navigation course. Once I turned around and retraced my steps, I found the bridlepath leading off the road and steeply uphill towards the tarn at Grisedale pass. I followed it upwards for a few miles. The ground was uneven and there was a race being held that day with runners in shorts wearing numbers on their vests hurtling down towards me at speed. My slowness, which on the first days of the walk had felt gentle, meditative and dignified, started to feel clumsy and ungainly in comparison to the runners. At times their motion looked more like falling than running; a constant lurching as they threw themselves downwards, their feet slipping over loose stones, their arms and hands flying outwards to find a handhold in thin air, as very young babies do when you lift them from the cot. The path ran alongside a gill that bubbled and foamed. I'd planned to turn and enjoy the view back down to Grasmere but didn't want to get in anyone's way so went on slowly, against the flow of the prevailing traffic, until I reached the tarn.

Wainwright calls Grisedale Tarn 'a large sheet of water in a bowl formed by bare hills'. His utilitarian description captures something of the bleakness of this place, the suddenly exposed water – black and uninviting – overlooked by the craggy eastern edges of the Helvellyn range. I watched geese gather and bother each other on the opposite edge, worrying at the wet long grass on the tarn's outskirts. I counted the runners as they were ticked off on a clipboard by stewards in high-vis vests, disappearing down the track I'd just come up. I found myself waiting for a gap in the traffic and a camera angle that would allow me to photograph this lonely spot as if nobody else were there. I couldn't find it, so I took off my boots and inspected the bad ankle, which was swollen but not getting worse, strapped it up with bright pink tape and ate my sandwiches. I'd been looking forward to eating and waiting here, imagining that as there were only eight miles to fit into the day, I'd be able to spend an hour or more at the tarn. Instead, the runners thundered by at regular intervals, calling and cheering and high fiving the stewards as they hurtled past. One of the stewards had a megaphone and used it to shout encouragement. The flow of runners showed no signs of drying up and I began to feel a distinctly Wainwrightian sense of offended ownership. It was as if the gill I'd been walking up, the tarn I'd just arrived at, every blade of grass and cairn and crumbling sheepfold I'd seen along the way was mine. I was no tourist: I'd *walked here* and because I'd walked here this had become my garden and my slow and solitary peace was being disturbed by trespassers. I got sick of myself, tied my laces and moved on.

Erling Kagge – a better walker than most of us by all measures (he was the first person to reach both the North Pole, the South Pole and the top of Mount Everest on foot) – learned, while testing his kit and preparing for a polar expedition in Iqaluit (a town in the northeast Canadian Arctic), about an Inuit tradition. If you're in such high emotion that you can't control your feelings, 'you are asked to leave your home and walk in a straight line through the landscape until your anger has left you. You then mark the point at which your anger is released with a stick in the snow.' The world is not just a dumping ground for feelings we don't like having, but the concept of measuring our griefs not by time, but space, appealed to me.

I wasn't really so many miles away from the house I'd left: Grasmere is only an hour's drive away from home. How many miles would I have to walk before I was ready to put my own stick into the ground? What would a ten-mile tantrum look like? A 192-mile mid-life funk? The lockdown rules about exercise outside the house had only allowed me to place a stick in the ground, so to speak, half an hour away from home. That got me as far as the Lune Viaduct some days, other days a nature reserve on the other side of town. I'd found other ways to weigh and measure my walking. While I was out, I listened to audiobooks, often using my one monthly Audible credit to purchase the longest book I could find in the hope that it would last me the month. The Audible edition of *Being and Time* by Martin Heidegger was nearly twenty-five hours long. I told myself I'd listen to it for one hour every day during my circular lockdown walk and once the book was done, the pandemic would be over and I would have come to some understanding of the nature of existence and death and a plan for how to manage being-towards my end.

It was overambitious of me.

On the north edge of the tarn, the route splits into two again: the hard path zigzags up Dollywaggon Pike towards Helvellyn and Striding Edge and the easier downhill route drifts along the Grisedale Valley, downwards towards Patterdale. The runners were coming up through the valley – they'd probably started at Glenridding – which was a point in favour of Helvellyn, but I never planned to take the high route: my ankle and my nerves were in no shape for it, and Helvellyn, all the guidebooks say, is not a fell for a beginner to tackle alone. Yet I dithered. Wainwright is strict about it: 'descend to the outlet of the tarn and make a decision'. I knew I'd only have this day once and, in the moments before I chose, the day was a field large enough to hold the possibility of everything – all routes, all views, all possible happy meetings and mishaps. When I chose, the other path would evaporate and something important would die. Knowing that this is the nature of all days is not news to anybody, but it mattered to me differently in that moment. The walk was making me pay attention: choosing *this* means letting go of *that* and letting go is always a little loss.

There's a famous stone near here my guidebook had warned me to look out for, and I saw many of the runners pausing to lean on it, catch their breath and glance at the inscription as they passed. The words were faded and almost unreadable, but I knew it was a poem by Wordsworth about his brother John, and that the stone marked the place where the two brothers said goodbye to each other as John left William and Grasmere and went to sea, never to return. I'd got impatient the day before, wondering if most of Cumbria would be stuffed with stones and plaques in memory of the dead – we were well on the way to filling up the entire world with a carved-in-stone card catalogue of those who had moved through it. But that day, the memorial landed differently with me, and seemed like a stick in the ground not to mark the end of a life or a relationship, but the start of a time of mourning. I wondered which route Clive would choose. I reckoned I could guess but banished the thought quickly because it irritated me. I was on my way, I thought, to becoming one of those women that, in my twenties, annoyed me. Handwringing, indecisive, moaners. Always seeking advice and reassurance. Terminally anxious and regretful. Nostalgia addicts.

I hope I'd be gentler with the paralysis a fork in the road provokes if I witnessed it now. It had become clear to me that I had been assigning this irritation that regularly bubbled up in me to the cumulative effects of too much work, a lack of time alone and too many people needing too many things from me. But yesterday's tender realisation of how much I had been given and how bad I was at receiving it meant that the alibi for my prickliness I had been giving myself had worn thin. And here I was, alone, doing what I wanted, every single runner that passed me minding their own business and wanting nothing from me. Even the land itself – with its innocent memorial plaques and stones, its endlessly forking paths – had the capacity to get on my nerves. There was something else going on here: some loss or lack I was bearing, something I wasn't even allowing myself to know that I wanted.

I took the valley path and joined what was nearly a procession of walkers slowly picking their way down a very rocky and uneven path by the side of Ruthwaite Beck, in the shadow of St Sunday Crag. Up high, walkers who chose differently scuttled their way along the ridge, their tiny silhouettes bobbing against the brightness of the sky.

A couple of miles down the path there's a little stone house, once a traveller's resting place, now locked up and bolted and owned by Sheffield University's mountaineering club. There isn't even an outside tap, but the sun was high, the house cast an oblique rectangle of shade on to the ground and I sat in it like an overheated dog, consulted my map and practised the exercises I'd been taught about measuring distance with the edge of my compass marked up with millimetres. You can use this measurement to calculate time to arrival by knowing how many paces you do per 100 metres (72) and adjusting average walking speed for incline and load. It takes longer than you'd think to walk a millimetre but knowing how long it should take you to reach the next landmark can help stop you getting lost. Even though the way was obvious, I spent a bit of time over this, doing the sums in my head and not my phone. I needed the practice: there were some harder navigational challenges coming up and I had such a fear of getting lost.

I wasn't alone in taking advantage of the shade: some of the runners had stopped here too, panting and sucking water from the spouts of their bottles, or leaning over, their hands pressed against their thighs and retching noisily as they tried to catch their breaths. The runners poured upwards through the valley, and I imagined an inexhaustible supply of them released from a spring down at Glenridding. They'd be at Grasmere to have a pub tea and catch their lift home before I'd reach Patterdale. That spring, as I tried to learn about walking by reading about it, I'd written Nan Shepherd's quote about competitions reducing experiences to the status of 'mere games' on a Post-it note and pinned it to the board above my writing desk. I have always pretended to be too high-minded for competitions I have no chance of winning. I sat on the stony ground, leaned against the cool wall of the house, and opened the letter from Clive that had been waiting for me at Grasmere.

The note was typed on the back side of a photograph of a huge old tree. Its gnarled and misshapen trunk takes up most of the image, its lower branches heavy and drooping and propped up by big planks that have been wedged into place. The crown of the tree is out of shot and because the photo has been printed in black and white and the sun was so high and bright, it took me a moment to focus and see that the tree is in a cemetery. The stones are crooked, half covered in ivy and drifts of leaf litter. The note begins,

Walking and Mourning

'Sometimes, walking, I think I really *am* alive,' and tells a peculiar story about walking in farmland outside Lancaster in bright midsummer.

The timeframes Clive moves between in this letter are complicated: there's a walk he's just taken up Little Fell, near where we live – a walk he might have taken just before sitting down to write to me, though it isn't clear. This is a walk he's taken many times before (I think he's describing a similar route to the one he'd taken when he'd found the suitcases and the Charles Atlas course), and as he tells me about it, it starts to overlap with the memory of some other walk in some other place, then a conversation with a farmer he's known for a while that prompts a memory about a different day and time again. It was hard to follow so I stopped trying and enjoyed the mind's porousness, the way times and places collapse into one while walking. I came to understand that this is one of the things Clive means by the sensation of aliveness he often speaks about: the way a moment spent in walking can hold so much more than itself, the way there can be no difference, as the feet slowly, slowly, cover their distance, between now and the last time he came through here, or the time before that.

There's also something indivisible about the teeming life Clive witnesses on his midsummer stroll: the 'curlews are going crazy, wild and dipping in tight circles'; the 'young kids belting up and down in great diesel tractors weighed down with black plastic bales of the good stuff and piles of grass for silage'; 'the air, the fields, the sky are all so alive, and these labourers who are capitalising on the longest days of the year, are a seamless part of the landscape'; these joyful summer sights – and the signs of sickness, death and decline that he welcomes into awareness in the same way. There's a farmer he knew a long time ago, now sick and in the aftermath of a stroke, 'confined to his upright, threadbare chair'. There's a meeting with a 'blind sheep dog', no longer working, but just along for the ride with his owner, who is shifty with guilt as he and Clive watch the curlews together. It turns out the birds aren't wild with the rapture of the summer's day, but mad with grief because, according to the farmer, 'it can't be helped and every year it's inevitable that ground nesters . . . get caught up in the machines.'

The moment of walking had become spacious enough to hold what is and what is lost, what lives full of youth and exuberance and what declines, grows sick, dies, is murdered. Clive ends the letter by showing me the birds in mourning: 'just standing on the lopsided walls', and remembering his first girlfriend's twin sister, who fell to her death in the threshing blades of a combine harvester. The letter is vivid, curious, strange – an act of mourning itself, or celebration. I turn it back over and examine the photograph, trying to be the best reader or listener I can be for my friend, but on that day it is too hard to look at the vibrant life of summer that Clive wants to show me – the lively profusions of the working countryside – and not be overwhelmed by the mourning curlews, the blind sheep dog, the farmer whose life is now spent in lamenting lost times.

The path down towards the next navigation point – Glenamara Park – is long. However quickly I walked eastwards, most of what my mind did when it wandered that day was to haul me back westwards, taking me home.

* * *

Walking and Mourning

When I moved away from Preston to go to university, I planned to never go back, but when I discovered I was pregnant with my daughter, Ben and I came back together – it was his hometown too. Nobody in either Cambridge or Oxford, the cities where we'd lived in the intervening years, had ever heard of Preston so it became a place that didn't quite exist, except in the way we remembered it. We used to say 'near Manchester' or 'near Blackpool' or 'south of the Lake District' and took private bets on who among our new acquaintances would know which part of the anonymous North we were referring to. The return happened so quickly after the grand leaving to go study 'down south' that I sometimes made jokes about it. My friends were starting their graduate trainee positions and internships and master's degrees, and I got knocked up and sped back home as if I was a dog on a retractable leash. The slightly cruel, self-deprecating joke was more acceptable than the truth, which is that I didn't really like it down south. It was too flat and windy in Cambridge, and the water in Oxford tasted weird. I wanted to go home, and I wanted to have a baby too.

That same year we came home, which was 2004, Clarks the shoe shop did an ad campaign featuring a young woman with nice hair and black tights gallivanting around Preston Flag Market in her new boots. The strapline of the advert was *Preston is my Paris* and the point of it seemed to be that this stylish young woman's solidly clad feet would have absolutely no problem at all with the rigours of Northern street paving. We wondered if the advert had run nationally, or if there were versions of it set all over the place, each town having their own advert, because at first we could not

The Parallel Path

imagine what use the rest of the world would have for Preston. They'd made it just for us? Was there a *Macclesfield is my Madrid* out there too? A *Blackburn is my Berlin*? We decided not, and wondered what it was about Preston that made an advert like this funny.

If there was a joke and we Prestonians weren't being over-touchy about it, it was definitely at the expense of the young woman in the advert who was having a rare old time of it in the city centre. Here's a woman who, unlike me, is able to take pleasure in the state of wanting, and is capable of enjoying what she gets. We see her getting dressed, trying on lots of different outfits, looking at fancy cakes through a window, gadding about in front of the Harris Library and Museum – the city's most prominent landmarks. The narrative shape of the thing is loudly telegraphed: pride always comes before a fall. Walking might coax us into imagining we know the world and shape our routes through it according to our will, but falling reminds us we're merely passengers on a turning earth, and have never quite perfected the art of keeping ourselves upright.

In Preston there's a civic logo known as the lamb and flag that shows St Wilfrid's lamb with the initials 'PP' underneath. This image is everywhere in Preston, including rather ignominiously on a lot of the manhole covers and litter bins. We tell ourselves that the initials stand for 'Proud Preston' and that this is where the city's motto comes from, but the old-timers will remind you it really means *princeps pacis*, for the lamb, the prince of peace. Pride is like that: something that both forgets and contains a gentler, softer thing. The Prestonian in the advert was, it was implied, a woman who had forgotten herself, who had ideas above her station.

Walking and Mourning

The Clarks advert wasn't a million miles away from the Boddingtons Bitter adverts that ran in the early 1990s, Enrico Caruso's 'O Sole Mio' warbling away as Anna Chancellor enjoys herself in a gondola in Venice, looking sexy and glamorous. She spies a good-looking man with a pint in the next gondola over, swipes the pint, necks it and smudges her lipstick as she wipes the foam from her top lip. Here's another woman who sees something she likes the look of, reaches out her hand and takes it. The tension of incongruity is relieved when the camera pans out and we see that we're not in Venice after all: they have canals in Manchester too. Ben and I liked this advert better. Sure, one reading of it might be that putting feminine glamour and European culture together with Northernness was so incongruous as to be hilarious. Imagine a Mancunian woman in an actual dress, sitting in an actual gondola, enjoying herself in Venice! That's why the PG Tips adverts with the chimpanzees wearing clothes were also funny, but our Anna never left home, you only thought she did, so the joke is on you. The other reading of the Boddies advert and the one that I like is this: you can put a Northern woman anywhere, wearing anything, and she will be entirely who she is – comfortable with her wanting – no matter how acceptable or not it might be to others. The Northern woman will never forget herself.

This woman in the Clarks advert, which was broadcast a decade later, seems to have forgotten herself. A grave error. She looked the type too – a bit flighty and insubstantial – twirling around in her daft boots and beanie. A bit of a wally. A woman who might even be tempted to try a baguette at some point. The soundtrack to the Clarks advert is 'Mimi' by Maurice Chevalier, a song sung in French about a man so in love he's got his shoes on the wrong feet and his trousers buttoned up backwards – the idiot – and the song, this silly girl's inner soundtrack, is interrupted by the exaggerated Northern accent of an old woman who bumps into her and brings the kid back down to earth. 'Are you all right, love?' The implication is that she is off her rocker. The camera pans away from her and what might be Paris dissolves into what it is: a Northern market town largely unknown until some shoe shop decided to take the piss out of it. We see a couple of kids eating chips out of a cone, two women holding carrier bags – everyone staring at dreamy shoe-girl in derision. *You are most certainly not in Paris and you should bloody well stop acting like you are.*

A version of the advert that made no sense without the context of the story ran in women's magazines showing the woman from the advert admiring her shoes on the steps of the Harris Library with the strapline printed below: *Preston is my Paris*. We'd moved back to Preston to find friends of ours a couple of streets over had torn the page out and put it up on the wall in their bathroom. This seemed to me a specifically Prestonian angle to take on the matter: it is not possible for someone to take the piss out of you if you enjoy it, and you can't be accused of getting above yourself if any dream you had was only a foolish impression of a dream, for entertainment purposes only. I'd grown up seeing the two interlinked Ps on lampposts and buses, but pride and an unashamed desire for comfort and pleasure would always be a complicated thing, based in not making too much visible effort, remembering where you came from, and never, ever imagining you could pretend to be someone you weren't and not get found out.

Walking and Mourning

Before I knew anything about psychogeography I understood that I did not own nor have a hand in shaping the places I moved through but had been formed by them early and there was a moral imperative involved in remaining as I had been created, though the way I had been created was more complex and beautiful and more related to the world than people who were not from our place would ever see or give me credit for. Proud Prestonians got the joke and were the butt of it at the same time. This kind of pride is not easy, it is not simple, and it is not unknowing, though we must take care it should look like all of these things.

Coming home to Preston was specifically intense because I did not only come home to the town, but to the street. Finding a house to rent while one of us was thirty-four weeks pregnant and the other was still looking for work was not straightforward. The house we moved into was on the street where my father lived and where I had lived with him until my parents' relationship ended very suddenly, when I was thirteen. The street was close and narrow, two rows of tightly packed terraces with people's living room windows staring at each other, front doors opening directly into the street. When I'd learned to ride my bike it had been on cobbles, though sometime in the 1990s a truck had come and covered them up with tarmac, which was already in a bad state. My dad lived on the evens side, us the odds, and the rented house was a mirror image of the one I'd grown up in: when I went to the toilet in the night, I turned the wrong way on the upstairs landing and bumped into the wall because something in me had returned to the wrong house – the one over the road – the one I hadn't set foot inside in over a decade.

The Parallel Path

We unpacked. Ben built a cot, and we watched the 2004 Olympics. We were getting ready for the next part of our lives, and it was already becoming obvious we'd be doing that separately, together as parents but not as a couple. I got bigger. The midwife visited and asked what my plans were for the birth. I began to dream about moving house again and not being able to get the settee out of the front door because it had somehow become too big to fit. I dreamed about getting a new job – and that job being to fill a huge bucket with milk using only a teaspoon. In the fortnight before the baby was born, I walked – to pass the time and to bring the labour on. Once our daughter was born and turned out to be one of those babies that didn't sleep, I walked even more: she would rest in a sling and, with a bit of manoeuvring, I could even feed her while she was strapped on to my chest. The slowness of walking, spending an entire afternoon going nowhere in particular, being held in relationship to the same street, the same tree-lined avenue on the park, the same route backwards and forwards to pay my rent, returned me to home. The edges of Preston hadn't changed much in the years I'd been away studying, but I had, and pacing the alleys returned me to myself, like a library book being slotted back into its correct place on the shelf.

The last few miles of the track towards Patterdale were undemanding enough to allow me to indulge my nostalgia, walking along obvious routes through fields of sheep and on tarmacked roads cutting through a pine plantation. If I'd taken the Helvellyn route, my mind might have wandered in a different direction, but those moments were as lost to me now as the ones I'd just experienced. I got into Patterdale in the middle of the afternoon, much earlier than I expected and long before I could check into my bed and breakfast for the evening. There wasn't much there – a couple of pubs and a shop famous for having a cashpoint and being the first to sell the original copies of Wainwright's book. I'd planned to stock up on sweets and postcards, but it was closed: another Covid casualty. So I found a pub to wait in and drank three pints of lime and soda, one after the other, and recorded the background music and chatter going on around me for Clive.

I felt guilty for gobbling up his letter – intricate and beautiful and strange – and having nothing to return, no evidence of my reading and attention. The best I could do was this noise: chatter and cutlery clattering and the barman talking to someone about the traffic along the A592, and someone else asking where the red squirrels were this year, and a fruit machine playing an electronic jingle, and the muted sounds of a television overhead playing some shopping channel, ignored. I put the phone on the table and held my breath and tried to drink my soda water quietly so there'd be no evidence, when Clive played the sound recording back, that I'd been there at all.

I had a phone, a book in my bag (Basho's *The Narrow Road to the Deep North* – a gift from a friend), there were newspapers in a pile on the edge of the bar: plenty available to distract me from the moment I was in if I wanted it. But Clive's letter and catching a glimpse of what really lay under my own anger that day – an unfulfilled longing for something I still could not name – had altered me a little and I was more content than I had been to just turn up to the moment without distraction. Walking had provided a lesson in what the work of mourning is: making a home in the present for what has been lost through either time or carelessness. I came to know mourning – an engagement with wanting what was not there – as a work of care and courage. Easier to be annoyed and irritable, closed off and taciturn, than to be sad about not having what I did not yet know how to ask for. There were hours to kill, and I was glad to be off my feet and happy enough to sit and listen to the sounds of the pub going on around me. I may have saved Helvellyn's Striding Edge for another day, but the truth is that I may not go that way again.

Walking's paradoxes multiplied as I paid attention to them: each step emptied the moment ready to provide a welcome for the new. Every step was also a goodbye. As for our steps, so for our days. There's no going home, not really – and of course we don't ever leave. My walking had helped me to understand some of the things Clive had said about the intensity that living as honestly with death as he's been able to has given him. Though I didn't know Clive before he was ill, I suspect this ability to welcome whatever comes – whether that be the wild profusion of summer or the can't-be-helped grief of mother curlews and blind sheepdogs – is more to do with who he is than what cancer has required of him. I can't imagine him struggling with boredom and restlessness the way I do: the wholehearted nature of his curiosity is one of the things about him I am most envious of. It is an ability to be at home inside each moment. A way of inhabiting all the homes – especially the ones lost – the time spent walking have to offer.

DAY SIX

A Spare Macaroon

Patterdale to Shap (17 miles)

When I left Patterdale I took a route that was roughly familiar to me: up the side of Patterdale common on an uphill but paved and well-maintained path to Boredale Hause, which is a flat, high piece of grassland that forms a pass and is the place where several trails meet: by the standards of Cumbria, it is almost a busy junction. I'd been here on one of the mountain navigation training days I'd taken in the spring: this was the place I'd learned to take a bearing and set my map. Because of this, finding Angle Tarn, a flat glossy sheet of water held in the grip of Buck Crag and Satura Crag, was easy enough: I was even asked for directions from a group of women who had come up from Patterdale behind me and become tangled in the profusion of paths at the Hause. Being someone else's expert, if only for a few seconds, was thrilling. This is the way I habitually am with people: wanting to help, wanting to be useful. I got out my compass and detained them for some minutes, demonstrating how the tracks through the grass related to the dotted lines on the map. 'You can take a bearing from anything,' I said, 'even the corner of a sheepfold.' I was showing off: this is exactly the phrase the trainer had used with us when he brought us up this way.

People camp at the tarn and even swim out to one of its little islands and spend the night sleeping with the geese.

The Parallel Path

But it was still early in what would be a long day, and I passed by it quickly, stepping over piles of goose shit on the path. A hot bath the night before had done the trick: my ankle felt great, my legs strong, the morning was cool and breezy and I knew where I was going and what I was doing. Today would be an important day because I'd climb up (and down) Kidsty Pike, which was the highest point on the whole walk, and emerge from the eastern side of the Lake District National Park.

After Angle Tarn, the track is clearer and follows a drystone wall, making it easy enough to navigate. The first time I was there, on the navigation course, I saw deer – or rather, I'd seen indistinct flitting shadows – tricks of the light – rushing up and down Buck Crag. The navigation trainer noticed me squinting and told me I was seeing herds of teenage fawns. Now I was alone, I stopped and looked for them again, but if they were there that day, I couldn't find them. Far below, Hayeswater sparkled, the water collected in the rut of the landscape like dregs of tea in a tilted green cup. It's a little lake, not to be confused with the bigger Haweswater Reservoir, which I'd walk alongside later. I passed a dead sheep lying against a wall. It had been there long enough that it had started to fall apart: a ribcage, a fleece, a jaw studded with blackened, serrated teeth. There was a cloud of flies and a bad smell, so I hurried away along the track, which turned softer and grassier as Kidsty Pike came into view. I climbed, counting my steps, trying to keep my pace steady and even, enjoying my ankle not hurting, and the pleasurable pull in my thigh and calf muscles. It got hotter.

* * *

A Spare Macaroon

The summit of Kidsty Pike is subtle and marked out by a rickety-looking cairn that is difficult to distinguish from the rocky and uneven terrain at the top. The day was bright – perfect conditions for admiring what came next. Haweswater shone back at me, deep and blue. I'd walk the length of it that afternoon. Further out, some industrial works on the outskirts of Shap – steam spouting from tall chimneys, lorries coming and going. Beyond that, the grey and purple shoulders of the Pennines. I felt a little afraid about how much further there was to go and concentrated instead on the next few steps. Getting down involved slipping and scrambling down an awkward path. The cumulative effects of many booted feet had gouged great holes into the dried-out and stony soil, my own feet kicking up dust that stuck to my sunscreen and insect repellent and made my eyes itch. I worried about my duff ankle and went slowly, taking some parts of the descent on my backside. It took a full hour before I was at the second stage of the day's walk, the bottom end of Haweswater Reservoir.

Before I set off, one of my friends had told me I might have a chance of seeing a golden eagle somewhere around Haweswater, and if I had binoculars, I should think about taking them. I didn't, but kept my eyes peeled as the sun rose higher and I slowly made my way along the shore. There had been a breeding pair of golden eagles in the area for a long time, though ten years ago or more the female had disappeared, leaving the male eagle alone. He and the RSPB's volunteers they encouraged to keep an eye out for her had watched for many years, but she never came back. Nobody would be searching for her anymore; that eagle must be over twenty years old now and had probably died.

The RSPB had since leased a couple of farms in the Mardale Valley from United Utilities, which owned the reservoir itself and much of the farmland around it. The RSPB were trying to attract the eagles back to the area. I can't look at these places as an ornithologist or a naturalist or a geologist and I quickly gave up taking pictures of interesting plants and rock formations I meant to find the names of later. A quick google of what I could see wouldn't turn me into an expert, wouldn't help me to encounter where I was more fully. I could learn more in the months to come, but how to invite in the stillness I had allowed myself a glimpse of yesterday and be here today, just as I was?

It felt impossible to walk along the shoreline of this reservoir, attending to what is there – the breath-caught shocking blueness of it all – and not try to see or imagine what was not there. In the late 1920s the government granted the Manchester Water Board permission to dam and flood the valley and create a reservoir that would provide Manchester with drinking water. The houses were evacuated, the village church dismantled and rebuilt elsewhere, the bodies in the cemetery exhumed and reburied at Shap, where they remain. The reservoir now provides 25 per cent of the Northwest's drinking water. The summer I walked the Coast to Coast was shaping up to be one of the hottest in years, and the water level in the reservoir was lower than usual.

Clive had water on his mind today too. In the first part of today's letter, he remembered a walk we took together where I tested the surface of a boggy area in Bowland with the toe of my boot, poking at the wobbling surface, the ground like nothing so much as a 'water filled blister'. It is a moment that has stayed with him. 'What would have happened if you had popped the surface? How could I have explained your disappearance?' It is a melancholy thought – imagining my friend, who spends more time than he'd like watching those who love him imagine a future without him, taking a turn at imagining me, suddenly not there. Perhaps this is what friendship is – a delicate testing of some surface tension between two people – a wondering what the rest of the walk would be like if your companion was not there. Worse, or better?

In another couple of weeks, with no break in the weather, the village of Mardale Green, submerged in a grave that is as shallow as it is watery (and referred to by some as a 'Lakeland Atlantis'), will be exposed to those who pass by. The humpbacked bridge and remnants of the old walls will creep out of the water like stone ghosts. Most of the houses are shattered beyond recognition because, once the village was evacuated, the Royal Engineers moved in and used the buildings to test their explosives. Wainwright came here sometimes to look at the water and remember the old village, mourning especially the loss of the pub, which was demolished brick by brick. I didn't see the ruins on the day that I walked the length of the reservoir, but I did see the crusty tidemarks on the shore where the water had receded, the cracked and dried-out mud, the yellowing and thirsty grasses and reeds high above the waterline. Beneath the surface, the broken edges of the old village hunched deep in the blue.

Back in Patterdale earlier that morning, the landlady of the B&B had shown me a large textured map pinned up in the hallway and outlined to me the route I'd be taking. She'd said the day would be long and hard, the weather was forecast to be very hot and I should take more water than I thought I needed. It might help, she suggested, to think of the walk as coming in three sections: the first from Patterdale to Kidsty ('have your lunch up there,' she'd advised, and I didn't); the second down from Kidsty, across a little bridge and along the whole length of Haweswater, a 'nice easy stretch'; then from the top of Haweswater ('you'll go through Burnbanks but there's nothing there') through several fields and across many stiles and little packhorse bridges, to Shap. She'd traced her finger along the crooked diversions, bumps and ridges of that last section and I could see the mucky marks on the map where she and her guests had done this before: using the tips of fingers to trace the path their feet would take, as if this picture of the world was Braille. 'You have to get your head on straight here. Don't go thinking that once you do the reservoir you're finished: it's another few miles after that and that last stage is the hardest,' she'd said, helpfully. 'There's a good chippy in Shap, though.'

She was right: there was a relentless ease to the walk along the edge of the reservoir: just endless, slow trudging, the brightness of the sun coming off the water making me squint, a little scramble over a rockfall that covered the path but must have been there for decades because it was mentioned in one of my guidebooks. I want to say it was quiet here, but it wasn't – the air was thick with the lively din of birds swooping low over the water to catch insects and looping heavily overhead. The water was still but I heard regular plopping sounds I thought were fish jumping: I never saw them, only their traces, the ripples appearing after the sound and circling outwards until my eye could no longer catch them. It got hotter and hotter. I put suncream on, sweated it off, put it on again. Walking became sleepwalking: my feet knew what to do and the steady lurch of step, fall forwards, step again and the stretch and flex of muscles became something I only hazily observed.

When I was younger, I thought my body was some mechanical thing, like a crane, operated by a little man who lived in the sealed cab of my skull, controlling everything with an array of switches and levers. I don't believe that now, and walking reminds me what a strange idea that is. When I walk it feels not that the body is the mind's servant, but that the mind is, at best, only the body's passenger, a misty side effect, a by-product, like sweat and shit. After half an hour or so of walking along the reservoir path my usual inward chatter stopped and even my looking became different. I was no longer searching for the path nor measuring a distance nor counting my paces. My gaze became softer, less of a laser beam flickering over the landscape collecting useful or novel detail and moving on, but more receptive: the world started to come to me, what was 'out there' oozing inwards. I had tramped myself into a state that was both totally relaxed and pin-sharp alert, the mind finally content to fall into line and allow the body to lead with its own felt, silent intelligence.

This is another reason I enjoy walking alone: I can get myself into this state of mind with my dog (I can't know for sure, but I suspect dogs live in this state permanently), but walking with friends brings other, busier pleasures. This type of soft attentiveness comes with the slow clattering unfurl of typing at a keyboard on those days when it feels like I am watching a story emerge from my hands rather than writing one with my brain. I experience it during the careful repetition of difficult knitting or sewing, my fingers managing to do something I'd struggle to explain to someone else. And, on good days, during the present-but-absent state of careful and complete listening that sometimes happens in teaching: a double awareness of how students are sitting, breathing, how exactly their bodies are attending to what is happening in the workshop and how I might be totally there with them, but not at all in the way of what they want to do. There's no reason why a body shouldn't think, shouldn't come up with something new, why consciousness should be held in the head but not in the hands, the feet, the lungs. Walking reminded me of that truth, but like all states, it passed. I got to Burnbanks and, as promised, there was nothing there, and that final stretch needed some careful navigation, crossing farmland and choosing between equally likely-looking paths.

The second part of Clive's letter was about water too. He remembered the house he grew up in in Morecambe, growing up within sight of the sea. He nearly drowned three times, he writes, but the time he specifically wants to tell me about happened in 1981 – the year before I was born.

'Morecambe was awash with kids who had got into punk and couldn't get out of it – sniffing glue and downing cheap bottles of cider in bus shelters on the prom,' he writes. We've walked along that prom together, Clive showing me places where he'd lived and worked, adding another layer to a place I already know well. This is the generosity of friendship: it more densely populates your world. Now Clive tells me about three school friends who decided to 'liberate boat number 4 from the boating pool at the West End'. The boat is not meant for the open water of the bay – it's a 'yellow and red fibreglass thing, designed for tourists'. The three boys are aiming for Barrow, or the Isle of Man. Clive doesn't say how old these lads were. I imagine my son, thirteen, my daughter, eighteen, myself as a teenager, knowing the bravado and stupidity of those hinterland years and how thin the ice between childhood and adulthood can be. I know how this story will end. Clive tells it quickly, brutally, without flourish.

'Gary was spotted floating face down in Heysham Harbour by the skipper of the Belfast Ferry eight days later. Tony took another couple of weeks to reappear and was found over near Silverdale on the shoreline, hunkered down amongst the crabs and sandhoppers. Mounted police searched the area for Philip, who I think is still out there to this day.' The rest of the letter reflects on what it was like as Clive kept a kind of internal, solitary watch from his bedroom, waiting for the boys to come back. Clive's present is watchful and full of water too; he must drink pints and pints of it to 'flush out the muck I am force fed each day by the medics'. I got a sense that Clive was asking me to imagine him – still ruminating about those missing boys, scared and sensible, chugging gallons of water – his life a kind of afterlife to his near-miss moment, a watery existence accompanied by the 'bad things that bide their time in my body'.

By this time it was late afternoon. I'd drunk all the water I'd been carrying and had drunk the extra water I'd unwisely filled my bottle with from a spring on the edge of the reservoir. It was hotter than it had been at lunchtime up on Kidsty Pike and the insect repellent I'd put on my face was dripping into my eyes. On the banks of Haweswater Beck, the meadows had not been cut and the grass was waist high. The walkers who had been here before me had either trod lightly or had found another route; the path was not obvious. Neither were the boggy areas the long grass disguised: I found each of them the phenomenological way. Bog water is surprisingly cold, even on hot days. And it stinks. I pulled my boots free, wiped my eyes and trudged on. The water in the beck was flowing fast and was treacly with huge knots of crowfoot. There were more green fronds and white flowers on it than I'd ever seen before. I stopped to look, sank into another bog, and a horsefly landed and bit my hand. I kicked a nettle with a sodden boot and swore.

Clive's letter had made me think about a girl I knew at primary school. She was a year older than me and lived just around the corner so would do the walk to school with me and my mum sometimes. I'll call her Alice. A couple of weeks before Christmas, when I was ten years old and she was eleven, Alice died in a horrible accident. She'd been getting off the bus after Christmas shopping with her mother but as the doors of the bus had slid closed, the belt of her coat had become trapped and when the bus had set off, she'd been pulled under its wheels. Alice's grandmother lived on the same street as us and was a retired nurse. A while later we'd gone into her house: my mother took me because I'd fallen while climbing the wheelie bin to get up on to the back wall of our yard and she wanted her to examine me.

A Spare Macaroon

I was invited to sit on the settee, and Alice's gran went into the back kitchen and returned with a bandage wrapped in paper and a mug of water. She unwrapped the bandage, unrolled the first part of it and dunked it in the mug, then wrapped it around my ankle tightly. I wonder now if this was like the 'magic sponge' my friend's dad used to bring out – just a flannel wrung out in water – whenever any of us came off our bikes. Adults would often care for us like this while we played out, the neighbours and the relatives of friends ready to dole out sweets and stories and ice pops to the almost-communal children of the street. I had my foot up on the pouffe, and Alice's grandmother wrapped the bandage around my ankle and secured it with a safety pin she brought out from a little enamelled tin with pink flowers on the lid.

I'd been to Alice's gran's house before to ask her to sign sponsorship forms and deliver Christmas cards and spare Sunday dinners, but I had never been invited inside so I took the opportunity to look around at everything. My mum was standing in the vestibule, watching the medical treatment take place with her 'behave yourself' look on her face. As I'd already fallen off the bin trying to get up the wall and could have cracked my head open and so was in disgrace, I knew not to say anything when I saw, on the mantelpiece next to the enamel tin, the framed order of service from Alice's funeral. I recognised its blurry photocopied reproduction of Alice's school photograph, which because she was in her uniform, looked just like mine: royal blue V-necked jumper obviously handknitted, a white shirt, a yellow and blue striped tie.

I'd been to that funeral too – my first one ever – and though I'd been quiet as I was being bandaged, I must have

The Parallel Path

asked later why Alice's grandmother had the order of service framed in her living room instead of a real school photo like my granny had (like *everyone's* granny had). My mum told me there'd been some family fall out, a years-old argument, and though they lived so close to each other, Alice's mother and grandmother didn't speak and Alice had never been inside her own granny's house or sat on that floral sofa. 'And that's why she's got a soft spot for you,' my mum had said. It made sense to me at the time. Alice and I were both dark-haired girls with wobbly teeth, handknitted school jumpers and done-at-home fringes. My mum helped me back along the street – we were just four or five doors down – on my sore ankle, which must have been quite badly sprained because, thirty years later, it is sensitive and always the first thing to start hurting on long walks.

I don't remember any sense of mourning or grief in the days or weeks after Alice died, though I do remember my mum's manner when she told me was so delicate and gentle it let me know I was expected to be upset. There was a girl in my class whose dad had died, and she'd drawn a picture of him in his coffin in her News Book with zeds flying out of his open mouth like he was only sleeping, and she didn't cry either. At Alice's funeral I'd been more interested in the altar boys swinging incense from balls on chains than in the white coffin, which our class teacher had described to us in advance so that we'd know what to expect. In our house we were Mormons and my mum had always kept us at home from school on Holy Days of Obligation, so the funeral was the first Catholic mass I'd ever witnessed, and it was exciting, and I felt like knowing all about that and not like crying.

Later, I'd taken the copy of the *Lancashire Evening Post*

that had printed Alice's school photograph on the front page and secretly cut out her picture. I hid the newspaper and screwed up the two-inch damp square I'd cut from it into a tiny pellet and put that inside a plastic bottle with a childproof top that fluoride tablets had come in. I distinctly remember the secrecy involved in this; I wasn't sure what I would say if anyone asked me why I had cut out the photograph or what I had done with it so I needed to make sure nobody ever asked the question. I distributed the spare fluoride tablets into the other bottles (my brother, sister and I had a bottle each: issued by the dentist) and as far as I know, what I'd done was never discovered. I wonder about this now. About what I thought would happen if I cried, as some of the other kids and teachers did. Someone would have been there with the brisk emotional equivalent of a mug of cold water and a bandage and a safety pin: the adults around us were standing ready, so keen to help it looked, from my child's perspective, as if they *wanted* us to be sad. What was I locking into that little bottle? Not Alice, but something soft about me that had stayed there for a long time.

Much later, I told Clive about this, told him the girl's real name, said he could google her if he wanted. If he did, he might, eventually, have been brought to YouTube where there is a poor-quality video of the 1992 Preston Guild schools' procession. Sitting through the entire video with an eagle's eye, he might have seen Alice in her little blue satin dress and navy sandals and white knee socks, walking in a procession from the gates of our school – which is now a community drug and alcohol service – through Preston's town centre, around the ring road and Flag Market, and down Fishergate, Preston's high street, towards Avenham Park and the river.

I was there too, in that group of girls. We'd been asked to walk nicely, clasping our hands demurely in front of us as we really would if we were attendants of the Virgin Mary, who I imagined as a kind of Catholic princess. She was actually a sad-looking statue with a dusty face in a blue cape surrounded by plaster lilies and carried by men I thought were porters from the Harris Museum because they were wearing waistcoats and bowler hats. The Preston Guild was a city-wide civic celebration that happened only every twentieth year and teachers kept telling us to walk nicely, to smile, to not complain when our sandals rubbed and the blood soaked through our ankle socks. We'd be in the newspaper. We might even be on the television. And when the next one came round in 2012 we'd be thirty years old and nobody would ask us to be in a procession for the Virgin Mary then, would they?

When people in Preston say 'once in a Preston Guild' they don't mean something only happens once every twenty years, they mean something is very unlikely to happen at all. The future is always like that: an improbable afterlife to the dreams of the present. When we imagined the 2012 Preston Guild we didn't picture ourselves as wives or mothers or checkout ladies in shops or dinner ladies or nurses or teachers. How could we? 2012 would be a decade into The New Millennium. We imagined space travel and time machines, hoverboards, phones you could carry about with you, cars you could plug in and all meals coming as tiny tablets in tinfoil packets. I was going to be a writer or a detective. Alice might have imagined herself in a gauzy, glittering ballroom dancing outfit, foxtrotting on the television for an audience of thousands, like the high school kids did in *Grease*, which she loved.

I suspect on entering Shap, you're supposed to take a few moments or longer to enjoy the views of the twelfth-century ruined abbey, think some thoughts about ruins, time and the impermanence of all human endeavour, and take some photographs. The abbey – once home to a group of contemplative monastics known as the 'white canons' because of their pale woollen cloaks – certainly counted as a church, and as a pilgrim, I probably should have popped in. But by the time I'd reached it, I was in the 'head down and let's get on with it' stage of the walk: the Sistine Chapel would have failed to capture my attention. I was what they say of toddlers and drunk people: tired and emotional. I stopped only for the paper shop, where I bought a bottle of Lucozade, found I couldn't open it, lost my rag and went back in and bought two cans of Coke. I sat on the tarmac in the car park, drinking the first can while crying over the horsefly bite on my hand, which was red and angry and swollen. How would I tie my shoelaces tomorrow morning if it was still like this? A man driving a red sports car pulled up at the front of the shop, glanced at me out of the corner of his eye and looked away quickly.

Getting to the bed and breakfast I was booked into that evening meant walking through the village, past a couple of pubs (one having some kind of party involving a bouncy castle and some really loud music) and the chippy I'd been warned to look out for. I drank the other Coke and limped along, the soles of my feet burning. The bed and breakfast was wilfully old-fashioned: net curtains brandished from every window. There was a boot rack and a pile of newspapers to stuff soaked and muddy footwear with and a heavily patterned carpet. I was greeted by the owner, who I will call Barbara, and who was wearing a flowered apron.

What I wanted more than anything was to shower and lie down on a bed. Now I'd quenched my thirst I could feel how hungry I was, but that felt like a problem I could put off until I'd had a good ten-hour sleep. There was almost pleasure in exhaustion like this: a safety in giving in so entirely to wanting what I knew I could provide for myself easily enough. Water, soap, sleep. This was not a type of exhaustion the life I had chosen called me to feel often: the simplicity of what care I needed now and my capacity to arrange it for myself was another type of relief.

Barbara led me to my room and spent a little while fussing at the light switches and towels, checking that all was in order. I won't guess at her age, but her relation to me felt grandmotherly and I imagined this bedroom had been decorated to her own taste: there was a lot of peach and floral fabric and the unfashionably powerful smell of fabric softener. I fidgeted politely while she chatted to me, waiting for her to leave. She opened the drawer of the yellow pine bedside table to show me a hairdryer and pointed out a little round wicker basket with three cakes of wrapped soap resting on a nest of shredded paper. She gestured towards the view from the window – the dark angular hump of Kidsty Pike – and let me know there would be tea and scones served downstairs in the sitting room in a few minutes and I should have a shower and come down, then she'd tell me where the best places to eat in the village were.

A Spare Macaroon

The atmosphere was different from the other places I'd stayed: it felt like she was putting me up in her home, and because the hospitality was more intimate, I felt duty-bound to receive it in a particular way. Which is to say: I didn't want to hurry back downstairs for my scones, but I felt I had to because I didn't want to hurt her feelings.

Downstairs, scrubbed and changed, I went to find Barbara. She was in her private living room at the back of the house sitting on a sofa, watching the telly and, from where she sat, operating an old-fashioned press through which she was quickly threading pillowcases in a way that looked both complicated and effortless. I had to poke my head around her door to let her know I was down and ready for my scones, and she got up and led me to where I was supposed to be. The front room for guests was all plush sofas and tassels and magazine racks. There were framed pictures of dogs. There was a folder of printed-out poems about the Lake District written by previous coast-to-coasters, each poem protected by a plastic wallet. Once seated, she brought out a little coffee table then returned with a tray on which lay a doily, a floral tea service for one, two large warm scones with butter, jam and clotted cream, and a spare macaroon in a paper case.

Barbara was right: I *did* want scones. How foolish of me not to know. I wanted – without the sniffy irony I'd been surveying the place with up until now – that comfy sofa and the doily and the tea in the flowery cup and the peach curtains and the three little cakes of individually wrapped soap. I ate everything, scraping the butter dish clean, and flicked through the poetry folder and looked at the pictures of the dogs. This place was a home and being there made me suddenly homesick and guilty about leaving my children and Duncan. I finished the spare macaroon and became luxuriantly, unattractively sorry for myself. The horsefly bite on my hand had continued to swell and now I couldn't move my thumb. I'd walked across the entire Lake District, and I still had the Dales and Vale of Mowbray and the North York Moors to go. I'd done hardly anything and look at the state of me. Sick of the whole enterprise, I went back up to my room, shut my curtains against the view and put myself to bed without any tea.

DAY SEVEN

A Girl from the North Country
Shap to Orton (8½ miles)

I left Shap behind quickly, following a lane leading eastwards along the north bank of a beck, the verge choked with brambles and cow parsley and weedy young sycamore saplings. The path led over the railway line and towards the motorway, which I'd cross from west to east. Today's stretch was one of the first watershed moments of the walk: as well as crossing the M6 I'd make a small foray into the Yorkshire Dales National Park (though, confusingly, Orton is still officially within the county of Cumbria).

I passed the working quarry I'd seen from the top of Kidsty Pike. Even early in the morning, its white chimneys were spouting clouds into the air. I stopped here and took videos and pictures for Clive because he'd told me that his father, who drove a lorry and made deliveries across the North of England, had once brought him here. The place is special to him in the way that Morecambe is: a physical location that holds inside itself a left-behind time to do with childhood and his parents. I texted him some pictures and he told me that *Withnail and I* was filmed around here. It was warm that day and though I detected none of the dank, rain-soaked shabbiness that the humour of the film relies on, the air itself felt different and it was a relief to have finally left the national park behind me. The fence nearest the motorway footbridge was decorated with the fluttering silvery corpses of moles and on the other side there were more quarry pools and a gravelly track I shared with yellow trucks going back and forth about their business. The mood was different here: the national park had the air of a place where I should have bought a ticket on the way in and picked up a leaflet about the health benefits of Romantic Poetry in the gift shop on the way out: beyond it, the labour of industry was undisguised.

There were only eight miles to walk and no rush to do it in, so I sat on a wall and let a man wearing binoculars around his neck and a camera bag on his shoulder stride on ahead of me while I opened the letter from Clive that had arrived at Shap the day before. His note was typewritten and attached to a page from an artbook showing a picture of a scary-looking mask and, tucked inside it, another note that looked like it had been torn from a training manual meant for nurses. The paper of the manual was thick and yellow, the writing letterpressed on to it in a way that I could feel from the underside. It describes the correct procedure for changing and making beds for the benefit of 'certain surgical cases' and remarks on the amount of 'invisible' perspiration a patient in bed might exhale daily: the breath both measurable and of interest, but the body that exhales it present only by implication. The reader is advised how best the bedclothes (rolled or pleated, but always pulled tight) should be arranged to expose various parts of her patient for a doctor's examination. The sheets are described; the body within them, not at all. If there is a middle way between discretion and erasure, looking but not staring, then this training leaflet misses it.

A Girl from the North Country

I could see why this pamphlet had caught Clive's interest: he had told me before how obliterating the creaking systems of hospital care could be. The regular counting of what is happening in his blood is so precise that, though the progression of his illness is exposed, he himself fades out of view entirely. Who or what is being masked when we do care like this? I flipped the page, looked at the mask again and thought about Clive ripping pages out of his books and sending them to me. I thought too about the way my own body had made itself known to me the day before: the hazy flowing ease of the long walk along Haweswater, the easy pleasure in wanting and getting food and a hot shower, and the strange and sudden depression that had landed on me and sent me early to bed.

In Marina Benjamin's memoir *A Little Give*, she explores the unpaid work of domestic, familial care. The chapters list some of its varieties: *cleaning, pleasing, feeding, safeguarding*, and trace the peculiar intensity of this work during lockdown: how many more meals were eaten at home, how it was to be a teacher as well as a parent, to ricochet from screen to sink and back again. As I'd read it, I felt again the pleasures and the burdens of domesticity I'd planned a walk across the country to escape: the way the locked-down days were divided by the length of time it took the dishwasher to complete its cycle, the alarmingly short period between clearing up after one meal and starting the preparation for the next. Benjamin examines the costs of this kind of care: the drudgery and confinement, the way it requires a woman (and it still is most often a woman) to be unnoticed, and generally unpaid. 'The success of housework turns on its invisibility, on the quiet conspiracy of the women who do it and then hide the fact of its doing, denying the physicality of their own labour.' There's a long history of this kind of caring invisibility, dating right back to Florence Nightingale, who in 1859 suggested that 'the best service a nurse can give *is* that the patient shall scarcely be aware of any – shall perceive her presence only by perceiving that he has *no* wants'.

I replayed the uncomfortable moment of blundering into Barbara's private sitting room and disturbing her as she ironed in front of the telly. Because her bed and breakfast had been decorated for her own comforts and tastes, and only peripherally to please her guests, it felt like I was a guest in her home, and not a customer of her business (though that too, of course). Barbara had been so powerfully present in all of those rooms that even when I was alone, her body was there, her hands arranging the soap in the dish, her skill with the old-fashioned ironing machine pressing the pillowcases, her patterned knife arranging little curls of butter in a floral dish that almost but didn't quite match with the cereal bowl.

Barbara had asked me as I had sat in her front room and while I attempted to delicately gobble my scones under the eyes of the dogs in the pictures, if my feet hurt. The question was too much. I had nearly cried, feeling my powerful desire to throw myself on the spotlessly hoovered carpet to wail and demand plasters and hot water bottles and brushed cotton sheets and basins of warm water spiked with Dettol. I'd taken another selfie in my bedroom before getting in the shower, wanting some record of the impression that the day's hiking had made on me. My face was red and dirt-streaked, my hair so filthy I didn't need a clip to pin my fringe back, the skin under my eyes sagging with dehydration and exhaustion. There was something satisfying in witnessing the absolute state of myself: I actually looked like a woman who had walked across the entire Lake District during a gathering heatwave. I'd cleaned up a bit by the time I'd gone down to be fed, but Barbara must have detected the urgency of my need for care when she asked that question all the same.

'Yes,' I'd replied. My feet bloody *did* hurt.

Seventeen miles on a hot day and the cumulative effect of all those letters from Clive, gently bringing me towards the parts of myself I had locked away in that little bottle with the picture of Alice, had been enough not to throw the floodgates open, but to lever them apart a little. The gentle intelligence of my body knew what it needed and the words bubbled into my throat before I had a chance to grit my teeth. I was about to give Barbara the whole spiel. About running out of water and having to fill my bottle in Haweswater. The clegg and my swollen hand. The sunburn. The insect repellent running into my eyes. The way the straps of my rucksack had made red and purple marks on my shoulders, the fact my bad ankle was still bad, even though I'd strapped it up with pink tape and tried my best to be brave. The final indignity of not even being able to open the bottle of Lucozade. Duncan had been doing everything for everyone in my absence so I couldn't even moan about my trivial, self-inflicted miseries when I phoned home. There was something about Barbara, or rather, in the way I insisted on noticing this woman (you'll know more about me than her from the way I describe her, of course), that called out the part of me that was crying out for nursing. It was the scones that had done it, the old-fashioned tea set, the spare macaroon and the floral curtains. I wanted to be mothered, and broadcasting some suffering seemed like the best way to elicit that.

'My feet *do* hurt. And my ankle—'

She'd interrupted me briskly, laughing a little. She had a traditional Cumbrian accent, a little Geordie, a little lowland Scots. And she had noted my accent too.

'You'll have no problems. A girl from the North country like you?'

My readiness to be mothered and receive the pity and fussing I was certain were coming was punctured abruptly. Though ideas about Northern grit were ones I'd meet again and again on this walk: there were coast-to-coasters who'd flown in from Europe and America, from as far away as Sydney. Most evenings I'd endure some version of polite chit chat with tourists from far away in the pubs where we'd compare route plans and mileage, and there would always be a laugh raised at the idea that I'd been walking solidly for days now, was a third of the way across the country, and still only thirty miles away from home. It made what I was doing both more strange and more pointless than the same walk undertaken by someone who'd had to fly in to start it. I expected the fact I was a woman on my own to be relatively unusual and was surprised that my Northernness was the real rarity. As Barbara's words suggested, the general thinking among locals and visitors was that this walk would pose no particular trouble to a Northerner: a girl from the North country would plod on, unsentimental and tough, immune to pulled muscles and blisters.

A Girl from the North Country

One of the most famous and most erroneous ideas about Northerners is that we are resistant to the effects of the landscape. The body of the Northerner, so the stereotype goes, is hardly a body at all: it famously never feels the cold and is capable of running all day on a bowl of porridge and a half cup of strong tea. The message – impressed on me in so many ways through childhood, and I felt an echo of it again that night, in Shap – was that it was a sin for a Northerner to be 'soft' and I was heading perilously close to committing it. Barbara's housework, her creative heart-labour of *homemaking*, had inspired a moment of unmasked neediness in me. I had felt both embarrassed and at home, embarrassed *because* of needing to feel at home – my secret wish to be something other than a paying guest suddenly revealed. She had not been unkind, not at all, but I'd met my unexpected bout of wanting, the clue to what had lain beneath the anger I'd been feeling for months, with enough unkindness of my own. I'd laughed at my own sore feet, dismissed myself as a whinging, delicate, fussy little flower and anaesthetised it all with sleep. I'd woken to shame, and carried it with me out of Shap that morning, feeling brittle and sour.

My route tracked roughly southwards in the slim sliver of land by the side of the motorway and between the edges of the Lake District and Yorkshire Dales national parks. The route was almost a diversion – I'd be back heading eastwards to Kirkby Stephen the following day – but that day's walk was so easy it felt as delicious as cheating and I dawdled, dreamy and inattentive. This was when I got a sense of what walking for many days in a row might feel

The Parallel Path

like: a letting go of the idea of progress, of making good time, of being finished; at the end of today's walking lay only some more walking, so why not dither for a while? I enjoyed the slowness of my limpy, lopsided plod and the gentleness of the landscape. I didn't look at my map much.

The colours were different: the bright greens of the Lakeland fells and drumlins replaced with the shaggy, coarse yellowish grasses of the moors and the greyish clints of the limestone pavements. Even the weather was gentler, the bright heat of yesterday gone, the sky watery and clouded. I felt my eyes and the muscles in my face relax: the views were washed out, smudgy and watercolour. I forgot to look out for the stone circles, dating back six thousand years, wandered obliviously past the place on Crosby Ravensworth Fell where Wainwright promised me a proper view of the Pennines, blundered right past a famous cairn supposed to be Robin Hood's grave, and without worrying too much about it, got lost between an old lime kiln and some farmland on the outskirts of Orton. Too lazy to get my map out of my bag, I made do with walking steadily downhill, probably trespassing, and kept what I presumed was the church spire at Orton roughly in sight.

Marina Benjamin understands this conundrum between the presence and absence of the carer and the cared-for. When visiting an elderly aunt, Benjamin cleans her kitchen. The maintenance of surfaces is a substitute for a more intimate kind of encounter that the aunt, made silent by dementia, remains in need of. But more significantly, Benjamin in her role of carer is herself in need of something: 'I want to leave a physical marker, a totem of shiny pots and pans, a cairn. I want to bequest a commemorative gift that says, "care has been lavished here."' Imagine a cairn inside a house! What need do we have of guards against getting lost when we're in the buildings that contain us while we eat and sleep together with those closest to us? Sometimes the care of housework, the relentless tending to of objects, is how people who love each other find each other and how they make themselves available for being found.

Clive told me once he remembered me cupping my hand under his teaspoon when we were in a café in Morecambe. I think I wanted to save the tablecloth from being marked by his squeezed-out teabag in case it fell. The bag didn't fall, and – because I know he's careful about Covid – I didn't touch my friend nor his spoon or his cup. Clive was moved by this gesture and mentioned it later – he had received some sense of being noticed by me. I remembered again Melvyn Bragg's fussing with the items Dennis Potter wanted by him during the interview, the moments where he made sure the seating was just right, the table at the right distance from the chair – that sense of care at one remove, a love that preserves autonomy and allows for distance and allows both parties to show up.

Though housework might be a way of building yourself and the people you love a cairn, a record of some effort to care without smothering, cairns are more or less permanent. They're a kind of totem: a version of the memorial plate bolted to a rock I'd seen on my way up the Langstrath Valley or the sentimental poem carved into a piece of Westmorland green slate I'd taken a photograph of at Honister. Housework is not like that. During the pandemic

The Parallel Path

I had defied the sudden shortages, ordered flour on the internet and baked, hoping my son and daughter's memories of me making them homemade puddings would somehow overshadow the global trauma and social deprivations they were living through.

But lockdown had taught me again what I already knew: in a few days the floors I had just cleaned would become dirty again, the soup I'd left in a pot on the stove would be consumed without relic, and the bedsheets I'd laundered and folded and put away nicely in the cupboard would make no specific impression on the world. If the purpose of care is to solve or wash away someone else's suffering, it wasn't working, and the repetition of it all started to feel like a one-woman battle against entropy and the only thing the work left its mark on was me. I had experienced a specifically safe and privileged pandemic and I had worn myself out trying to rinse any of its remaining discomforts away for the sake of my children. And as I battled uselessly against the way things were, I misjudged things: inevitably, repeatedly.

The interplay between invisibility and presence is complicated. Housework might, as well as being the thankless drudge women are told is about the sacredness of relationship only to encourage us to carry on doing it smilingly and for free, also be a way of advertising the self in a way that resists the centrifugal, obliterating forces of marriage and children. *Look! I was here*, the clean sheets and hoovered skirting boards and chocolatey pear pudding say. Picture me: an armful of home-baked goods proffered to someone who didn't want them and hadn't asked for them. I hadn't particularly wanted to stand at the cooker making them, either. This is the work of growing up: the child declines to be mothered, the mother, shut out, seethes and rages (and bakes). We did it during lockdown, and neither of us had anywhere else to go.

The letter that Clive had sent along with the page from the nursing book was typed – the shaking in his hands must have been difficult that day – and part of what he wanted to talk about was how his treatment was going. Clive told me things in these letters I had not asked about and would never ask about and that always felt like a gift, though the news he wanted to tell me was hard to read: 'Now when I see my consultant, they are less ebullient, their eye contact is more furtive as we talk about "experimental" treatment. I understand from observing friends' eventual deaths following cancer treatment, that *experimental* and *trials* are words that they held on to tightly, nearer the ends of their lives.'

I imagined Clive examining the faces of his doctors for information about what was happening inside his own body, the way part of how he knew himself in these moments was in his observation of others. Clive went on to talk about how it felt to see the fear in his partner's eyes when she heard this news, and it was painful to be let into the privacy of a moment like this and to know again that what happens inside someone else's body can hurt those who stand close by. Clive said he was going to take a walk after he posted the letter. He was going to head east and feel the sun on his skin, 'walking a strange parallel path with you'. I liked the idea of that: of having company, close, but not too close – connected, but not touching, with space to

The Parallel Path

say what you wanted to say but only when you felt like saying it. The lag on these letters meant that Clive had already taken his walk, but that felt irrelevant.

I remembered that moment at Morecambe Bay, when Clive first told me he was dying. He talks more often about living with cancer, about what it is to be fully alive to his diagnosis of incurable illness. But in that moment, he'd chosen, because we didn't know each other all that well yet and he didn't need to worry about hurting me, a kind of abruptness to his delivery that left me staring at him, my curiosity undisguised. The way in which he'd required me to perceive his presence had caused something in me to change. And yet I still hadn't written back to him: not properly. I'd been walking a week and I hadn't taken the paper and envelopes I'd brought with me out of my rucksack once. I had been telling myself that the photographs and sound recordings I'd sent to him, trying to absent myself from the view, the frame, holding my breath so he could hear the trickling beck or chattering of birds in the trees but not me, were a way of getting out of the way and giving him the walk he wasn't taking. But Clive's resistance to becoming an invisible patient and his insistence that those around him showed up to an encounter that was about something more than the transaction of work was calling something else from me; he was gently asking me to show up.

Despite my dawdling and frequent stops to rest the dodgy ankle, I arrived in Orton just after lunch and far too early to be let into my room at the George. The pub was closed too. Someone had turned an old bus shelter into a kind of community book exchange, and I spent half an hour

A Girl from the North Country

leafing through yellowed paperbacks, killing time. Up a hill just outside the main village the All Saints church, whose blocky bell tower I'd been using to navigate during the last couple of miles of my walk, seemed worth a visit. That was closed too, though the church had a stained-glass baptistry window designed by Beatrice Whistler, the wife of the American painter James McNeill Whistler. I stopped to take a look.

The window shows three long-haired angels, one praying, one watching, one holding on to the shoulders of a young child. Everyone is wearing nice white sheets, draped on the empire line like maternity dresses, with bright blue sky behind and a green flowery meadow in front. There was good 4G reception in the churchyard, so I did a bit of googling and tried to find out what Beatrice Whistler's connection was to Orton. She was very definitely *not* a girl from the North country. She was born and educated in Chelsea and after her marriage lived in Paris and designed furniture, patterns for tiles, wallpaper and crockery, and administrated the manufacture and sale of prints of her husband's work. The only connection I could find between Beatrice and Cumbria was the fact that her husband famously sued John Ruskin in a libel action because Ruskin disliked his paintings and committed his thoughts on them to print. Ruskin was living in Brantwood, near Coniston, at the time – fifty miles and two big lakes away.

The Whistlers returned from their home in Paris to London long after the libel trial was over: Beatrice had been diagnosed with cancer. She was treated while living at the Savoy Hotel, and it was there that her husband made portraits of her in her sick bed, taking her likeness while she lay dying. His sketches and portraits of her are smudged and dreamy – she's already out of reach and insubstantial. In *By the Balcony* and *The Siesta* her clothes and body are not quite distinct from each other nor from the blankets and coverlets of the bed she is lying on: she has already become part object and her artist has paid a brutal equality of attention to her failing body and the rented hotel sheets that enclose it.

The window she designed for the church at Orton, however, is precise and bright, the colours strong and startling. She'd been commissioned by Jane Holme, a widow from Kendal, to design the glasswork in memory of her daughter Mary, who had died at only eight years old. Jane knew Beatrice as she'd commissioned her once before to design and decorate the interiors of her house. So the little girl on the centre panel, surrounded by angels and dressed just like them – all that white laundered creaseless linen the handiwork of someone – must be Mary. I thought of my daughter at eight, felled and furious by the news of Ben's sickness, delicate and angry, grief crackling around her like electricity. The inscription beneath the window names both the girl and her mother, and quotes from the Psalms, 'they shall bear thee up in their hands'. It was finished in 1892, just a couple of years before Beatrice first started complaining of ill health. She was probably gestating the cancer that killed her while she worked on it. Her husband, apparently, was disparaging of the work, calling it 'the widdies' windy'.

There's a famous chocolate shop in the village where you can peep over the counter and watch the chocolate being made. I stopped there too, bought some chocolate for my children, then lay down on a bench outside the shop on a little village green, deep with shaggy grass, and ate it myself. Orton is a village well used to walkers passing through, but I'd made myself conspicuous by setting up camp there on a midweek afternoon, dangling my legs over the edge of the bench. If I'd been reading a book or talking on the phone it would have been better, I think: the alibi for loitering would have been obvious. I'd got out of the habit of being in public and it hadn't taken long to exhaust Orton's visitor attractions. Eventually, a man came out from the closed pub and asked me if I was booked in to stay, and if so, did I want to get into my room early? Disappointed to have this new experience of conspicuous uselessness brought to such a sudden end, I followed him through a heavy door and into the dim coolness of the bar.

DAY EIGHT

Brown, Blue, Black

Orton to Kirkby Stephen (12 ½ miles)

The eighth day of the walk would take me eastwards out of Orton and over what appeared to be mainly featureless moorland towards the market town of Kirkby Stephen in the Upper Eden Valley. I got lost almost immediately. Wainwright's directions are confusing, often remarking on what is not there, or what is disappointing, rather than outlining where exactly you are supposed to go. Sunbiggin Tarn is 'little more than a large reedy pond in the middle of a morass' and the Bronze Age cremation trench at Rayseat Pike is noted, but not described; I probably walked right over it. Wainwright gives a 'clue' to where the next part of the path should be joined, but notes that back in 1971 it was barricaded by a corrugated iron sheet. 'The author's experience here was unhappy and he has no advice to offer.' I thought it was unlikely the obstruction would still be there, but could find neither it nor the path I was instructed to follow across open moorland, looking out for the hawthorn trees that dot the terrain. The heather was shin-deep; walking became wading.

There's a lot of talk in Coast to Coast forums about Wainwright's *official* route – and lesser, easier or newer alternatives. Wainwright had said his aim was to inspire others to find their own way across the country, but I'd really wanted to do this thing properly, which meant doing it exactly as he said he'd done it. Though all the promises I thought walking had made me – the peace of being alone, the soul-altering effect of an awesome view from a high place, the reassurances of strength and toughness – had proved themselves more complicated than I thought, and only brought me closer to what I was trying to walk away from: the discomfort of my secret desire for care and comfort. At least, I caught myself thinking, I could follow the route precisely. No short cuts, no half measures. (I explained away the ragged wander down to Orton the day before as a 'rest' day.)

From the moment I first allowed myself to desire this walk, the inner voices that told me I wouldn't be able to manage it reminded me that left and right were still a challenge for me, how often I took the wrong turning at roundabouts on routes I've driven on many, many times before, and how confusing and labyrinthine I still found the university campus I'd been working on for over a decade. Duncan can draw a mental map of any place he's been, can find his way across the country and to a specific building after a brief glimpse at the A–Z, can ask a person for directions and – miraculously – remember them well beyond the end of the conversation. He's been in charge of our navigation for nearly two decades and whatever direction-finding skills I was born with have atrophied. The walk was an absurd idea: I knew this even before I started. I would not be able to do it because I did not have a mind designed to manage it.

Rebecca Solnit has made a virtue of this deficiency and I've tried hard to believe what she says about the matter in her book *A Field Guide to Getting Lost*: 'To be lost is to be fully present, and to be fully present is to be capable of being in uncertainty and doubt. And one does not get lost but loses oneself, with the implication that it is a conscious choice, a chosen surrender, a psychic state achievable through geography.' Because I like the sound of this, I've shared her guidance with my writing students: not knowing what happens next, being tangled deeply in a work that has not revealed its form to you, setting your hands to type before you know what you think; these are all essential practices for writing and involve a letting go of orientation to welcome in a more creative bewilderment. But the times I had to pull over and set up the Sat Nav to show me how to get to my own mother's house, I was not making a conscious decision to surrender my topographical certainty in exchange for a finer spiritual truth. I just have a talent for disorientation. I have always found this tendency humiliating and revealing of some inbuilt deficiency: a child's dependency on others. For someone like me, this walk was both hubristic and irresponsible. But I would not listen to my own voices of reason. I wanted to do it and so very badly wanted to find my way without help – hence the two-day mountain navigation course I'd signed up to earlier in the year.

The first day of the course we met in Dunsop Bridge, a former lead mining village in the Ribble Valley – the heart of the Forest of Bowland. (We'd only be let loose on the gentle fells above Patterdale and left to find Angle Tarn on the second day, later in the spring.) The bridge the village is named after marks the confluence of two rivers, the Dunsop and the Hodder, and is, according to the Ordnance Survey, the nearest village to the exact centre of the British Isles. A nice reminder that to be in the North of England is to be at the heart of things. We were also within spitting distance of the famous Salter Fell Track, which is the route that some say the women from Pendle accused of witchcraft took as they walked to Lancaster to be tried at the castle fifteen miles away.

We began by sitting around a picnic table outside a café learning the map symbols that would be useful to know on a day's hike, then 'navigating' round an obstacle course in a field next to a car park to illustrate the importance of 'setting the map'. This means holding it so the top of it points north according to your compass, rather than holding it the 'right way up'. After an hour or so of this, I'd been impatient to be off: the fells rose up quickly outside the village — it was one of the first bright days of the year and the entire world was calling.

There were four of us on the course, all women, and we navigated upwards, testing ourselves with increasingly difficult instructions and enjoying stories of mishaps in the Cairngorms from the trainer. The moral of these anecdotes was simple and useful: foolishness and unpreparedness can sometimes mean death, and at the very least can be an expensive and embarrassing drain on the resources of the mountain rescue charities. We trotted off to find markers in the long grass and hid things for each other to find. Through the day we started to share the reasons why we'd signed up for the course. One woman had, after saving for years, just bought a camper van (it was parked up in the village: we'd all admired it before we set off) and was keen to get outside on her own and feel safe doing it. The other had always meant to learn navigation from her father, who was an experienced outdoorsman, but he'd died unexpectedly before she had fully grown out of her teenage uninterest in what he could do. The third said she'd only started walking to cure 'a broken heart' and had a plan to get up Ben Nevis later that year, though she'd never done anything like it before. 'When I do that,' she said, with an emphatic gesture, 'I'll know I can do anything.'

Of all of us, the heartbroken woman was the best at taking the compass bearings, figuring out her pace count and estimating how many minutes it would take her to walk between two or three points. I was – and this didn't surprise me, though I felt sore about it – definitely the bottom of the class. I noticed how good my broken-hearted walking companion was at mental arithmetic, and felt slow and stupid as I fumbled with the numbers, getting my map twisted and dropping my compass as she confidently pointed towards the place she'd already worked out we should go. She told me she'd had lots of practice because she worked as a carer in a residential home for elderly people. I didn't follow, and she explained how many times a day she'd count and measure in the sluice room when taking a record of urine output from the catheter bag she'd just emptied and how she would write down the running totals for her patients in biro on the back of her gloved hand. When it was my turn to say why I was there and what motivated me to learn to do something I obviously wasn't very good at, I told the group I was planning to take the Coast to Coast Walk, that I knew large parts of the route across the Lake District and the moors were not signposted and that I really wanted to do it on my own without having any help from *anyone*. The others, disclosing their hopes for an emotional and personal journey as well a physical one, might have been disappointed in me. I was here to learn how to read a map; the heartbroken woman, who'd already had to help me with the adding up, looked sympathetic and doubtful.

Wandering around the moors, my thoughts spiralled. Maybe I wasn't lost at all. I'd get to Kirkby Stephen one way or another – I was just taking an alternative route. And anyway, my urge to copy Wainwright *exactly* didn't make sense because I didn't like reckoning with my daily sense of cliché either – of being instantly recognisable with my still-shiny boots as a latecomer, all-the-gear-and-no-idea walker, a hobbyist, just playing at it, trotting along doing what thousands before me had done. If being original meant taking a way nobody has ever taken before, and discovery follows a period of being lost, then perhaps being lost was okay?

These were self-comforting excuses but they held a little truth. A fear of unoriginality comes from my work as a writer, of course, where getting off the signposted route is part of the job description. Maybe one day I will take my reader somewhere they both recognise as true and haven't ever been to before: writing well means to guide someone towards that fully present state of lostness that Rebecca Solnit describes. For writing as for walking, the risks of humiliation lurk nearby: something being 'new to you' isn't good enough – not if you're only rediscovering a thought or an idea that someone else had and wrote about earlier, but you were too poor a reader to uncover. This drive to break new ground is good and by the time I set out that summer, at the end of the first post-Covid academic year, a part of

The Parallel Path

me had grown weary with it. I'd started to wonder about the other type of work – where no new paths are forged or territories discovered, but what is already there is cared for, maintained and protected.

The year before I'd discovered the work of Mierle Laderman Ukeles. She's best known as the self-titled artist in residence at the New York City Department of Sanitation. She's done this for about forty years and her work bridges an interest in places and spaces, labour, feminism and environmentalism and most of all in what it is we mean when we talk about art being radical, of making something new. In the late 1960s Ukeles spoke about being torn between mothering and making, nurturing and creating, cleaning and caring and bringing new works of art into being. 'I literally was divided in two,' she told *Art in America*. 'Half of my week I was the mother, and the other half the artist. But, I thought to myself, "this is ridiculous, I am the one."'

Ukeles didn't address her problem by trying to get a better work/life balance. Being dismembered – that 'divided in two' is an appropriately gruesome and visceral description for what it feels like to exist in this state – needed a bolder solution than merely managing her diary more competently. Instead, in 1969 she wrote the 'Manifesto for Maintenance Art' in which she insisted that acts of care, of sheltering, of nurturing and nourishing were also acts of artistry. The manifesto understands the dichotomy between the selfless mother and the selfish or single-minded artist is a false one. And with this manifesto, she proposed a number of projects and exhibitions that showcased her work dressing her children, cleaning the museums in which her artworks were exhibited, and engaging by touch and listening with the sanitation workers who maintained health and cleanliness in the city. Care work became art work. To be radical – which for an artist is a stance most often associated with newness, or a breaking away from what has gone before – also implies a rootedness; a secure attentive belonging to the landscapes that hold us and have formed us. When Ukeles got on her hands and knees and cleaned the steps of the Wadsworth Atheneum Museum of Art in Hartford, Connecticut, in 1973 something necessary and fertile happened – she was cleaning and creating, caring for what was already there and making something new. She was exactly where she should have been: the artist was in the art museum – and she was sort of lost too.

The hours passed. Any sense of where I was in relation to where I was supposed to be was long gone. I'd made the mistake of imagining that on terrain like this there was no need to use the map as there was nothing to do but follow the path through the grass, but then the path disappeared, or I'd accidentally followed what the Cumbrians call a 'sheep-trod' and ended up nowhere, or back where I started. It might have been something to do with the landscape too – the new flatness almost featureless to a set of eyes trained to pay attention to pikes and fells. I had not learned to like walking in flat places yet. On that day it still seemed to me that the secrets of the landscape were giving themselves up at all once and with nothing left for the eye to anticipate, the topographical narrative tension I'd enjoyed in the Lakes dissipated.

Is there a way to be good at walking? To excel at it? To bring some artistry to the practice? If the biggest challenge for the Coast to Coast walker was in finding the right path, sticking to it, and putting one foot in front of the other until the next stopping point was reached, I had already proved to myself it was impossible to do that perfectly. While walking races and other kinds of competitive walking exist, I can't help but find the concept bizarre: if you want to get somewhere fast, run, or call a taxi. To be *pedestrian* is to be unremarkable, average and nondescript: I only joined the slow traffic of the thousands who followed Wainwright across the North since the early 1970s.

I trudged onwards; Seamus Heaney once said that writing on lined paper made writing feel like ploughing – that sense of constriction and of following the rules was inherently a bad thing. Art work is not farm work and the blank page with no route to follow marked out by someone else's hand was the surface the *real* artist committed their poems to. I thought about this as I tried to plough the dotted line of Wainwright's route across that day's moorland on the map. I was safe enough: the weather was fine, I had loads of water, there were no sudden drops to injure myself on or animals that might want to harm me. Being lost was annoying, but not dangerous. And as I calmed down, what the paradox of excelling or marking oneself as extraordinary in the discipline or sport or art of walking might look like started to intrigue me.

On the mountain navigation training day we'd been warned that all maps are only approximations: once printed, their marks are permanent but the world itself oozes and crumbles and is constantly in the process of reconfiguring itself.

Brown, Blue, Black

Humans are forever turfing things up, moving barns and walls, diverting water courses – even in national parks. So, I was told, when a walker is lost, she should remember *brown, blue, black*. That 'when' was reassuring: the enterprise of navigation was defined for us by its failure – the whole two-day course assumed that we'd get lost, and took a problem-solving approach to the teaching – here's what to do when it happens.

First, you try to find yourself in relation to anything that shows *brown* on the map: contour lines, mainly. The outlines of fells and pikes and dales are unlikely to move during a few ordinary human lifetimes. If that doesn't work, try *blue*: lakes, reservoirs, tarns, ponds and water courses. These do move, from season to season and year to year, but the big tarns and lakes won't dry up or dribble away, and if big changes do happen, as in the case of Mardale and Haweswater, even the most casual of walkers would have heard of them. When all else fails, think *black*. Black is for buildings. Churches, stone circles, barns and walls and farmhouses. Navigate by these only when desperate, and only if you're certain. I was not a good navigator, but I'd been a good student and memorised all of this and repeated it to myself as I circled and zigzagged over the moor.

Brown. There were no high fells to be whole hours in the company of. A few gentle rises covered in haze, but nothing I could match up with the map.

Blue. Definitely no ponds or lakes gleaming in a valley bottom, nor white foaming gills chattering down a cleft between two crags. I'd seen Sunbiggin Tarn an hour ago but had mislaid it since then.

Black. Now and again, there was a dry-stone wall to peep over; on the other side, meadows, and pastureland of the same type as the one around my ankles.

Back in Orton, there had been another letter from Clive waiting for me, and while I circled the moors, I remembered how badly I think when I am hungry, so I'd sat on the damp heather and opened my packed lunch and the envelope that had been getting bashed about in my rucksack. I'd eat, read the letter, maybe lie on my back and rest for a while, then look at the map again and see if I could find myself.

Inside the envelope was a taped-together pamphlet. It looked like he'd cut illustrations from a children's book: on the first page there was a woman in a bonnet walking towards the viewer down a garden path. The flowers behind her had faces and someone, either a figure at first I took to be the gardener, peeping at her from behind a wall, but who on closer inspection turned out to be a winged cherub in a summer hat, or the flowers themselves, was singing 'How does my lady's garden grow?' On the flip side of this page was a music score for a song called 'Natural History', the lyrics familiar. The first verse is 'what are little boys made of?' – slugs and snails, puppy dog tails. I didn't know the song had a second verse, sometimes attributed to Robert Southey. The young boy becomes a man, made of 'sighs and leers and crocodile tears', and the young girl becomes a woman made of 'ribbons and laces and sweet pretty faces'. It was the mood I was in – lost and ashamed about it – and the combination of the creepy faces in the flowers in the illustration and the depressing gender essentialism of the old song, but I was suddenly sad. I was reminded, I think, of what I'd read about women walkers – the street walkers strutting for their punters, the models 'scissoring' along the catwalk, the walking woman's vulnerability to the 'slap'. I was safer here than I was wandering around Lancaster on my night-time walks, but the sadness was about something deeper than that. To be available for care – which is what my stay in Shap had proved to me I wanted so secretly even I was surprised about it – also means being available to be seen. And some of the ways we are seen – all of us – are so often brutally diminishing it's no wonder allowing my vulnerability to be visible enough to be cared about, by anyone, felt as foolish as setting off across the moors alone.

Clive's letter was written on the last page of the pamphlet he has made and in it he is tentative. 'There is a danger when somebody is ill, or worse, that they become tirelessly self-indulgent. That is me, here, using these letters as a way of expunging things. To connect, to feel cared for – and to care.' Maybe he felt he'd said too much and presented too much of himself for viewing, though what choice had I given him with my lack of reply? He alluded to the difficulties in childhood we both had in common, and how we – by lots of yardsticks – both flourish now. Our own 'natural histories' had not become our destinies and both of us amounted to more than we ought to have been, more than was expected of us. *Socially mobile* is the phrase for what we are: forever lost between then and now even though we've both settled a stone's throw away from where we grew up. This kind of mobility comes with a kind of self-inflicted homelessness you're not allowed to grieve. We're both entertained by the way we pass as middle-class now, though we're not, not really.

Clive's letter hinted at wanting to hear more from me, in the gentlest of ways. 'You know there are many things I'd like to ask you about, but feel I am digging too deeply – but we'll see.' In conversation, or over email, Clive will often preface what he wants to say with an apology – a worry that because of my work and my children still at home my life is too full for an extra friend. It seems that it feels difficult for him to break into the flow of life and to trust that his interruption will be welcome. I do know what that is like. When writing feels difficult for me the problem is not caused by the inevitable lostness of not knowing what happens next but by temporary loss of faith in the friendliness of a listener. I have to be able to imagine that the message will be cared *for* and cared *about* before I can imagine anything else. I had been struggling to find in myself an ability to be available for this friendliness for some months. Blank pages and empty Word documents had been staring back at me. I packed away the letter and the wrappers from my lunch and promised myself and the moors that I would send Clive a postcard from Kirkby Stephen.

Once I got off the moors the way became clearer and I found an obvious track, muddy and rutted in places, with a relief so sudden and all-consuming it felt like joy. This track led me through some farmers' fields, beneath a railway bridge on the Settle to Carlisle line, through another couple of farms. I was so pleased that I called out a greeting to a man cutting hedges at the point where the track turned into a road that turned into a street that led me on to the road into the town. 'I should have been here two and a half hours ago,' I said, as if he'd asked me a question, and he nodded politely and turned back to his work.

In town, I found the Coast to Coast chippy Wainwright liked so much. When the Eric Robson documentary was filmed, Robson brought him here, and Wainwright's popularity was such that he was recognised in the street – to his obvious discomfort. In his guide, Wainwright calls Kirkby Stephen an ideal place for 'licking wounds' and the chemist on the main street must have read this because, as I passed it, I noticed a window display full of antiseptic cream, kinetic tape, Compeed, insect repellent, boot insoles and even a couple of comically placed crutches. On the way in, I passed the old Temperance Hall – built to serve travellers who had taken the pledge and didn't want to stay at one of the tiny town's seventeen pubs and licensed premises. I wasn't quite halfway yet, but most of the packhorse companies operate from Kirkby Stephen and people who want to do the walk in two halves often leave their cars here. A couple I fell into step with on the last half hour of the walk told me they were going home and would get the train back in the autumn to do the rest of their miles during cooler weather: today had been merely warm and humid but much hotter weather was forecast for later in the week. I stopped at a newsagent's and spent a long time choosing a postcard for Clive.

That evening in one of Kirkby Stephen's pubs, I took up too much room at the bar and opened my maps and guidebooks and tried to work out what had happened. The footpath was supposed to link up with a farm track I never found, and, after a long period of wandering within sight of Sunbiggin Tarn, trying to keep it at my back and head east but somehow turning and finding myself heading northwards whenever I checked my compass, I caught the path again as it crossed the north side of Smardale Fell, roughly using some bumps on the horizon to take a bearing as I had been taught. Whether I did this accurately or found my way to the path as it met a B-road by sheer luck, I don't know. There were no signposts and the one information board I passed was faded, the map on it illegible. There were sheep. Dry-stone walls that weren't in the places the map said they should have been. Rises that didn't match up with the contour lines I had learned to measure and factor into my pace count.

In *Walden*, Thoreau says, 'Not until we are lost, in other words, not until we have lost the world, do we begin to find ourselves, and realise where we are, and the infinite extent of our relations.' Maybe the eighth day could have been the day I learned to be grateful for an interruption to my solitude; other walkers would surely have offered help. But there weren't any, only sheep who were either fearful of me and ran away, or who stood their ground, staring and chewing as I kicked through the thick long grass and annoyed them. I forgot to enjoy the pink blooming heather, though it's there in the photographs I took. I did not attend well enough to the colours of the lichen on the spotted dry-stone walls, the flowers blooming in the meadows and on the roadside verges I passed. Though I'd read that around this area there were lots of rare sandbowl snails and had even saved a picture of one on my phone so I knew what to look out for (they're red-brown and their shells are pointed, like whelks), I was too panicky and unmoored to look out for them. I might have been foiled by Ravenstonedale Moor or the rough pasturelands between Brownber and Smardale Bridge: there should be no shame in that; but I still wanted to know where the wrong turn was. Being able to plot my footsteps on the map and know where I had been felt important: how could I make myself available to be found if I had no idea where I had been? In the pub that night, my courage evaporated. I turned the postcard I'd bought over and over and thought for a little while about how I might show up to Clive. I copied out a quotation from a book about walking I'd been reading in the evenings before sleep: it was the best I could come up with.

DAY NINE

On Walking Well

Kirkby Stephen to Keld (13 miles)

I left Kirkby Stephen, down the high street, past the church and chemist and diverted to the sweetie shop to buy Mars bars and post the card for Clive. Then I crossed the River Eden and walked eastwards along the north bank. The route today would take me out of Kirkby Stephen, along the Eden, past another quarry then over moorland towards Nine Standards Rigg, named for a series of mysterious, carefully constructed rock cairns lined up on the fell's summit. Passing them would mean I'd crossed the North of England's backbone: the Pennines. These cairns also marked the North country's watershed, and east of them, all the running water would flow in the other direction, towards the North Sea.

I was still a little bruised, my ego worse off than my feet. When I'd called home after my pub tea I'd described the mishap and called it 'an adventure in navigation', though being lost had revealed something to me I had preferred not to know: part of the motivation for doing this was about finding a way to excel at being a walker even though this relentless drive for improvement was one of the things that had left me so careworn in the first place. In the early spring, a year after the first 2020 spring lockdown, the Conservative government had published a paper called 'Build Back Better'. For a while, 'build back better' became a sticky little catchphrase I heard on the radio most mornings as I supervised breakfasts and the finding of PE kits. While all of us had reasons to be cynical about what kind of 'better' that government was offering, and to whom, one of the reasons I couldn't stand the phrase was because I was so bloody knackered. It felt like another task to add to an endless to-do list. *Improve everything, always.* The world certainly needed fixing, and I did too. But must everything always be better? Could I not just walk? Only walk? Evidently not, though this inner urge to flog myself onwards towards impressiveness was hardly something I could blame the government for.

There are several different routes up to Nine Standards Rigg, and which you take depends on the time of year, the state of erosion of the delicate peat bogs, how recently it has rained, and so on. They're signposted but the waymarking is erratic and generally considered useless: the long grass grows quickly, the bogs are subject to sudden heaves and collapses and new desire paths made by both animals and walkers trying to avoid the wettest places abound. Even Wainwright calls this stretch a 'rough journey' and urges the walker to have a celebratory can of beer ready in his backpack for when he completes it. Beerless, I instead decided to save a Mars bar for the approach into Keld: I definitely wasn't going to get lost. Even though I understood that my perfectionism was causing me more weariness than the walk, I was not yet ready to give up the hope that today my walking would be flawless.

I paused by a dry-stone wall to orient myself on the map and take a bearing, which is a very basic navigational technique that involves twiddling the dial on your compass casing until the 'direction of travel' arrow points at where you want to go, then walking in as straight a line as you can manage. You can leave your compass on the palm of your hand and follow it like that but staring at the dial means you miss everything else, and a walker should be able to aim herself at some intermediary landmark that aligns with it and check her compass again when she gets there. There are various techniques you can use to accommodate for the fact that it's nearly impossible to walk in a straight line without a path to follow, especially on an incline or over uneven ground. I took my bearing, identified a distinctive-looking lump in the tussocky grass, and proceeded.

To walk like this, belligerently marching in a straight line no matter what transpires underfoot, is reckless, damaging to both ecosystems and ankles, and it isn't much fun. There's no adventure, only obedience. Our language reflects this too: we 'toe the line' when we behave ourselves and when we're 'falling into line' we go with the crowd and do what everyone else is doing. Lines feel like certainty, but they obscure what is true; we 'spin a line' when we lie or seduce, and a line of language – a sentence or plot or argument – is one of the ways we tidy up the three-dimensional blur of experience into story. This kind of walking was tiring, effortful and at the time I didn't appreciate how silly I must have looked as I strode blindly upwards, my face turned only to my compass. I waded through long marsh grass and stomped across slippery chunks of mossy limestone when finding a way around would have been easier. I was so determined to be better today than I had been the day before.

On Walking Well

I climbed Hartley Fell, the clouds gathering in a way that suggested rain. Wet weather would be disastrous if it came down heavily while I was crossing the boggy section on the other side. There was no point worrying about that, though; I was too far along the track and even if I turned back to Kirkby Stephen, I'd still be knee deep in bogland when the clouds opened. I went on. The Nine Standards themselves are obvious from some distance away; persisting with the compass started to get embarrassing, though I carried on and at the fell's rocky summit the wind blew like nothing I'd felt before. I'd half planned to eat up here, take out my maps and double check my route to Keld, but it was impossible to do anything except plant my feet hard on the ground and listen to the howling.

The neat cairns – in the North Pennines they're more accurately called curricks – aren't the usual raggedy toppling piles of stones you get on summits or at places where the way is unclear. These large, conical mounds were built like dry-stone walls; the local limestone slotted together in a perfect feat of engineering. Nobody knows why they are there. One theory is that from a great distance, the tall shapes on the horizon could be mistaken for soldiers by the marauding Scots, though that seems a stretch. Another is that they mark the line between Westmorland and Swaledale. They appear on maps from the eighteenth century, were considered ancient then, and one theory is that there used to be thirteen of them, that they're over eight hundred years old and that they might mark the site of an enormous long barrow dug into the top of the fell. The patient industry it must have taken to find and slot every single stone into place snugly enough to withstand centuries of the wind's rough attentions amazed me.

Before I'd set off, I told a friend that my two-and a-bit weeks of being away might end up being the longest period of time I'd not been touched by another person since my daughter was born. It was something I looked forward to; being the sole owner of my own skin again, knowing what sleeping and eating by myself would feel like. Isn't that how writers are supposed to live? I had not been lonely on the walk, but being alone had not offered the transformation into a person impervious to the world, needing nothing, that I realised I had been hoping for. There, on top of Hartley Fell, the world put its hands on me. The wind became intrusive, almost intimate. I felt it inside my clothes, insinuating its way through the zip on my cagoule, turning my pockets inside out and snatching my tears away. *Alone* had become *untethered*; I was a balloon about to be whipped away into the air and I wasn't only standing in the wind, I had come to the wind's place and made myself available for it to manhandle me. Two men arrived to take photographs and because the wind was too loud for small talk we pointed and grinned at the view together, circling the massive stone cairns and looking back to the Lake District fells and the rest of the Eden Valley. I didn't linger long; the wind drove me onwards, towards the peat bogs that I'd been warned would be hard going. The rain held off, and by mid-afternoon the change in the weather was dramatic. It had always been another warm day; the force of the wind had just been hiding it.

* * *

On Walking Well

During the second part of the route I softened and allowed the ground to teach me the way I should walk. Wainwright calls this place, of pools and quagmires and fissured limestone, an 'upland wilderness'. There are gullies and craters, the black peat and grass roots exposed by the movement of water or the damage caused by hundreds of pairs of feet. This place is delicate: sometimes the path disappears and is replaced with great standing pools of brackish water that need to be navigated around, leaping from one wobbly tussock of grass to another. Slabs have been laid over some of the worst bogs. I knew the map I had with all three possible routes marked out and colour coded was more or less useless. The calculations I'd learned to do on the first three Ds of navigation – direction, distance and duration – could only be approximate. There was no point searching for the way that Wainwright took because in the intervening years there had been so much churn it had already gone. The landscape taught me to meander, to tiptoe and leap, to shuffle down into craters on my backside and clamber out of them on my hands and knees. I was hurting this place: the tracks hikers had left through the terrain were sometimes great water-filled ruts in the peat – but I was going to tread as lightly as I could. This surrender to what the ground required of me made me feel playful and daft. I was going to jump and scurry and I was going to get muddy and I would be okay. It wasn't hard work – not if I didn't make it so. I had fun.

Finally, out of the bogs and past a few grouse butts giving a clue as to what this landscape was now used for, I entered the Yorkshire Dales properly. The mossy tans and browns of the peat bogs turned into gentler, greener inclines. I reached Ravenseat, a large sheep farm on Whitsun Dale. Here I stopped and bought a cream tea from a van parked in the farmyard. This little corner of Swaledale has been made famous by the *Our Yorkshire Farm* television programme. At the time the farm was run by Amanda Owen and she lived there with her family and wrote books about her life as a shepherdess. I'd listened to her speak about her life at the Borderline book festival in Carlisle a few years ago and coast-to-coasters almost always stop here and like to report sightings of her striding about in her wellies with her long dark hair flying.

There were wooden picnic tables and benches to eat your scones at, but this was a family house – someone had left two children's trikes and a bicycle propped against a barn door. A little white dog came and rested his head on my boot as I drank my tea and demolished my scone. At a table near me a couple, both wearing Tilley hats, argued loudly over the different directions their two GPS gadgets were suggesting they take out of the valley and towards Keld. It wasn't just the three of us; Ravenseat is on a couple of circular walks, and, thanks to the Owens' celebrity and the spacious car park, a destination in itself, most of the tables had occupants and I felt a stiffening, a mutual turning away from the couple who were rowing and towards the view of a ford over Whitsun Dale Beck. A teenage boy on a quad bike left the farm by its main track and crossed the ford; the sun made the water glitter, the dog rushed away from me to chase him and the splashing they both made cast up little rainbows. I got out my compass to check which way the water was flowing and, yes, it ran towards the North Sea. Something behind my ribs turned over; the moment was an unexpected gift and I waited a while, grinning for no reason, before opening the day's letter.

Clive had sent another mini-pamphlet, this one made from pages razored out of a wildflower identification book. The names of these flowers were a treat: Alpine Barrenwort, Fumitory, Pheasant's Eye. These had been bound together with the title page of the manual, *A Handy-Book for the Rambling Botanist*, sheets of Clive's handwriting and some cyanotypes he'd made from a handful of laburnum seeds he'd found in a stream up in Littledale. Later, Clive will explain to me how he'd made these images. The 'sun print paper' is soaked in chemicals that react to light: anything laid on it while it is exposed to the sun will leave a pale 'shadow' as the exposed paper turns blue. The blue and white images of the laburnum pods were both vivid and ghostly – as cyanotypes always are. He must have been having a shaking-hands day when he wrote the letter because deciphering what he wanted to say today took effort, and I lingered over my tea and scone, trying to work it out without getting jam on the pages. Clive said he'd chosen these seeds 'to make a ghost' because the laburnum, due to the way its yellow flowers dangle towards the ground like strings of beads, is also called the Golden Chain tree. The name reminds him of 'these light chains that float recklessly around my body'.

He'd told me before about these light chains. His cancer causes his bone marrow to create abnormal plasma cells. These cells in turn create strangely shaped proteins: the doctors call them light chains. The unexpected lyricism of the name pleased him and him being pleased by it – an ability to find what hurts him beautiful – had pleased me. I hadn't fully understood the business about plasma and proteins but didn't want to interrupt my listening to ask, so I had gone home and looked it up, feeling a bit furtive, as if I was rooting through a drawer I had not been invited to open. My discomfort wasn't about the nosiness: my curiosity has always been with me, reliably cropping up at the worst possible time. It was about being curious about the wrong thing; distracted from my friend and attending to a mysterious and half-understood world of immunoglobulin.

Curiosity-as-distraction was happening again as I read his letter; the phrase 'light chain' sent my mind towards the bulbs strung along Arnside promenade in winter, or further back towards chips and gravy in a Styrofoam tray at Blackpool illuminations, or back further still, to home and the great Christmas Lights Turn On in Preston. We'd all gather on the Flag Market in the cold and count down as a Z-list celebrity flicked a switch and brought all the scraggy sycamores along the high street to life by illuminating strings of little yellow bulbs in metal cages. It seemed to me these laburnum cyanotypes were Clive's way of thinking about what was happening in his bones and blood. But I was using my curiosity as a way of going away rather than going towards, even as I sat there chewing on my scone and reading his letter. I thought about my postcard: how little I'd written, and how I'd copied down someone else's words instead of my own. This was an attempt to be clever, maybe. Or an attempt to distract Clive from his wish for me to show up in some way, to tell him something more about what I was doing and how the walk was doing its work on me.

It is possible to use anything as a means of distraction, and it is also possible to go towards your own death using anything you have available to you. Clive used sun print paper and seeds to expose something more fundamental. These cyanotypes were not mere decoration: he knew precisely what he was up to. 'The seeds are the most deadly part of the plant,' he wrote, and I didn't feel burdened, as he'd so often worried. Instead, I felt taught. Clive had shown me with these letters that the art of care is always a going-towards and that there is a way of attending to almost anything. He had demonstrated to me that what makes each of us who we are – that deadly seed of gratuitous particularity we call a soul – is formed in us and knitted into the world by these acts of tending. Had shown me that when a person tells the truth about what is going on inside of them, their listener is never burdened. For the first time, I started to think of the walk not as a thing I had trained for, but a kind of training in itself. Clive wasn't someone sick who needed to be listened to, he was a kind of teacher, showing me something I needed to know. There are lots of people who make art out of disease, and lots of artists and writers who have plenty to say about dying. But I don't know anyone else who would muck about in a stream with light-sensitive paper and poisonous seeds, who would become fascinated by light chains, who would turn dying into a series of gifts for a friend, a gift that both invited her into his bloodstream and generously waved her away as she wandered off to be differently knitted back into her old places: Arnside, Blackpool, Preston. I began to understand I was being bequeathed a different way of seeing. Laburnums and light chains will exist differently for me now.

Clive has written an essay entitled 'Present-Tense' that, before he became ill, was published in a book called *Mortality: Death and the Imagination*. In it he describes the fifteenth-century Latin texts *Ars Moriendi* that gave advice on how to die well and wonders what a contemporary version of a book like this would advise. Does dying 'well' mean that, even in a person's last hours, there is something for them to do? Should the person who gives a sub-par performance to the relatives at the bedside be sent for further training and guidance? No – Clive detaches the word 'well' from any sense of skill or achievement and instead wonders how a sense of 'wellbeing' can be entirely unhooked from a medical understanding of 'health' and instead be something available to the sick and the dying. What wellness in the approach to death might look like is as particular as the soul but Clive has long been curious about art's role in all of this. This is not about art offering some kind of cure or distraction – Clive is as suspicious of this as he is of the nature cure, or of those who use either science or religion to evade the fact of their own mortality – but he suggests that we can 'learn something of the numinous from our deep immersion in others' vision'.

In his letter he goes on to tell me he is also 'horrified of having a last photo taken, all cancer chic and ever so brave'. I think he wants to fight his way past the cancer patient clichés and have dying be something that he does with the sensitive particularity he does everything else – like being a father or partner or teacher or filmmaker or friend – rather than something that happens to him. Clive knows that artists 'provide us with traces of themselves and fractured biographies of others' and what he is offering in his letters, containing these traces of his life, beckons me towards another kind of care; a commitment not only to remember a person's work – their photographs and letters and cyanotypes, all those stories of a childhood in Morecambe, the high jinks with his friends, building bonfires, digging holes – but to inhabit 'someone else's vision'. He was still worried about saying too much, and I still only dimly understood that he was asking to know something deeper about my vision. I sent him a photograph of the ford I sat by as I read his letter, trying to show what I could not tell: just how entranced and happy I'd been made by being there with him and the boy on the quad bike, the dog, the sun shining into the water.

I left Ravenseat and continued, along the east bank of the beck, towards Keld. I was staying at a lodge just outside of it, perched on the rolling edge of two dales and reached by a maddeningly long looped lane: it was almost a mile between the front door and the post box out on the main road. The lodge was a beautifully converted three-hundred-year-old barn – or cow-house, as the locals call them (it's pronounced 'cowuss'). Because there was no nearby pub to go to for your tea, the evening meal was served at one long table where everyone sat together. If I was going to write a country house murder mystery where culprit, collaborators, bystanders and sleuth were all shut in together, trapped by snow or high water, until the crime was solved, I'd set it here. There were two couples: the pair in the Tilley hats I'd run into outside Ravenseat (who merrily told the story of marital strife caused by their conflicting GPS devices between the starter and the first course), an older couple I'd not seen before, me, and one other single man who I admired immensely for putting his headphones on and ploughing through his entire meal without saying a word.

I was seated next to Patricia — this is nothing like her name — who introduced herself as a recently retired GP from the Midlands (this isn't true either) who was walking in the Dales to train for the Highland Way, which she was planning to do in September once the worst of the summer heat was over. She was with a friend, who sat opposite her and didn't say much. I asked her how her pandemic had been, wondering if she was walking to recover from what must have been a horrendous period in her professional life. She'd been lucky, she said, and had been working part time and from home, so had been able to spend a lot of her lockdown doing solo marathons through the emptied streets. When I asked her, thinking of my own strange locked-down loops, what it was like running through her city when it was empty, she told me how wonderful it was to have the pavement and riverbank paths to herself, but also how terrible. Why weren't the streets busier, she'd wondered. Why wasn't everyone who'd been furloughed out running, cycling, cityhiking and doing what they could to improve their health and reduce the burden on the NHS? 'Poverty is no excuse,' she said. You didn't need to pay for a gym membership to get out and move your body.

Patricia had found her captive audience and for the rest of the meal (which I ate gluttonously, and asked for extra pudding, as if to spite her) I listened to her thoughts about sugar, processed foods, smoking and the working classes' propensity to fill themselves with expensive ready meals when porridge and cabbage were cheap enough. 'So many people didn't need to die from Covid,' she said.

I tried to listen with kindness and reminded myself that this woman had spent years at the business end of suffering. I didn't like what I was hearing, but most of my discomfort was caused by a growing understanding that the part of her I was meeting now was too much like a part of me for me to have any business judging her. Had I not been the one to stand over my daughter in her long grief and tell her that she'd feel so much better if only she'd open the curtains, clear up her room a bit, got outside for half an hour, eat more vegetables and find something constructive to do with her day? We're all made up of multitudes: there was more to Patricia than what I saw over dinner and more to me than the brisk, efficient listmaker I had become. Still, the part of this woman I objected to was the twin sister of the part of me that approached my locked-down children with a list of improving activities they could do each day to make the most out of this 'special time'. I ate my pudding, observing Patricia and learning that this part of me that does what it thinks is care – and gets so exhausted by its efforts it becomes furious at their fruitlessness – acts the way it does because it finds being helpless when someone else is suffering too difficult to bear. I tried to listen for Patricia's vulnerability as she spoke and searched for an opportunity to acknowledge the grief that I believed – and maybe this was just wishful thinking – was trapped in there somewhere. It was difficult: the least-appealing parts of me are the ones that need caring for the most, and because I'd not yet learned to forgive and be kind to the part of myself that was just like Patricia, I went to bed feeling like I'd done a full day's work – more wrung out from listening than walking.

DAY TEN

To Accompany a River

Keld to Reeth (12½ miles)

From Keld, there's a choice – the high route that follows the old lead mining tracks across exposed moorland, or the low route through the valley along a path that clings to the banks of the River Swale. Wainwright is peculiar about this stage in a way that reveals something interesting about what walking meant to him. He admits the path along the Swale is more beautiful but urges the reader to take the high route anyway, utterly failing to sell it as he describes what it offers: 'a graphic scene of industrial decay' scattered by the disintegrating wrecks of old mines and smelting works. The hills and dales were mined for lead ore by pretty much everyone from the Romans and the monks who ran the Yorkshire monasteries onwards until the industry collapsed in the nineteenth century. Wainwright describes the damage this industry did to the landscape in melodramatic terms: the gills, the fellsides and even the summits have all been 'torn asunder' and the spoil heaps and derelict buildings that remain are 'chaos'. Using words more appropriate to a gothic ghost story he continues at length: the landscape is 'pockmarked', 'petrified', 'gaunt' and 'skeletal'. And yet he urges the reader to avoid the valley route along the river, and despite his hatred of tourists, cars and crowds of day-visitors, spends a precious half page of his guide urging a university or archaeological society to preserve one of the abandoned mines, with suggestions for how the finished exhibit should look.

It is clear that the ugliness or otherwise of the landscape is nothing to do with Wainwright's interest in it and his walking is about something other than sightseeing. Neither route is particularly arduous or tricky to navigate so he isn't pep talking the reader into a feat of physical endurance or map-reading prowess either. Instead, he urges the walker who follows in his footsteps to become a witness to thwarted human labour, the collapse of a community and the end of what he sees as 'initiative, industry and ingenuity' in this area. The tone here is different from the crabby, depressed state of mourning I detected in him when he appeared in the Eric Robson documentary. He wrote the Coast to Coast guide as a younger man, one who was still able to take the high routes, to clamber over a dry-stone wall, to navigate around the remains of the lead mines. For this Wainwright, walking is a way of remembering or even restoring to the present what we have foolishly, through our liking of cheap foreign imports and our taste for urban living, managed to let slip through our fingers. For a man obsessed with timekeeping and history (what he likes about Keld is its sleepiness, its resistance to change: 'a sundial records the hours, but time is measured in centuries at Keld') one of walking's primary attractions for Wainwright is the way it seems to allow the walker to keep hold of time itself. 'We have lost too much of the past through concern for the present,' he writes, as if a walk can revive old ghosts and restore long-forgotten ruins.

Wainwright doesn't describe the alternative low route in any detail so I decided to work it out from my maps and took the path along the Swale instead. I hoped that because he was so dismissive, it would be the road-less-travelled. And, despite his lavish descriptions of the 'dismal wreckage' available to me up top, I had more interest in the river than I did in the ruins of the Yorkshire lead mining industry. After taking the long loop away from Frith Lodge and back on to the main route east – a singularly maddening trek to have to do twice – I joined a wide and obvious path and oriented myself eastwards again. There'd been no letter at Keld from Clive that day, so I wandered without him, the day feeling emptier because of it.

Lots of sources describe the Swale as one of the fastest flowing rivers in the country, though on the day I set out to walk beside it the weather was bright again, there had been no proper rain in a few weeks and the water moved along lazily, slopping through green meadows and catching itself in foamy whorls that spun in the shallows. Most people allow around four hours for the low route; I'd make it last more than six because I was taking my own time. Maybe I was still smarting from my encounter with Patricia and her vigorous commitment to her cardiovascular health, or maybe I was discovering – gently, deliciously – that it is nearly impossible to be bored by walking. All my plans to improve each shining hour of the day by listening to novels and podcasts on my phone, stuffing every moment with worthwhile activity, had been abandoned before I was an hour away from St Bees. The Swale made its own chatter, the ducks and heron and sheep lent their voices to the air, and I needed no other entertainment. The tenderness of the landscape guided me to calm my steps to a rate much slower than the river's flow. I let the river and every walker I met that day overtake me.

The Parallel Path

Eventually, I arrived in Muker, where I'd been looking forward to visiting the Swaledale Woollens shop, the other reason for me taking the low road that day. If you're a knitter – as I am – it's a nearly famous shop, set up in the 1970s with hopes of reviving a traditional knitting industry that was lost as the villages emptied when the lead mining stopped. The owners of the shop take fleeces from the Swaledale and Wensleydale sheep I'd been swapping dirty looks with since Ravenseat and send them up to Scotland, where they're spun and finished in the hydro-powered Lanark Mill using a traditional nineteenth-century spinning mule. They come back to the Dales as skeins of yarn ready to be turned into jumpers, cowls, shawls, hats, mittens and scarves by a network of home hand knitters from across the Yorkshire Dales.

There was no room in my bag for a jumper but I'd planned to eye up the goods in person then order online later. As it turned out, the shop was closed and I had to be content with spending a few minutes staring through the windows at the Reeth, the Richmond, the Shunner Fell. The jumpers were named, like the east-coast and Scottish ganseys are, after the places where they were made. The intricate interlocking of cables and twists and areas of moss stitch and rib, according to some, represented different aspects of the wild and agricultural landscape that is home to both sheep and knitter. Knitting has always reminded me of the way a place can seep its way into the body's muscle memory, then flow outwards again, into the objects that body creates. Even the way the knitter holds her needles can let you know where she or the person who taught her to knit came from. Sometimes you can tell something about origins just by looking at the knitting.

To Accompany a River

A couple of years ago my friend Hilary trusted me to finish a lopapeysa – a beautiful Icelandic yoked jumper made from lopi, wool from Icelandic sheep. Her mother, who had died, had left the work unfinished. Picking up her needles and continuing her work felt like learning to finish a letter using someone else's handwriting and I couldn't merge my own stitches into the work already done until I taught myself to hold the wool 'continental style', in my left hand. It's sometimes called 'German knitting' but only by the English, I think; children learning to knit at school during the 1940s had their hands slapped for trying it, even though it's easier if you're a left hander.

Yarn's intimacy with landscape and body ties the two together: to 'knit' means to join and we talk of broken bones knitting themselves together as they heal. My granny taught me to knit when I was so small I was still wandering around Preston speaking with the Scottish accent I'd learned from my mother, despite being born and brought up in Lancashire. You can tell by the way my granny held the yarn, the needle held still and tight against her body as she worked, that she'd learned from someone who'd been taught to knit in the deep North. I never knew there was anything distinctive about the way she did it until I saw a documentary about Shetlander women, knitting as they walked from field to shore, holding their needles close to their bodies with the help of a knitting belt. When I picked up the needles again when I was expecting my daughter, peering over a book for beginners I'd got out of the library, I felt through my hands a different kind of belonging: I forgot I'd already been taught how to do this, and watching myself cast on, saw that my hands had remembered what to do and they were doing it Shetlander style. The wild untethered feeling the wind at the top of Hartley Fell had blown into me subsided, and beneath it was a happier awareness of being knitted into the nature of things.

I left Muker empty handed and carried on along the Swale, ambling through meadows full of buttercups and spotting two herons standing together on a rock on the river's opposite bank. Again, I let other walkers overtake me, standing aside from the path and gazing into the water, being careful to appear meditative and not excited in case they thought I'd spotted the Swale otters playing in the shallows and came to have a look at them too. The slowness of my day was intoxicating. I felt altered by it. Corrected, almost.

One of my most vivid impressions of lockdown was the sense of constant interruption. When I was with my children, my students or colleagues needed me. When I was with my students and colleagues, my children would call on my attention. Work time collapsed too: some of my students had gone home on the last flights out of the country and attended my online workshops in the middle of their night or asked for one-to-one meetings in the evening or before breakfast. The borders between work and home stopped mattering – it all took place in the same room, anyway. At night, my phone would buzz with notifications from friends who were in as bad a state as I was, insomniac, frightened, bored, angry. Time was no longer mine to spend.

I'm a creature of routine and did not adjust well to this collapsed, broken time. I started to wake in the middle of the night, fretting that I'd not washed a school blazer even

To Accompany a River

though it had been weeks since one was needed. There was no other building to go to; my office on campus had always been the most effective shield from the demands of home and intimate relationships I have ever known, and home – curtains closed tight, the laptop away in a drawer – has always been a closely guarded cordon sanitaire against my employer. With both of my refuges gone, I found myself vigorously resisting then utterly succumbing to the calls to care over and over again, brittle then soft, firm then yielding, until I was in a constant state of undoneness that felt like shattering and evaporating at precisely the same time.

Clive had already taught me about the double time of hospitals. Sometimes he'd send me messages during his endless hanging-around, frustrated by the enforced leisure and the requirement to linger in waiting rooms between tests, bored and idle while around him the overworked hospital staff breathlessly hurried, powerwalking between wards. An experience that is a once-in-a-lifetime emergency for a patient is routine labour for a nurse or doctor, their own time overstuffed with an impossible amount of work. Turning to my reading to better understand what this experience might be, I found 'Six Ways of Looking at Crip Time' by Ellen Samuels. This essay describes the way disability and illness might expand a person's understanding of time. '*Crip time is time travel.* Disability and illness have the power to extract us from linear, progressive time with its normative life stages and cast us into a wormhole of backward and forward acceleration, jerky stops and starts, tedious intervals and abrupt endings,' she writes.

I idled slowly, enjoying the rare experience of my thoughts unfurling at their own pace, with no particular mental destination in mind. As stressful as my home-bound lockdown experience of time had been, and as grateful as I was for my unrushed hours along the Swale, it seemed possible that during lockdown I had been experiencing one moment crashing into the next more truthfully than usual. The problem was not my circumstances, but only the effort I put into improving and resisting them. One of the vital components of the shared conversation that caring and being cared for involves is a willingness to make someone else's time your own and to step out of what Ellen Samuels describes as the 'sheltered space' of time as the 'well' experience it. This stepping out involves giving up your own sense of time for someone else's and letting the needs of their body dictate the movements and freedoms of yours. The metaphors we use habitually when we speak about time make it sound as if it is money – something we can use, or spend, or save, or waste, not something we can submit to. Walking reminded me that time is not a resource I own and that there were other ways of being with people than the frantic, fix-it attempts my conversation with Patricia the day before had made obvious to me.

On that day, I felt held by the valley – tucked in somehow – neither breaking nor disappearing, but gently guided onwards by the steady flow of the water. I allowed myself to be taught by its flow and learned to move with as much pleasure as a living being with no sense of anywhere else to be can move. The paradox available in having somewhere I wanted to get to and choosing to get there by the slowest means possible created a little friction: walking across the country doesn't quite make sense, and because it doesn't, it allows other things beyond my sense of the way things ought to be to happen. Walking alongside the river for miles – around twelve of them that day – felt very different to crossing it. The rivers I'd crossed so far had become obstacles or way points. 'Let's get the Lowther out of the way,' I'd caught myself thinking, on the way into Shap, and now when I want to think about it, I have to flick through my guidebooks and photographs because the Lowther made no impression on my memory. The gentleness I experienced on my day along the Swale was contained by the consistency and firmness of my commitment: I would go where the path took me, and the path would go where the river took it, alongside, but keeping its distance too – the way I might one day learn to walk with a friend.

A few miles on, I reached the little village of Gunnerside, where I stopped to admire and envy the miners' limestone cottages, treated myself to a fancy coffee in a traditional Yorkshire Dales tearoom and sat at a splintery, weathered picnic table to squint at my maps. There was a choice here: the walker could carry on following the river right into Reeth, or she could detour slightly. I fancied a change, so I left the eastern edge of the village through a small wooden gate and temporarily abandoned the river for open moor again, the wide space around me a quick shift from the sensation I'd had of being held close by the Swale Valley. The horned, arsey-looking Swaledale sheep took a good look at me: this was their moor and they had cropped it with their long nicotine-stained teeth; the vegetation underfoot was as closely woven as rough carpet.

I know myself to be a person inclined to slowness: I was still bearing my little grudge against Patricia in Keld, who surely had forgotten all about me and had no reason at all to be concerned with my opinions. I am slow to let go of things, slow to process what other people seem to digest if not with ease, then at least with a pace that looks to me like alacrity, or even alchemy. Round the corner from where I live in Lancaster there's a tiny post office, and when walking past it a couple of weeks before I set off on my Coast to Coast, I saw a queue that snaked out of the door and into the street. It was just an ordinary queue but it reminded me of how things were for a while: those days of waiting outside the supermarket in a socially distanced line watching people shuffle carefully forwards, feeling like an extra in an end-of-the-world film, trying not to see a never-before mix of shock and boredom plastered over everybody's faces. That time was gone but not all of me knew that: my body reacted as if I'd been hit and tears prickled behind my eyelids. I do not think a reaction like this is either proportionate or deserving of special pity. It was just a post office queue. Everyone else seemed to have got through this – whatever *this* was – very quickly – and parts of me were still frozen, stuck in the river whose onward flow had paused.

The change in my mood once I got up on to the moor was bracing: the North York Moors were still ahead of me, but now I got a sense of space, of distance, of how little of the country I'd tiptoed over that day. Treeless now, with only the softest rise away from the Swale and Gunnerside, I got a taste of the route not taken and the vastness of the sky overhead. Why hadn't Wainwright mentioned this? Had his eyes been so drawn to the crumbling old limestone buildings that he'd never thought to look up? It was as if there was an abrupt increase in how much air there was and how much I was capable of taking in, and I trotted around, losing the path and enjoying being blown to bits by the wind. I had to root out my compass to find east again, and once I did, I walked quickly, out of breath and with the wind at my back – as if outrunning something – to come down from the moor and rejoin the river on its way into Reeth.

Not for the first time on the walk, I wanted to laugh – laugh the way a toddler does, with a bubbling-over sense of joy at being alive, at being upright, at moving inelegantly through a world that is indifferent to her preferences. The sense of stuckness and of being in a body caught in a time that had passed long ago blew away. I promised myself that as my moods were so obviously and easily swayed by my environment, I would take all of them – the heartsickness and the fits of depression, the anger over minor irritations, the sometimes overwhelming despair and sense of a life utterly wasted that comes over me at each tiny setback (or when hungry) – much less seriously.

I make these giddy promises to myself often.

In Reeth the little streets were packed with cars and all the pubs were full. Because I wasn't with a big group who had booked a table I had to wait to be served and ate conspicuously alone amidst the din of a party. I expected the B&B to be full too, but when I got there it turned out I was the only guest, and the owner told me that everyone in town was there for a wake and would not be staying the night. Because it was just me the owner was standing by ready to be lavishly hospitable, so I went out again, sat at a table outside the pub and fed crisps to someone else's dog, drinking pint after pint of lime and soda.

I should have been able to work out there was a wake happening and one large enough to be dispersed across several pubs. Almost everyone else around me was dressed smartly in black dresses and suits and shiny shoes and had neat haircuts. Some of the women were dressed up to the absolute nines: black wool coats, even in the summer, and diamonds on their fingers. Lots of the men had proper waistcoats under their suit jackets and every tie was black. Even the children were in their dark-coloured Sunday best. I enjoyed the opportunity to people watch, to speculate. The vibe was celebratory, rather than tragic. Maybe it was a very old person who had died – sad, but not unexpected. Some other place I had been stuck in and waiting a while came back to me.

After a private family funeral in a church near their home in Preston, Ben's family booked Blackburn Cathedral for a more public memorial service. Ben had worked for Blackburn libraries before he'd taken his medical retirement, and this was the only place big enough to hold the crowds that his family knew would come. They'd hired some AV equipment with speakers and big screens to make sure everyone could hear and see everything. There were talks from the oncologist who'd treated him, the BBC radio and television presenters who'd helped him to tell his story, members of his family, his running club. A huge television screen at the front of the church showed a slideshow of a life condensed to a minute or two: there he was as an awkward kid, hanging out at Christmas with his brothers and sisters; hugging his mum in the kitchen on the day he went off to university; getting married to Louise; holding his babies, one by one, as they arrived. There was a photograph of us too, looking teenage and unlined and taken during that Lake District camping trip where we'd argued about the best way to walk along the screefalls at Wast Water.

This was the sort of service where you weren't supposed to wear black: Ben's friends came in their running kit and the non-runners wore bright colours. I sat on the front row with Louise and all the girls wearing what I now judge to be a quite horrible dress with a big green and yellow floral print and, for reasons I have now forgotten, a very orange cardigan. Some of the children had flowers in their hair, as if at a wedding. Someone from the press must have been there because there were photographs, and for a long time afterwards I'd google them and see how many people I recognised. I think I remember some of these photographs being taken, or at least I remember feeling my body was in the way of something, which is the sensation I generally get when someone brandishes a camera. I wanted to see and hear everything like everyone else, but I didn't want to have to be there in order to have that happen. The desire manifested itself in a physical sensation I experience often, a not knowing where to stand, my limbs and face heavy and redundant and quite frozen. At times like this, my feet always feel not quite right – as if I have forgotten to put my socks on, my shoes too cold and too hard against the soft flesh and delicate bones.

The shape of Reeth – laid out in a kind of triangle around a green, with far too many pubs and teashops for how small it is – made it ideal for people watching. Four men in their shirt sleeves crossed the green, from one pub to the next. Their suit jackets were swung over their shoulders, held by a finger hooked through the loop inside the collar. Maybe they were the hosts of the wake and were paying the bar tab in each place, or looking for their wives, or doing the rounds, thanking the distant relatives for coming and making sure those who had travelled a long way were in a fit state to drive back. Belatedly, I realised I was seeing a pub crawl, and once I'd clocked these four men coming and going, I realised how much movement there was between pubs – people were trying to work their way around the village and take a drink in each place.

There was a pleasing ritual to this, like the Catholic tradition of observing the stations of the cross that I'd once inadvertently participated in as a child. School had taken us across the road to the big Catholic church that I'd later sit in for Alice's funeral, and we'd been given a tour, then had to follow Father Denis and Sister Margaret and our class teacher around, dipping our fingers into water and curtseying in a complicated way at regular intervals as we circled the edges of the church. My mother almost certainly would not approve of this; my granny and granddad, who were nominally Church of Scotland and my grandad specifically in possession of some opinions about Catholics that even I knew about, would certainly have something to say. Mormons aren't that big on crucifixion; they never have crucifixes on display in their churches and I'd received the message there was something unseemly about them. The images of a tortured half-dead man were a little too hammy, the naked chest and weeping wounds distasteful and indecorous. It was also the working-class Northern and Scottish culture of my household that taught me the best way to take your whipping was to not make a song and dance about it. But Preston is Priest-Town, after all, and the Catholicism seeped into my childhood: exotic, forbidden and thrilling. I followed the stations of the cross around the edge of the church, lapping it all up. As far as I could grasp at the time, this ritual was a kind of walking prayer to do with counting out pictures of Jesus, who in these pictures was taking his own walk, mainly carrying a cross, or having the familiar (to the child I was then) experiences of being shouted at and getting his face wiped. We went right round, curtseying and listening to the priest.

Older now, I wondered if being on your feet as you remember a death was about changing something – not the fact of the death, but your own feelings about it. But what kind of 'moving on' and letting go sent you in a loop and brought you right back to the same church door you'd started at? It had been a long time since Ben had died. The funeral was over. But inside me, it carried on. I lingered at the pub most of the evening, watching the people at the wake get rowdy then start to disperse. It was getting dark. I let the dog that kept me company lick the inside of my crisp packet. It might have been the pub's dog: it had its own water bowl and someone came and poured a half pint of shandy into it so carelessly the fluid frothed over the sides and ran along the paving stones. Someone else shouted and jeered at the man who had done the pouring. A little girl ran across the green chasing a toddler, navy ribbons flying from her hair, and was told off for squealing.

DAY ELEVEN

The Green and the Grey: A Difficulty in Staying Upright

Reeth to Richmond (14½ miles)

The route from Reeth to Richmond required one more day along the Swale and is, in Wainwright's own words, 'short and easily accomplished'. Before setting off, I'd marvelled at a fourteen-mile walk being described in this way, but now comfortably into my second week of walking, the prospect of it had become hardly anything at all: almost a rest day. I spent much of the first hour or two on quiet roads and stony farm tracks, looking down at the gently bubbling Swale, wider now, from higher up the gentle and grassy valley edge. I remember a bench next to a shiny red post box, and bramble leaves, brown at the edges and spattered with berry-flecked bird shit. I climbed a stairway cut into the sloping edge of a dark wooded hill; there are over three hundred steps, apparently, though I lost count of them in an absent daydream as they took me away from the tiny village of Marrick and its ruined priory. The crumbling ruins were clasped together by knots of ivy, shiny in the sun. There were swifts in it, I think, or some other speedy bird, diving in and out of the foliage as if it were water. The walking that morning was a way of chewing up the space between here and the afternoon's destination of Richmond, where a pub tea was waiting. I plodded easily, as if I'd always known how to do it.

* * *

My daughter was a late walker. Not that I knew anything about babies or the order in which they were supposed to do things. Early motherhood did not leave much time for googling milestones or consulting books. That first year we were together in the world was like a walk through a darkened room: concentrating on each shuffling, sleep-deprived step through the washed-out daytime hours was enough. The news came from the health visitor, who'd mentioned my daughter's lateness to walk in the context of reassuring me.

First children are often a bit lazy to get going because an attentive parent with no other child to run around after will bring them anything they want, she'd said. The implication was (this is what I heard, but sleeplessness makes you paranoid and I was always sleepless then) that my attentiveness and the ways in which I had learned to anticipate my daughter's desires had prevented her from developing as she should. It made sense: my daughter was a late talker too because there was no need to say 'cup' or 'ball' or 'biscuit' when pointing did the trick.

When I was pregnant, I'd read a book about attachment parenting and somehow understood that if babies were parented properly, they didn't ever need to cry. I was twenty-one and the last serious thing I'd read was Samuel Richardson's *Clarissa*, a novel too long to risk for my finals, but one I saved for a treat the summer I graduated. It wasn't much of a preparation – nothing about my degree was – for the attachment parenting book. It suggested that babyhood was supposed to be another trimester of the pregnancy and the baby should be kept close to the mother's body at all times. The hard fact of the child's existential aloneness

The Parallel Path

should be introduced gradually. In some cultures, the book said (the book never specified which cultures: they'd call it racism now, and it was – lots of mention of 'tribes' and 'native cultures' as if, in some other, hotter country, perfect parents uncorrupted by 'civilisation' existed), a child didn't put its feet on the ground until it was two years old. At least.

I held my daughter close: she slept with me, was carried rather than wheeled around in a pram, was fed on demand and tried on solid foods late. She (having not read the book) still cried, and when she did, I felt a bolt of cold terror about the suffering I had failed to prevent. And now I'd made her into a late walker because I was carrying her too much. I tried to explain to the health visitor what I'd been doing without letting her know I was sharing a bed with my child (because that wasn't allowed) but she only repeated what she had said. My daughter would *never* learn to stand on her own two feet unless I did something about it. And I did want her to walk (*you do, don't you?*), though I really, really didn't want her to cry. I understood I needed to withdraw and leave a gap in the world for her to reach into and then walk towards. I started putting her toys out of reach, and trembled, distressed and guilty, in the back kitchen while she screamed and raged.

I spent the morning crossing fields, squeezing through slot gates and gaps in hedges taller than I was, and was still fresh and full of beans when I arrived in Marske. There's a twelfth-century church in the village: St Edmund's. Inside, I ran into the pair in the Tilley hats I'd first seen at Ravenseat and then again in Keld. The church was pale and cool and smelled damp and heavy, like a cellar. The pews were a polished dark wood, the red kneelers fringed and dusty.

'We must stop meeting like this,' I said, into the whitewashed and still interior of the church. My voice was too loud, too pretend-cheerful. The atmosphere I'd blundered into was brittle: the man had his boots and socks off and was resting his feet up on the pew. He'd rolled up the bottoms of his trousers and his feet were so battered they looked like they'd been skinned; even the air must have hurt them. Other than a nod to acknowledge my presence, neither he nor his wife responded. How much he must have wanted to get to the other side, to walk his feet into a state like that? Hikers talk a lot about blisters: there are all kinds of home remedies for hardening the feet and I'd been sleeping every night with mine soaked in Vaseline. St Edmund's had a table laid out with treats for walkers: cereal bars and boxes of juice and plasters, and, knowing there'd be cash machines in Richmond, I left the last bit of my cash in exchange for a Mars bar, resisting the urge to go back to the couple and point out the little tubes of antiseptic cream and blister dressings that were also available. I sensed the pair would welcome no intrusion into their fertile marital silence. The two of them sat quietly, not touching and in some kind of stalemate. Maybe they'd just had another argument about their GPS gadgets, or – this is my fantasy – she'd encouraged him to continue when his feet weren't up to it with such vigour that her support had started to feel like control and, by coming to this standstill, he was resisting her.

* * *

The Parallel Path

Applegarth Scar is a limestone cliff that the path contours around on its way towards Richmond. Eleven days in, and I had not become immune to the views. Sometimes I sent photographs to Clive, nothing more of me in the shot than my shadow. Most nights I phoned home and talked to my children and Duncan about what I'd been up to. But during the day I hoarded the experience, tucking it inside myself, feeling nourished by my happy secrets: the steps only I would take, the sights only I would see. *Mine, Mine, Mine*, I thought, as if I was eating it. Greedy with euphoria, I looked back over the gently wooded dales I'd just walked through, the foothills around the villages I'd passed, the Swale, its banks sometimes densely covered in trees, sometimes flat and grassed, meandering its way towards the town. I hurried on, powered by my desire for the metropolitan offerings of Richmond, the biggest town I'd visit during the whole walk. I imagined streets lined with second-hand bookshops, cafés and laundrettes, hoped for sweetshops and anticipated the anonymous churn of pavement pedestrians that I had started to miss. The path led me higher, towards the stony shelf of Willance's Leap.

You'd expect – given its name – that Willance's Leap would be a startling and remarkable precipice, something to approach with caution, but it's only a rocky slope and I'd hardly have noticed it except for its little monument: a weirdly out of place-looking obelisk, about as tall as a big man, tucked behind a set of waist-high iron railings that seem to be there in case, having come up the bridlepath, you were tempted to nick the finger of stone and carry it away across the Dales with you. The Leap earned its name in the early 1600s when Robert Willance fell from his horse in a hunting accident. Wainwright says Willance was uninjured, though other sources claim that his nervous horse, misjudging the steepness of the slope in a sudden mist, was killed in the fall and Willance himself suffered a badly shattered leg and was stranded overnight in the freezing November mist. As he awaited rescue, he apparently slit open the gut of the dead horse with his hunting knife and inserted his injured leg into the cavity. This piece of gruesome quick thinking was credited with Willance avoiding gangrene and later surviving an amputation.

The story is one of those cheeky fictions of success we like so much. Willance didn't 'leap' anywhere, after all; his horse stumbled and fell in bad weather, and he, perched on its back, fell right along with it. The monument doesn't mark a site of athletic achievement, only everyday human disaster. How sticking your mangled leg into the opened guts of a horse is meant to protect you from infection is beyond fathoming. The story feels like an overegged myth circulated by the politician himself, aimed at turning poor horsemanship, bad luck, a nasty tumble and ordinary human disability into a triumph of ingenuity and endurance. Beyond the self-mythologising of a rich seventeenth-century draper – a fine politician and a poor horseman – the story also constitutes a kind of foundation myth for modern Richmond itself. There are local ballads and poems about the fall, and about what happened afterwards. Robert had his leg buried in Richmond's main churchyard and would go on to be the town's first alderman. He gave regular and lavish gifts to the town to celebrate his survival, some of which are still kept and displayed in the Green Howards regimental museum. When he died, he was reunited with his amputated leg and buried at St Mary's, where it had been waiting in the grave for him.

After Applegarth Scar, I took out Clive's letter. He'd been thinking about the pictures I'd sent of Shap's quarry works. The memory of his father driving the tanker to Shap quarry has set Clive off on a reverie and his gift for me today is a list of what he loves, starting with another reminder of home: the pylons down by the River Lune with 'their great loping electrical twine that feeds all our greedy day to day needs' and the 'deadwood and drowned dogs' on the wide shallow banks of the Lune Estuary. I've walked down there too and, during times of avian flu, counted the dead swans and geese, their balding wings and empty ribcages spread over the terrain they've washed up on: untidy mounds of bleached driftwood and broken polystyrene, tangles of blue and orange rope, hundreds of mud-filled crab shells.

There are some beautiful green and blue views where we live, but in this letter, Clive looks in the other direction and remembers the 'demonised cooling towers' and 'giant wind farms whose shadows move across the land, better than any sundial to mark out the number of our days'. He's romantic in his nostalgia, remembering the 'everlasting flame that belched from the chemical works on the banks of the Manchester Ship canal' and the 'giant blocks of cement that hold all that exotic simmering fission'.

Clive's letter is attached to a copy of John Davies's 1983 photograph of Agecroft Power Station in Salford. The original photograph is in Washington DC's National Gallery of Art in the British Landscape collection. It shows the power station's new cooling towers and pylons sitting in their razed patch of cleared land. This picture captures a North poised between modernity and redundancy: the old redbrick colliery buildings visible behind and between the great pale cooling towers, which dominate the frame. There's a football game happening in the foreground. In the left-hand corner, there's a man with a horse doing some sort of business half hidden by the dark shapes of the scratchy and crooked trees. This photograph acknowledges one of the ways in which the North is imagined: the post-industrial spoil, greyscale and dirty, former producer of textiles and coal. But it shows something else too: the way we layer up, keep hold of ourselves, remember. We've got wind farms and nuclear power stations now, but this modernity is haunted by what persists in the landscape as well as the culture. Clive has written a love letter to the defiant and capacious ugliness of the North, and to the way some of us can only imagine it in greyscale. I sat in the boldly alive green of the countryside in high summer, the air around me chattering with insects and bird life, and was transported.

After lunch, there was a light shower, the first on the walk. It clung to the long grass in fat strings of beads and dripped heavily from the corrugated edges of barn roofs. I didn't bother with my cagoule, which I'd been carrying uselessly for well over a hundred miles now. The water was warm on the back of my neck and I let it soak through my hair and drip down the back of my T-shirt. It dried up as I made my way past East Applegate Farm and I stopped to count an uneven row of rusty horseshoes nailed up over a barn door. I saw a man and a younger boy – probably his son – peering at their maps and looking around. The better part of me was glad they were there. I'd noticed the horseshoes weren't nailed on that securely, and a thought about nicking one of them for Clive had arisen. The audience kept me honest, and I stopped to chat for a while.

These two had the look of experienced coast-to-coasters about them: there was something at ease and unworried about their bearing and, like me, they'd been on the trail long enough to have submitted to its discomforts without much in the way of complaint. They were dishevelled and filthy and they too hadn't bothered putting their waterproofs on when it rained. We started to reminisce, each knowing intimately where the other had been, and compared notes on how we'd managed the bogs after Nine Standards and, before that, the steep descent down Kidsty Pike. There was an easy camaraderie between the two of them, wordless and intimate, and I stood in the damp glow of it, wondering what it might be to take a walk like this in company. They were looking around for somewhere to wild camp and teased me a little about the soft bed and hot shower I'd be looking forward to that night. When I waved goodbye to them, the father promised to buy me a drink if he saw me out in Richmond that evening.

Along with the letter, Clive had attached, with a paperclip, a note about *Edge of Darkness*. Broadcast around the same time as Davies took his photograph, this is a 1985 anti-nuclear drama by Scottish writer Troy Kennedy Martin. Martin was influenced by his concerns about the safety record of the Sellafield power station, just south of St Bees and home to Britain's worst ever nuclear accident, the Windscale fire in 1957. The whole series is set in the post-industrial North of the popular imagination: there's plenty of shots of windswept moorland, wet pavements and dirty trains carrying containers of spent uranium away from sinister-looking power stations. The miners' strike is on the television, every meal involves brown sauce and most scenes feature lots of men with Yorkshire accents standing around smoking. The local Labour councillor is attending a discussion held on a university campus, ready to explore alternative futures for the energy-producing North.

This apparent realism is coupled with a magical folkloric evocation of landscape as a complex set of systems resulting in something like consciousness. This living, pissed-off landscape constitutes a traditional view of the rural North too, where anything too far away from the urban centres becomes a vaguely sketched-in marshland, populated by weirdly hostile locals or marsh-goblins. *Here be monsters!* This is the place where Craven, a police detective, begins to investigate the sudden death of his daughter, Emma. Martin's inspiration for this magical Northern landscape is modern as well as folkloric; the series is in lively dialogue with Lovelockian ideas. Before she died, Emma had been a member of an anti-nuclear group – Gaia – and the Lovelockian possibility that the world is alive and objects to what humans are doing to it haunts each episode. This mystical view of the world's living systems prepares the reader for the main character's ending: Craven dies of radiation sickness on a Scottish hillside covered with black flowers. This is a reference to James Lovelock's Daisyworld, a computer programme simulating the growth of white and black flowers as a way of testing the Gaia hypothesis.

The Parallel Path

Clive and I had talked about this show before and his note was a reminder of previous conversations. I knew what a fan he was, and how the way the show imagined the North had influenced his thinking. When I watched *Edge of Darkness*, I saw in it all the things that Clive loves: the grimness of that traditional North, the tenderness of working-class men, the hope as well as the filthiness of a time I can't quite remember but which shaped the ways my parents lived and raised me. But I, carrying my worries for my daughter and my own losses into every new encounter, could only meet it as a story about parental loss and helplessness. The sudden death of a daughter on the brink of adulthood triggers a fresh bout of Craven's grief for his wife, who had died many years previously. We learn the two of them, parent and child, have always been together, the daughter as keenly attentive to her father's grief as he has been to hers. One scene shows them walking together behind their wife/mother's coffin. This is a slow, sad walk to the grave's edge and the beginning of their navigation of a wifeless, motherless landscape.

For me, *Edge of Darkness* would always be about grief work and not police work. After Emma's death much of the action follows Craven as he investigates her murder, unpicking collusion and corruption, nuclear espionage and political cover-ups. But Craven's search is not about the ends of justice: restitution or restoration. He seeks to know the rooms where his little girl slept and the places she walked and his searching becomes a process of remapping a life without her in it, finding new bearings, taking a set of co-ordinates from a radically changed, yet still magical world. Understanding his daughter means understanding the place she was investigating; a key moment in both the investigation and Craven's grief occurs when he's able to access a three-dimensional map of Northmoor. (Northmoor is a fictional place, though Martin's notes make it clear he imagined it in proximity to the real-life Sellafield.) For Craven, his daughter's body is indivisible from the nuclear waste facility her Gaia group was interested in. In the mortuary, he takes a lock of her hair from her corpse: later, he discovers, like the landscape itself, it is contaminated enough to set a Geiger counter rattling. Craven's investigation feeds him: he becomes as contaminated by the life of his daughter as she had been by the radiation at Northmoor. Even in death, she's with him, her voice giving him instructions about how to work the washing machine and accompanying him through unfamiliar cities as he retraces her footsteps. The father aches to know his child, rooting around her bedside drawer, and in a shocking and well-observed moment of parental intrusion, discovers and handles her vibrator. It becomes unclear if he's grieving the fact that she's dead, or that she grew up. In death, he seems to understand her better and hear her voice more clearly than he did when she was alive and off being a teenager, staying out late, keeping her secrets. Clive has sent me to this show for his own reasons, but it taught me that grief is not about coming to terms with absence, but in accommodating presence differently.

After I left the man and his son, who were still vocally amused by how easy a ride I was giving myself by not camping, I carried on alone along a muddy path that passed through a gate and into Whitcliffe Wood. The cloud had come in again, and the branches of leggy ash trees met overhead; the place was cool and dim and quiet: it felt like walking into St Edmund's; the sky disappearing, the air held more closely around me. I was getting tired, slowing down and looking around at the trees, maybe a bit gormlessly, when I tripped and muddied my hand in breaking my fall. Nobody witnessed this, nothing hurt and I wiped my hand on some grass and carried on. A few more paces along the path and I tripped and fell again.

The path was churned up and a little muddy after the recent shower, but not *that* muddy. For someone who'd got across the peat bogs in one piece, this gentle track should have presented no problem. I stopped and looked back at where I'd been. There were no wobbly rocks or exposed tree roots: no obvious reason why I'd fallen. As I turned my head to scan the ground and find what had made me fall, dizziness swept over me: as if the path itself was tilting or had become soft. The ground had become a living thing, reaching up to snatch me into itself. I could easily have fallen again. Not a trip or a slip but a tipping over, as if I'd suddenly forgotten how to balance on two legs. I reached out with one hand, swiping through the moist air as if for something to hold on to, then the sensation passed, and I was fine.

I'd been more worried about my difficulty in staying upright being observed than I was at the possibility of injuring myself in a fall. We get embarrassed when we fall because we're supposed to grow out of it: like getting lost, a controlled navigation of the body moving through space is a marker of a rational being, and to fail at it is to fail at being human. That's why Robert Willance had to make a myth out of the fall from his horse and why a whole town joined in and raised a monument that obscured vulnerability with valour. While they're learning to walk, which for most children takes place between ten and twenty months, a child falls on average seventeen times per waking hour, spending more time on the floor than on two feet. Learning to walk means falling, but we don't want to know about it, not really; there's been more research done into language acquisition and object permanence – those other milestones of infant development – than there has been into how exactly children learn to walk.

Walking may be powered by desire – that's why the health visitor advised I put my daughter's toys out of reach to get her going – but it is made possible by balance, which is a fantastically complex set of operations involving not only muscle development in the head and neck, the core muscles in the abdomen, lower back and buttocks and the feet, but also an even more complex interplay of messages about orientation and location from the eyes, ears and a set of nerves connecting the inner ear to the brain. In *The Vestibular System: A Sixth Sense* the authors argue this system also controls our ability to direct our gaze (essential for everything, from strolling to flirting to reading), to judge distances and navigate between fixed points, contributes to the reliability of our reflexes, our ability to know which way up we are when we close our eyes, and how we visualise and remember routes we've walked along before. A functioning vestibular system is even involved in the way we develop higher levels of consciousness, theory of mind and empathy. We're not fully able to be ourselves in the world, and to understand ourselves as selves, moving through a variously configured and ever-changing space which other people also move through, without the proper functioning of this whole-body vestibular system. When it starts to go wrong, the symptoms can be subtle, and easily missed. It's no wonder I didn't really notice this fall meant something was wrong with me: I'd walked myself into the fittest state the sedentary, desk-bound version of myself had ever been in. I vaguely put my sudden struggle to stay upright down to low blood sugar. I ate a handful of nuts, drank the rest of my water and carried on.

When walking did finally come for my daughter, it came quickly. One morning, she got up on her feet and took a trip along the edge of the sofa. This is a typical stage in development; a halfway house between crawling and unsupported walking that is called *cruising*. My daughter was after the cat, who was sleeping on the back of the sofa. Her first proper word came at around this time too – *gentle* – which is what she heard me say whenever she got within reach of him.

This, according to that attachment parenting book I was still too young and knackered to think critically about, was the official end of the fourth trimester: my child was now old enough to bear the truth that she was no longer of my body, but alone inside her own. A few days after I first caught her cruising cat-wards, I went into the kitchen to fetch a drink and when I came back, she'd teleported from the blanket she'd been sitting on, surrounded by carefully placed just-out-of-reach toys, to the front door. There she stood, unsupported and swaying, eyeing the gap in the letterbox hungrily. The expression on her face was both defiant and furtive and when she saw me, she started crying. This looked like frustration at the locked front door and fear at her new sense of aloneness. She looked angry too, as if I had been the one to walk away from her.

We will do this walking-away dance many more times: at the start of school, when she both wanted me to hold her hand and walk her across the playground and into her classroom, and – at the same time – not to touch her or speak to her. It will crop up over and over during her fierce grief after Ben's death, when I sleep on her bedroom floor for a while and am berated both for being there and, when I give her privacy, for going away. During the pandemic, I will be so anxious about her asthma that I decide to take her out of school a week before it closes and the country goes into its official lockdown, robbing her of those last days with her friends, some of whom she wouldn't see again. Once I have her at home, I confine her to the house and try to force her to wear a mask when we walk the dog in the park.

I hope I was doing what I was supposed to do. I know my daughter did what she was supposed to do too, which was to tell me where to go and what to do with myself when I got there. One night she left the house in the dark without her coat, returning soaking wet several hours later. She refused to say where she had been wandering. Our paths diverged.

Balance of all kinds is something we only really notice when it's gone. So it is for the ways in which we choose to accompany someone else; when the journey is effortless, we barely notice it. More often, we lurch and stumble. At one of care's extremes, we find control: an excess of attentiveness fuelled by fear that serves the needs of the one caring and constricts the one cared for. At its other extreme are neglect and abandonment, a method the overwhelmed or ignored use to care for themselves by running away from what it hurts them to be in relationship with. Care's route between them is more of a tightrope than a highway and most of us will lose our balance and fall over and over again.

I am late to learn things too; maybe leisureliness is a family trait. As I'd been walking I'd started to understand that care's failures were stitched so closely into its fibres that to know care was also, inevitably, to know control and neglect. Every single offering of care is muddied with the everyday human clutter of self-interest and control and fear. But understanding this didn't take away the pain of personal insufficiency. My phone lines up all the photos I have ever taken in date order, and there's a moment, in the summer she was twelve and her father died, where my daughter stopped smiling. I saw it happen and told myself not to get grief muddled up with adolescence; one needed love and the other required a firm hand. There would be years to bring that smile back into being; all the time in the world. When I let myself know that in my daughter's grief I was only a good-enough mother to her some of the time, the knowledge is both brutal and kind because it puts me in need of the care of others and prevents the world falling into two halves, each impoverished by the lack of the other – the mothers and daughters, the ones who care and the ones who need it, the sick and the well, the grey and the green.

Richmond appeared, hugged by trees, criss-crossed with narrow cobbled streets. This is a place shaped (as human beings themselves are) by the apparatus of attack and defence. The old castle, perched on a cliff over the Swale, is an eleventh-century structure built in the aftermath of the Norman invasion and the focal point the rest of the town gradually evolved around. During the Civil War, Richmond was the headquarters of the Parliamentarians and in the First World War the castle was used to imprison conscientious objectors. There's still a fenced-in garrison and barracks in the adjoining town of Catterick. As the path turned to track turned to a road with a real pavement I spotted the Wainwright plaque, placed to welcome walkers and quote the nice things he'd written about the town. What he liked about the place is characteristic; in a world of flux and change, 'Richmond folk have always jealously guarded their heritage and consequently the town centre shows little in the nature of 20th century improvements.' This is Rishi Sunak's constituency, a Northern Conservative stronghold; even Nigel Farage is popular here. Wainwright's description of a place committed to 'true values' hits the ear differently in this post-Brexit, post-pandemic world. The plaque also offered some welcome accounting: I was 113 miles away from St Bees and had only 76 miles to walk before I'd reach Robin Hood's Bay.

DAY TWELVE

A Marathon with the Almost-Dead
Richmond to Ingleby Cross (23 miles/26½ miles)

The sun was shining almost aggressively through the little dining room windows in the Richmond B&B. I was too hot to be hungry and turned to Clive's letter for distraction from the joyless carb-loading. I got through my eggs and beans and accepted a bowl of porridge, trying to get it down before the day got any warmer and I began the longest day's walk of the whole trip – twenty-three miles over the Vale of Mowbray.

Clive had sent another lesson from the Charles Atlas course. In this lesson, Charles addressed 'a matter of prime importance', the 'great British complaint' of constipation. What followed were three pages of alarmingly specific advice on improved bowel functioning, including a graphic description of how best to administer an enema and some very arresting photographs of a nearly naked Charles demonstrating some exercises he promised would keep things moving along. I forced down the porridge, eying up the prunes and tinned pineapple sitting in Mason jars on the buffet bar.

The first part of the walk involved another stretch along the south bank of the Swale, a climb upwards through some dark, grubby woodland, the undergrowth a carpet of pale, ground elder choked with litter, and round the back of a

A Marathon with the Almost-Dead

sewage works. Once I emerged from the mucky edgelands I followed a track through fields and farms into North Yorkshire's agricultural flatlands. The dry-stone walls of the previous days turned into tall hedges and gates, each bearing a sign to remind the walker to close it after her, to stick to the path or the edge of the field, to drop no litter and to trample no crops.

After an hour or so, the path led me through a field in which there was a bull. There was no mistaking it: it looked exactly like the way bulls are drawn in children's picture books; the Platonic ideal of *bull* – a perfect black all over, spiky little brown horns (like the devil), red-rimmed eyes, wide square shoulders and shiny neat hooves. (All the better for trampling you with.) He even had a ring through his nose and the part of him that made him bull dangled ostentatiously beneath. I lingered by the gate and pep-talked myself. Was it even legal (I googled, knowing I was only killing time) for a farmer to keep a bull in a field through which ran a right of way? How fast could a bull run? How fast could I run? Could a bull crash through a hedge? Could I? I worked out an alternative route, avoided the field and the farm, and added a mile on to the day's total before heading onwards, flirting with the river as it ran through Catterick, skirting the racecourse and past a derelict pub.

By the Swale again, though a dirtier version of it than the last couple of days, I sat on a bench, drank from my water bottle and took another look at Clive's letter. His opening sentences were even more striking than nearly naked Charles and his enviable bowels. 'Was it uplifting letters you hoped for? Clive dancing naked around trees on a nature ramble?' he asked. Was this anger, or was he trying to make me laugh? Clive wanted to tell me what it felt like to start the work of dying. 'This business of dying is solitary too – the work of letting go – neatly/messily – slowly/rapidly – gently or with unwelcome violence. Others might float and fret with me with a desperate love (and god knows, we all need moments of that and we need each other), but it's down to the almost-dead to deal with the sticky ending.'

I found myself, as I sat there with bumblebees flitting around my head, long grass tickling my shins, admiring the sentences. I liked the feel of 'down to the almost-dead' and read it aloud a few times, feeling all those 'd' and 't' sounds in my mouth as if they were boiled sweets: a treat, a gift. But this clever fiddling about with words is one of the ways I pretend I'm attending to what someone wants to say to me while ignoring it. Clive raised a tender subject, angry that etiquette had left him alone with it: 'Because our country is prudish and doesn't want to really talk about the business of dying, and certainly doesn't want to do anything serious around assisted dying, people are forced to actions best described as suicide.'

Propriety is a kind of calcified and deadened version of care, as related to it as the fossil is to the soft, living creature it used to be. Clive has meant something – the design of these letters always means something – by writing on the back of the Charles Atlas lesson about bowel movements. If constipation is a specifically British affliction, then reticence around death is another. I started to get a sense of how lonely that reticence – which in the North is as often

A Marathon with the Almost-Dead

expressed through sarcasm and dark humour as it is through polite formality – had made Clive. We can be glib and dark together: it is one of the things I enjoy most about our conversations; once we'd tested the edges to check we weren't really going to be able to shock each other, we could get to the business of being friends. But this is not a loneliness that can be cured by a companion. Clive is skilfully loved by his family and loves them in return. ('We just like each other,' he'd said, shrugging and beaming, when once I'd asked him if he had any wisdom about raising teenagers that he could share.) No matter how much and how well he was loved, his death would be something that he would do alone, and the fact of that would hurt all his friendly bystanders too. In that abrupt opening, 'Was it uplifting letters you hoped for?', I heard my friend's Puckish, slightly sarcastic voice as a thin veil of care, covering but not hiding the worry that by committing these thoughts to paper, he may do me some harm.

I left the river and made my way towards Bolton-on-Swale, a tiny village with a little church. Like St Edmund's in Marske, St Mary's takes its responsibilities to the modern pilgrim seriously: here the walker may tend to her body as well as her soul. There was a table laid out with drinks and snacks, the facilities for making tea and coffee, boxes of plasters and antiseptic cream and an honesty box for donations. I took off my boots and let the cold flags of the church floor ease my hot feet, enjoyed the cassock hanging on the back of the toilet door (like a child, I tittered at the idea of a vicar taking a pee), made myself a cup of tea and rested in the cool of the church.

The Parallel Path

St Mary's is known for its memorial of Henry Jenkins. By most accounts, Jenkins was a poor and unremarkable man, utterly ordinary apart from his claim that he was 169 years old at the time of his death in December 1670. He said – under oath – he could remember the battle of Flodden in 1513 and, when questioned, told a tall story about helping out the English archers by passing them arrows. Seventy-odd years after his death his myth was already being formed: the village raised the obelisk in the churchyard and mounted a large black marble plaque in the church itself, adorned with a long text written by the Master of Magdalene College, Cambridge. You'd expect a memorial stone to emphasise the unusual achievements of a person but this text focuses on the poverty and humility of the life remembered. Jenkins was a man 'enriched with the goods of nature but not of fortune', and the ordinariness of his long existence is set up as a kind of example to the rest of us. God had bestowed on Jenkins 'a patriarch's health and length of days, to teach mistaken man these blessings are entailed on temperance, a life of labour, and a mind at ease'.

I detected here a much earlier iteration of the view I'd bumped into at Keld: health and long life are both a reward for hard work and self-control and could even be evidence of the person being favoured by God. It is difficult not to draw the intended conclusion: the sick, disabled and dying have only themselves to blame and are probably in God's bad books. A belief like this is self-care of the most toxic kind. We decide that hard work and good behaviour are enough to exempt us from suffering and death because the fact that even the good and rich will die is too terrible to contemplate. Equally, the fact that some of the suffering of the poor is caused by the rich and not some mysterious working of providence is something many of us prefer not to know. All of this effectively shuts the sufferer up and is another way of isolating them. Who'd want to talk about their illness or dying when confessing to suffering is tantamount to admitting to personal and spiritual failure?

Jenkins himself wasn't remembered by this plaque and obelisk: he'd disappeared almost entirely behind the sickly comfort of the life lesson for the well to which those who came after had reduced him. But still, I left St Mary's deciding I quite liked this man because I had resolved to imagine him as a penniless joker, entertaining himself by playing the fool and hoodwinking the rich and the pious into believing tall stories of his exploits at Flodden. I hoped he'd enjoyed himself.

Wainwright, preferring the rugged scrambles and climbs through the Lakeland fells, is dismissive about what the walk from Richmond to Ingleby Cross offers. Lots of coast-to-coasters agree with him; the most popular contemporary guidebook calls the entire route 'a tepid agricultural tract' and few break it up with a stay at Danby Wiske: the general attitude is that you may as well grit your teeth and get it over with as quickly as possible. It is true that farmland has been over-romanticised for centuries and today's miles were no grand tour through a Northern pastoral idyl. I saw broken-down and rotting farm machinery, thin dogs tied up in yards without shade, fly-tipped mattresses and burned-out cars on the edges of fields. Many of the old hedgerows had been pulled in favour of great swathes of grass monoculture, the native birds and insects decimated, the streams and rivers polluted with chemical runoff. But still, I was happy.

I got lost again. There are two routes: Wainwright's original, which offers a cheeky bit of trespassing – generally tolerated – and an alternative. Both involve some road walking, and I confused the two, missed a turning and was heading too far along a road towards Northallerton before I realised where I'd gone wrong. I had to go another couple of miles along a different road, walking into incoming traffic and dodging cars going too fast along a lane on which they didn't expect to see a walker. I waded through long grass and ragwort on the uneven verges, kicking through faded litter, sweating and annoyed with myself. That was another two and a half miles added to the day's total, and on most days that wouldn't matter, but today, when every hour it got hotter and I was already doing so many miles, it felt like a disaster.

I sat on a bench and ate my jelly babies. I must have looked pathetic because a woman in a car with two kids in the back pulled over and asked me if I wanted a lift anywhere. She seemed frazzled and the kids were red-faced and fighting. That car would have air conditioning. It wasn't my fault I'd missed my turning, was it? Nobody would know and getting a bit of help wouldn't exactly be cheating, would it? I wiped my face and told her I was fine and carried on, waving to the kids as the car disappeared around the corner.

In Danby Wiske, there's another church and, delinquent pilgrim that I was, I stopped there to rest, pulling off my boots and lying down full length on one of the pews. I'd done more than fourteen miles and the heat felt as brutal as a personal attack. My eyes were sticky, and I closed them, trying not to think about the ten miles left to go. To cross the country on foot felt ridiculous; the self-flagellation involved in getting from one side to the other self-indulgent and attention seeking. I must have fallen asleep because the whispering sounds of two women taking away some dying flowers and replacing them with fresh bunches woke me up a little while later. I won't have been the first walker that summer to use the church as a refuge from the sun and to rest on a pew for a while before moving on. I sat up quickly and tried to behave as you are supposed to in church, but these women only smiled at me and turned back to their work.

After Danby Wiske there were more farms. The landscape was measured and patient and the thought of Clive alone with the work of his dying was with me at every step. The postcard I'd sent him from Kirkby Stephen had a picture of a tree on it because I knew he liked them. Drawings and photographs of trees, often rotting, crumbling, or the standing dead, occurred repeatedly in his letters. He had a special tree: a dying, fungus-encrusted but still vibrant sycamore that lived behind a dry-stone wall outside Littledale in the northern part of the Forest of Bowland. He'd taken me there to see it on one of our walks and had shared many photographs of it.

But a postcard with a tree on it really wasn't much. A letter like this, two big handfuls of letters like these, deserved a better response. He'd written that death – his death, and the concept of it more generally – was just a 'fiction in people's minds'. There was a challenge here: to read this letter as if it was something other than a well-turned piece of lyric prose, though it was, and to refuse to admire it in bad faith, considering my friend's dying 'as if' it was true and with the bloodless kind of attentiveness I paid when bad or frightening things happened in books. It was important to hear, to read and, more importantly, to respond in a better way than that.

The psychologist Susan Silk specialises in the care of those traumatised by natural disasters and terrorist attacks. As she worked with people who had lived through Hurricane Katrina and the attack on the World Trade Center she became interested in the way suffering can leap from one body to another. Her work made it clear to her that the people who came to help, the paramedics and the nurses and firefighters and the family and friends of the traumatised, injured and directly bereaved, also required care. As these helpers witnessed and listened, a suffering that was not theirs started to inhabit them. Silk developed an idea she named Ring Theory, which is often depicted as a series of concentric circles with the person who has been hurt in the middle, those closest to them in the next smallest ring, colleagues and acquaintances further out still. The aim of it was to help those of us involved with a person who is suffering know where to both give help and to get it. The trick is to figure out your proximity to the blast and provide 'comfort in' to those nearest to it and 'dump out' to those further away.

It sort of makes sense. Nobody wants to go to their GP with a strange lump and listen to their physician's worries about their wayward teenage child. You want the person prescribing your chemotherapy to have someone to talk to about what it is to spend a working life trying to outwit death, but that person should not be you. Ring Theory acknowledges that those who care need to be cared for too, sometimes for wounds inflicted during the act of caring itself. There's a dignity to the idea: even in the midst of a crisis we are and can be responsible for weighing our discomforts, imagining the weight of our neighbours' burdens, and choosing carefully in which direction to send our own.

Ring Theory is sometimes borrowed by bereavement charities and counselling organisations and called the 'circle of grief', which is where I first read about it, wondering about how best to listen and help in those early days after Ben had died. With the 'circle of grief' the idea becomes about proximity to the dead person. The child or wife or parent is at the centre of the circle, those less closely related further out. Using relatedness as a rule of thumb, it is easy to work out whose turn it is to care and for whom and because I understood how peripheral my own thoughts and feelings were, I tried to keep them to myself. When I said my daughter's father had died, people asked about her and her sisters and her stepmother. It was right that they did. It was right that I stood to one side, and away, waiting for a practical job like tea-making or bin-emptying to become obvious. It took a long time for me to understand that this was a loss that had happened to me, as well as to everyone else. 'Your old friend died,' someone said to me, when I said, a few weeks later, that I couldn't work or sleep and I didn't know why.

* * *

The Parallel Path

After curing my sulk at Danby Wiske with more jelly babies and a cheese sandwich, I finally learned to love what a flat place could offer. I crossed field after field of yellow corn. Green pea plants with curly tendrils and fizzy-smelling unripe wheat swished past my hips. I lost count of the neat green pastures full of cows, safely gated away from me. With the extra couple of miles added on for getting lost and avoiding the bull, the day's total had been bumped up to just over twenty-six: the traditional distance of a marathon. The extra miles on the longest day had felt like a disaster but, after something to eat, I started to see the funny side. Today I would walk a whole marathon and I'd disapproved of them since Ben started running them.

At first, he'd wanted to do six marathons in six months: he ran in a red and white running vest with his name on, and 'six marathons in six months' printed underneath and a link to his website and his Twitter handle, which summed up his situation: @chemodadruns. Sometimes he'd post pictures of our daughter on his website, and I didn't like that. The donations started to come in, first a trickle, then a torrent. Six months passed, and he did it; he'd run six marathons and transformed himself from patient into hero. He carried on, signing up for more marathons, travelling around the country and sometimes to Europe to do them. He had some surgeries and long stays in hospital, did his chemotherapy and lived longer than we thought he might. I wonder if he thought of these extra months as borrowed, or a coda – some epilogue to the story of his life as a dad, as a librarian, as a man who did not have cancer? He spent a lot of that unexpected time running up and down the

A Marathon with the Almost-Dead

River Ribble in Preston or building himself up at the gym. He watched his diet and kept training records. There were times when he wasn't well enough to run, and during those he worked on the busy Facebook pages and attended to his media requests. We all prefer the terminal to be inspirational: thousands of followers on his Facebook page cheered him on. By the time he died he'd run twenty-four marathons in twenty-four months. It was extraordinary. He was so very well loved for it.

A few hours after he died, I took our daughter and the younger two girls out to the park. Duncan drove the car, and we bought the girls Happy Meals and parked near the swings under the shade of two sycamores that dropped their sticky yellow-green flowers on the windscreen whenever the wind blew. It was early July: the day was bright.

My daughter leaned her cheek against the car window and wouldn't look at us. She sucked the milkshake up through her straw, deliberately making a chugging noise that in usual circumstances we'd tell her to stop.

We talked about Ben and the fact that he'd died. About his running. If there was something to say here, and if it was my job to say it, I came up short. Putting one fact – that Ben had died – against another – that he'd done a lot of running – was a way of trying to feel how these two statements were equal to or different from each other.

The BBC News website did the same thing: ' "Marathon man" cancer patient Ben Ashworth dies' was how they'd announced his death that afternoon. They'd called him 'marathon man' when he was raising money too, and I'd wanted to ask him if that felt like a reduction or an expansion of who he was, but I'd kept my questions to myself

The Parallel Path

and now it was too late to ask them. There'd been five summers since then, but the sight of sycamore flowers always takes me back there.

The word 'marathon' has become a by-word for any extraordinary feat of endurance, though it is running we think of most often. When a person runs a marathon, they hardly ever expect to win it: making a personal best time might be nice, but completing the thing is enough: everyone gets a medal. There's something egalitarian and non-competitive about this that I should like. But as a non-runner, I'd watched Ben run and understood the fetishisation of his endurance as a sick kind of violence. Why should we award laurels to the runner who has been able to carry on doing something his body does not want to do? He has forced himself through pain and misery, past knackered knees and blackened toenails, to finish the race. There's no point to it really; no essential message carried, as in the myth of the first marathon in Greece. There's the money raised, I suppose, but what does it say about the rest of us that donating to fund cancer research is such a burden we need to be paid for our generosity by the sight of an unwell man running himself into exhaustion? The pointlessness of the marathon is essential to its greater meaning: if it can't be about winning, nor getting to the race's destination, then it becomes clear it is about pain and discomfort or, more precisely, about the special insanity of spending a long time doing something you don't have to do and don't really like doing. (For hoovering the stairs this morning, I award myself a rosette.)

This kind of endurance relies on us understanding the body as some dumb thing that must be flogged away from its own desires for rest and comfort by the mind, that cold, imperious entity who sits pretty up top and does not suffer the effort of the journey. I did understand the obsessiveness of persistence, the all-consuming fire of addiction, the complicated peace to be found in surrendering yourself entirely to something that is not you. But as his miles mounted up, it was not always easy for me to explain to my daughter where Ben was or what he was doing. For a while, I wished he would have run less and turned to face what was coming. Our city's marathon man became a hero, but he was our daughter's hero too, and I wanted him to stand his ground and help her to see what was going to happen.

Then the day came when I covered all those miles myself. Endurance slipped, opened out, became more spacious and gentler. Endurance became about friendliness, not force. I can't know what powered Ben through all those miles, not really. When I say I wish he'd have done his dying the way I thought he should have done it what I'm really saying is that I wish he was still alive. I would have liked the chance to carry on disapproving of decisions he made that were nothing to do with me. Was he running *towards* and not *away* after all? I was still heading east and away from home too, but that day endurance became a room to invite things into. When I felt euphoric to be crossing the corn fields under the bright clear sky, I walked. When I wondered about what I was up to, leaving Duncan (who had *definitely* had a harder pandemic than I had) to manage the kids and the house on his own while I indulged myself, I walked. When my feet hurt and I was thirsty and I wanted to call a taxi and get a shower, I walked. When I was lonely and wanted to divert to the nearest train station, I walked. When I was smugly drunk on a sense of my own walking prowess, I walked. When I was embarrassed about how much I wanted this, I walked. When the hugeness of the world, even my own local corner of it, and the slowness of my small steps across it made me feel vulnerable, tiny, protected, abandoned, cherished, lost, I walked. This version of endurance taught me a little more about becoming quietly hospitable to the changeable weather of that thing we call self and to befriend all of these inner visitors without preference. That's a lot easier to do when the decision about what to do next – take just one more step – has already been made.

I had learned to walk like this, but I wanted to be able to live like this.

Over the last couple of miles, however, it became evident that my own particular brand of endurance did not involve much in the way of stoicism. I can tell you that my feet hurt. Or I can say that before I walked a marathon, I didn't pay much attention to the surfaces of things. Most often I'd walk looking upwards or ahead, watching out for the next cairn, or gazing at the view as it changed. What was beneath my feet was of little interest to me and it was enough to know if the ground was muddy or the incline steep. When walking started to properly hurt, more than it had ever done before, I forgot what I'd been taught about erosion and sticking to the marked paths and walked on the grassy verges, the softness as delicious as rest. I avoided the dried-out ruts the tractors had left through the fields and the sight of a long, long gravelled track that looped between three farms on the final stretch was enough to make me shudder. I felt every piece of gravel through the soles of my boots for two miles, and they were the slowest two miles I have ever walked.

I texted Clive as I shuffled along, forgetting to be a good friend, a good listener, a happy witness for the walk that I was taking partly for him. He had hinted about wanting to hear more from me, hadn't he? In a series of texts, I finally let him see a little more of the walker he'd been wondering about. My turning up to be seen was superficial, but it was a start. I complained about what I'd chosen for myself as I watched the yellowhammers and skylarks flit across the fields and the sun dropped into late afternoon. I moaned about my feet. I made sure he understood precisely just how hot it was, and just what my feelings were about that. Clive is not, it goes without saying, an obvious candidate to hear my minor woes. He regularly has a procedure called a bone aspiration: this involves a nurse forcing a needle into his pelvis to extract marrow for testing. It is unpleasant, and he sometimes wonders about asking the nurses to retrieve a fragment of bone 'while they're at it' so he can make a reliquary. Should I have sent my whinging elsewhere? It seemed I'd decided that 'comfort in' and 'dump out' did not apply to the unique, self-inflicted sufferings of the long-distance walker.

I did wonder, when Clive and I first started chatting, if it was a good idea to be friends with someone who was going to die. It took me too long to realise that Clive was also signing up, quite willingly, to spend some of his precious and limited minutes listening to me bang on about my wobbly ankle and the strange new pain in my right arse cheek. I had made the same mistake about suffering as I had about time: it is not a finite substance that can be passed around as if it were money, weighed, measured, gathered up and given to someone else to care for. Ring Theory would only make sense if suffering was a solid matter we could pass from hand to hand and be rid of. The it-seems-to-make-sense equation just leaves all of us lonely in carefully tended bubbles of our own misery that the well-intentioned have constructed for us in the name of care. Letting go of it was a relief.

While exclusion from the usual human traffic of friendliness might be as isolating as reticence or politeness, Clive had considered his own solitary journey carefully in his letter. He described the apartness from others he experienced as he made that 'shift in my place along the conveyor belt towards oblivion' and the bleakness of the solitude he sometimes experienced at home, scouring the internet for information about assisted dying and the gentlest and most dignified ways of ending a life. The words available for a response seemed paltry and embarrassing. I could share my opinions on the legality of assisted dying: we'd talked about that lots of times before. I could rehearse my observations about the way our literary and popular culture deals with (or does not deal with) death. Maybe I could tell him what it had been like to watch Ben's slow dying, to linger near his finish line and witness the quieter, more private steadfastness of those closest to him. But as I considered these possibilities, none of them felt remotely adequate.

A Marathon with the Almost-Dead

Instead, I pulled Clive's letter out of the front pocket of my bag and decided, as I trudged those last hard miles, to commit parts of it to memory. Learning something off by heart puts words inside your body. I was volunteering for a kind of spirit possession where Clive's 'first person singular, that pregnant enormity' became part of my 'I' too. I didn't tell Clive I was going to do this because it felt alarming to me: someone else's words inside your skull, your mouth, your ribcage; foreign bodies welcomed home: this was an intimacy too far. Do any of us really want to be read like this? 'I am not at all miserable when I am writing,' Clive had written at the end of the day's letter. So I read and reread as I walked, and read again, keeping the present-tense moment of his writing alive, knowing friendship differently now, as both an act of trespass and a willingness to be trespassed into.

The path turned around farm buildings and the edges of fields, the endless distance broken up by stiles and slot gates. I was steadfast in cleaving to it. In the months to come, the day I walked across the entire Vale of Mowbray will become a kind of prayer for me. 'You did *that*,' I'd say to myself, looking at my photographs – the relentlessness of fields and hedges that might drive a person mad with the boredom of repetition, 'so you can definitely do *this*.' These days, when I say that to myself, what I am calling up is not the gritted-teeth mind-over-matter feat of violently forcing myself into doing something I don't want to do, but the soft memory of what it was like to notice what was happening as fully as I could, offer friendliness to it and allow it to inhabit me, to let someone else see it, and to take one more step anyway.

* * *

At the very end of the day's miles there was a final dash across the A19. There's no pedestrian crossing, no footbridge: you're supposed to wait for a gap in the traffic and run, though by that point I'd been walking for nearly ten hours and running was as likely as flying. I loitered a while at the garage, bought a few bars of chocolate because this would be the last shop for thirty miles, and was relieved to see the man and his son that I'd met on the way into Richmond the day before. Not too prickly to accept an escort now, the three of us crossed together. Hobble-running across the road as a group while the cars beeped their horns at us felt safer, meeting them a piece of good luck rather than an intrusion. They were camping in Ingleby Cross and on the way into the village I marvelled at how they'd managed the day carrying all of their camping things. The man was on his second crossing and insisted this one, despite the heat, was easier because he had company.

'I can't think about how bad my feet are,' he said, nodding towards his son who was wearing big headphones and oblivious to our conversation, 'not when I've got him to keep an eye on.'

It is sometimes true that caring for someone else can be distracting. I had seen the way I had made use of a busy anxiety about others (and resentment for the work that it caused me) as substitute for attending properly to myself. What the cared-for might have to say about being utilised in that way was another matter – the ways in which we ease each other's crossings are risky. That's one truth, and beside it lay another: friendship's traffic could always run in both directions.

* * *

A Marathon with the Almost-Dead

When I got to the bed and breakfast, it turned out I'd been given the most special accommodation they could offer: a little shepherd's hut away from the main house at the bottom of a beautifully tended flower garden. I felt treated and spoiled, and I liked that (hadn't my marathon *earned* me some special treatment?), though when I couldn't work the shower, I convinced myself it was broken and went grumpily back across the garden and down to the main house, shuffling on feet so sore it felt like I was walking across a carpet full of spilled Lego while every single muscle in my legs contracted with pain.

I complained huffily. Showers, especially showers in bed and breakfasts, should be easy to use. There should be hot water. Yes, *of course* I'd tried turning the dial to the left and waiting for the water to run for a while. The B&B owners both came down themselves to inspect what was happening, following me as I limped through their garden and between their flower beds. They turned the dial to the left and we waited for the water to run for a while and the shower ran hot, exactly as they said it would. They chatted to me kindly about their young grandson and how much they had missed seeing him during the lockdown as the room filled with steam.

I went to sleep with the windows of the hut wide open and woke in the early hours to heavy rainfall that soaked all the clothes I'd handwashed and hung out in the garden. I'd been dreaming about walking, moving in that effortless, gliding way through endless fields in different shades of gold and yellow, and as I walked through my dream, I'd been chanting some lines from Clive's letter. That's how you learn things off by heart: you've got to find some

The Parallel Path

rhythm in it, learn the beat by tapping it out with your feet and your hands, and slot the words into the space the movement of your body creates. I fell back to sleep easily, slept later than usual and woke to full sun, the rained-on kit already dry.

DAY THIRTEEN

Every Home a Hospital
Ingleby Cross to Clay Bank Top (12 miles)

At breakfast, my hosts eyed me with concern. Had I really gone to bed with no dinner last night? Nothing at all to eat? I told them, protective of my dignity, that I thought in retrospect I had been extremely dehydrated. Maybe I even had a touch of sunstroke. It had been a very long and hot day, after all. I hate to indulge in stereotypes – there are brisk and generous and unsentimental people everywhere – but what followed was a conversation that could only have taken place between a group of Northerners.

'Sunstroke. That'll do it. Did you not have a hat?' he said.

I shook my head.

'We did wonder. What with the shower . . .' she added.

'I just couldn't see how to get it going.'

'We couldn't work out what was wrong with you,' he said, putting a plate piled high with toast and butter in front me (to be 'going on with', before my 'real breakfast' arrived). 'We thought you might have been drunk . . .' and he paused, trying to find a well-mannered way for what he wanted to say next. Softened up by my walk, I helped him out.

'Or just thick?'

'Well, yes. Exactly.'

We laughed and carried on laughing. They sent me away with a cap from their lost property box and a large bottle of water he'd driven out and bought from the garage on the A19 while I'd still been in bed.

I left Ingleby Cross with the most painful feet (and arse) I have ever experienced in my life, limping steeply upwards through Arncliffe Woods for the first hour and enjoying the damp green air and the heavy, alive smell of the still-wet branches and mulchy undergrowth all around me. That morning a couple of friends had sent texts warning me that later that afternoon the weather was predicted to be even hotter than it had been yesterday. I should make sure to carry enough water, and consider shortening my walk, they said. I'd only half listened: I was in North Yorkshire, not the Med.

Advice is never more irritating than when it is correct: everybody knows that. I'd come across a meme while mindlessly doomscrolling one day during the pandemic. It featured Glinda the Good Witch from *The Wizard of Oz*, serene in her big pink dress, brandishing her sparkly wand. The text reads: 'If you say "I'm depressed" three times, someone with a "dance like no one is watching" T-shirt will appear and ask if you've tried taking a walk.' It isn't that the advice is wrong: there's so much research about the effect of walking on mood and brain chemistry that Glinda is hardly worth arguing with. What interested me more was Glinda herself, appearing in the woods with a smile and a magic wand right on cue. In the 1939 MGM film, Glinda is an amalgamation of several characters featured in Frank Baum's original novels. It might be why she's a bit much: she isn't just herself, she's also the Queen of the Field Mice and the Good Witches of both North and South. She turns up when Dorothy, on her own long walk, is lost, in trouble or tired. Because she's an amalgam, she becomes little more than a cipher for helpfulness in the face of distress. Clad in pink and eternally smiling, Glinda is the one who both shows Dorothy the yellow brick road that will lead her to Oz and, later on, draws attention to the specialness of her shoes and teaches her the trick of getting home.

Despite the warning of a heatwave, the morning felt soft and damp and close and I was, never mind the wear and tear making itself known in my knees, giddy with excitement. With the marathon crossing of the Vale of Mowbray (*all of it!*) under my belt, I'd spend the next three days crossing the North York Moors then I would be done. I had not allowed myself to picture myself reaching the east coast but that morning I did, and as I climbed, imagined what it would feel like to put my feet in the North Sea at Robin Hood's Bay. I was so close to finishing and going home that I wasn't going to miss a moment of it no matter what the bloody weather forecast said.

    I emerged from that relentlessly uphill trek through the woods on to Scarth Wood Moor, where there was nothing to see but heather for miles around, and one clear paved track through it, laid to protect the delicate ecosystems underfoot. The space hit the eye differently: empty of people, of farmhouses and barns, of sheep and cows, of hedges and stiles, and the easy drift of it into my gaze undid the tension in my muscles from yesterday's efforts. I knew the moor was not empty at all; the air was full of insects and birds: grouse hidden in the heather would regularly throw themselves untidily into the air and the ground was

The Parallel Path

writhing with life. But because of the absence of visible human industry and the lack of boundary marks or fences on the landscape the only point of focus was the single narrow path leading away and out of sight: the world felt enormous again. I fell into step with a group of women a little older than me who were doing part of the Cleveland Way together. This is another long-distance walk; a hundred-mile stretch along the east coast and through the North York Moors, and for a while, the Coast to Coast path shares its route. These women were happy and lively – giddy, almost. The group had the feel of a hen party about it. When someone tripped on the flagged path and tumbled into the heather, there was a lot of shrieking and friendly teasing.

'We'll end up carrying her, at this rate,' someone said. The falling woman had already been marked out as the clumsy one, the liability, the burden. She picked herself up and laughed; she seemed to be taking it well.

'She'll need a stretcher if she carries on like this, won't she?' They included me, and I laughed too, forgetting for the minute my own strange falling on the way into Richmond.

When the path narrowed and the group thinned out I came off the hot and breezy moorland and into the shade and green clamminess of Clain Wood. I left the group behind, and fell into step with a woman, another solitary walker like me. The woman asked me what I was doing on the Coast to Coast, all on my own. Although nearly a fortnight alone with myself had slowly revealed to me that something more fragile lay beneath my fierce urge to walk eastwards, I only told her some superficial version of the truth, which was that I'd spent the best part of a year shut in the house with my children, and if I didn't get outside on my own for a while, I'd probably end up going mad. I was flippant about it, not wanting to spoil the holiday mood, but she took me seriously and asked me about my children, about my job, about how it was for the students I'd been teaching via a screen during that time. After a while she told me about her daughter, who, in her early teens, had become very depressed. For a while it seemed she had been coming *past it*. That's the phrase she used. We think of these illnesses of distress as obstacles on the path, don't we? Something we can get over, or can be helped to get over? Healing looks like a successful hike: you climb the mountain or cross the bog, move on and leave it behind.

Her daughter had been doing well, she said. She seemed okay, then Covid happened. During the spring lockdown, her daughter took a step back, relapsed, went to her room, stopped speaking entirely. It became impossible to see the GP. The woman's words became a stream at this point and walking helped me to listen to her – her anxiety washed over us and into the heather. She was on the phone every single morning for hours, she said, waiting in a queue, listening to a recorded message about what to do if you had Covid symptoms. She'd get cut off at the same point in the recorded message each time, before it was finished, which made her think there was something wrong with the telephony system – but how to let the surgery know about that? When she did get through it was to someone who was working from home with a screaming kid in the background, and each day that person would tell her there were no appointments that day, and hang up on her before she could get another word in. She'd been in such a bind, she told me. Her daughter needed a referral to the Child and Adolescent Mental Health Service and that had to come from the GP, but even though she emailed the practice manager and waited by the phone every day, she could never get anyone from the GP's surgery to get back to her. *We thought about A and E but we'd have had to force her into the car and physically drag her there, and she'd have screamed, and fought us, biting and fighting like a cat, more strength in her than you'd have thought possible, given the state of her, given the look of her, a girl slowly fading away.* I listened. I wonder if anyone had ever told her or her daughter to get out on a nice long walk – though here she was, choosing one.

The path passed through farmland, and we waited for each other at the gates and lent a hand to lift heavy packs and walking poles over wobbly stiles. I'd not walked so long in company before and it was nice, throwing someone else's overloaded rucksack over the fence, and having a hand to hold on the way down from the ladder stile. After the farm, there was another steep climb up steps built into a densely wooded hill, and as we negotiated the incline, we clutched at each other's arms as if we were very old, or very young, and kept on talking. Eventually, this woman, this mother, this walker, told me that when her daughter did go back to school in the early summer, her teachers *took one look at her*. There'd been such a change in her, they said. They could see it right away. I thought of the couple back in Ingleby Cross who had been amazed and grieved by how much their grandson had grown in the months they had not seen him, astonished by what a body could do in six months and by what Zoom had hidden from them. *As if we hadn't noticed*, this woman, the mother, the walker said, *as if we hadn't begged and pleaded. I lost weight myself*, she said, because misery had become contagious.

After that the girl been admitted to a ward where she was kept for many weeks. And of course, this was when nobody was allowed to visit. They managed to keep her inside all that time, and though she hated it, and sent hundreds of texts a day hating her parents for it, absolutely raging, whatever they'd done to her in the hospital had worked in that she'd put on weight, she'd lived, she'd done well enough to be released from hospital, come home and begin again to withdraw from her family and fade away. I didn't need to ask this mother, this woman, this walker, why she was doing the Cleveland Way, just as I hadn't needed to ask the group I'd run into earlier why they were all acting like they were drunk, or at a hen party, or had just been let out of prison.

We walked a few miles together, up and down through woodland and emerging again on to Live Moor. Not being Glinda, I had nothing to say in the way of comfort or advice but the rhythm of shared walking was soothing. Roseberry Topping slipped in and out of view as the path curved around the gentle contours of the landscape.

'You'll go faster than me,' the woman with the sick daughter at home said. 'Don't let me hold you back.' She wasn't. This might have been a polite way of getting rid of me, but if it was I didn't mind: it was good to leave her as I wanted to be alone again to count cairns and watch out for the four-thousand-year-old burial mound that would mark the way on to Carlton Moor, where I'd be able to see, if I was lucky, the sea.

I *was* lucky. The forecast had been right: by mid-morning the sun had burned the dampness out of the air. The heather was dangerously dry; I passed many patches where it looked not only dead, but actually burned. Pinned to every post were warnings about the risk of fire and the importance of taking away any rubbish, especially glass bottles that might magnify the sun and cause a hot spot to erupt into flames on the desiccated ground. The haziness that had muffled the view on the moor above Gunnerside a few days earlier was gone: I turned slowly, seeing everything, marvelling. There, westwards, was the way back to the Vale of Mowbray's flat patchwork of yellow and green fields and I caught my breath at the realisation – coming to me as if it were news – that I had walked through *all of it*. I turned to look east and north over the moors – brown and purple and crossed with clearly visible paths – and found the blocky grey jumble of Middlesbrough and, beyond that, the North Sea.

It was only the North Sea, I know. Just a thin dark blue strip on the very edge of what I could see, melting into the sky. I couldn't even get a proper photograph of it. Was this what I had left home for? When people tell you they're going on their holidays to Filey or Scarborough you think of caravans and rainy weekends, not whole-body experiences of awe. I'd been priming myself for this view for nearly a fortnight: more than a hundred miles of walking, half a year in the anticipation, and this glimpse of my journey's end was more and better than I had hoped for. My chest fizzed; my eyes stung. It felt good to be alone because the only appropriate response to a sight like this was silence. No photograph for Clive. I nodded at what I could see, as if catching the eye of an old friend across a busy room, then carried on, downwards to Lordstones.

Clive's letter from yesterday was still on my mind. When someone tells you that they are experiencing the extreme solitude of the almost-dead, how best to be a friend to them? My hope that there was nothing a human could be that could not be befriended seemed sickly and Glinda-like; something pink and sparkly deployed in a way that would dishonour Clive's careful exploration of his own love-bounded solitude.

In her essay 'On Being Ill', Virginia Woolf makes a curious statement about the idea that all human feeling is, in some sense, shared.

> That illusion of a world so shaped that it echoes every groan, of human beings so tied together by common needs and fears that a twitch at one wrist jerks another, where however strange your experience other people have had it too, where however far you travel in your own mind, someone has been there before you – is all an illusion.

I'd felt that too – that isolating conviction that I was different from everyone else; that I was worst, the most awful or terrible, the unluckiest, the strangest, that something deep down about my humanity was utterly untranslatable. But I am not sure I have ever met anyone who has *not* felt that. Woolf's assertion that there are unique human experiences no other human can share is, ironically enough, almost universally felt.

As writers often do, Woolf resorts to the metaphor of a walk through a wild place to make her point about this unshared inner territory: 'Human beings do not go hand in hand the whole stretch of the way. There is a virgin forest, tangled, pathless, in each; a snow field where even the print of birds' feet is unknown. Here we go alone, and like it better so.' I thought of Clive's letter and my attempt to learn it off by heart. About the kindness of the B&B owners who had been patient with me while I told them their shower was broken and gave me a hat. About the woman who I had met that morning, who wanted nothing more from me than for me to walk alongside her for a while. I wanted to write back through the years and tell Woolf that we *could* go with each other, wrists tied together as if we were children on a school trip and that there was no tangled pathless thicket within, that the idea was a sickness, a delusion. But this – this urgent unlistening comfort in place of friendship – is what a Glinda does, I think. And after all, I was the one who'd hoarded my sea view and decided that I was not even going to try to share it.

At the Lordstones, which is a café, restaurant and a place to fancily glamp, I ordered coffee to have outside and resisted the urge to lie down on the cool polished floors of the slightly swanky café among the cleaner and better dressed. I didn't stay long, and pressed on, walking faster than was usual for me. I'd walked myself into fitness, the long stretches and steep inclines taking less out of me than they had back in the Lake District. The coffee was probably doing me a bit of good too. But really, my haste was caused by excitement; the pull of the sea hurrying me forwards and quickening my steps.

There were lots of walkers on this stretch, the path sometimes blocked with photographers taking a loop from Lordstones and trying to get shots of the kites flying above. The paths were layering up one on top of the other too; I was still on both the Coast to Coast route and the Cleveland Way but the fingerposts were getting confusing, the moor criss-crossed with routes through the heather, more or less official, more or less popular. Their names are eccentric, folkloric: the Monk's Trod, the Hambleton Hobble, the Crosses Road. There was a plaque just after the Lordstones in memory of Richard, who in 1979 devised a forty-mile circular walk he called the Samaritan Way and, the plaque says, knew 'the pleasure of walking to alleviate the pain for those in despair'. From time to time groups of Samaritans volunteers and their supporters walk this way too, to raise money for the Teesside branch.

For a while, during the time I was at university and for a year afterwards, I volunteered as a Samaritan. Because I was young and didn't yet have kids, I'd often do a couple of night shifts a month, sitting up into the small hours and beyond, making a commitment to offer befriending to anyone who happened to call. The Anglican minister Chad Varah set up the organisation in the early 1950s after he'd held a funeral for a thirteen-year-old girl who had ended her own life in shame and terror at the arrival of her first period. He believed in frank sex education, the healing power of conversation and that listening, only listening

– not therapy or coaching or psychiatry or any other professionalised system of helping – could keep people alive, and that people were worth keeping alive, no exceptions, no conditions. He called what the Samaritans offered 'befriending', which is a word out of fashion now, one that has the sanctimonious stink of charity about it, though at the time it gestured towards his most radical idea: no matter who you were, how you felt or what you'd done, friendship was possible.

Though I was young I was not innocent about suffering. Young people never are. But I still had the young person's idea that my own sufferings were a special case; a virgin forest nobody else could ever know. I imagined that in other houses, a steadier kind of happiness was normal. This happiness, I speculated, was as unremarkable as air, which is why people didn't tend to mention it. Working with the Samaritans unravelled and rearranged my little world in all kinds of ways and broke apart the easy logic I'd used to understand what people were like. Some people who'd done the most terrible things were funny and kind and likable and sometimes something as tiny as the morning post being late would be enough to send a person who was coping well with tragedy into the deepest despair. Some people loved to spin the most unbelievable tales, knowing you'd never call their bluff – the lies felt almost aggressive – and others, drenched in self-pity, complained about being abandoned by a long list of loved ones with whom you ended up sympathising.

Still, despite all that rearranging (the term for what was happening is 'growing up') I never outgrew my belief that Chad Varah had been right: radical and indiscriminate friendliness was no special charity, but only what each human absolutely deserved, just by virtue of being human. To decide if someone was likable or deserving of warmth or attentiveness became at first a silly and unnecessary calculation and then, as the weeks and months passed and my shifts mounted up, seemed almost obscene – like putting myself in charge of deciding which people deserved to have water. Listening became an active, creative thing, and during my listening, I had the sense I was constructing a shelter for a person, and welcoming them inside for a little while, as if out of bad weather.

At the end of the night shifts, I'd walk home just as the clubs kicked out, following girls in sparkly dresses and guys with undone bowties at sunrise along the Cam, reeling from being in touch with life beyond the rarefied or merely adolescent antics at Cambridge colleges. Ben, who I lived with then, would sometimes meet me at the door with a massive Sports Direct mug of over-sugared coffee meant to keep me awake long enough to shower and get off to work or to a lecture. *It's like the roofs have come off all the houses*, I remember telling him once – not being able to communicate my shock at the ordinariness of suffering, the widespread-ness of it, the feelings I had – a mixture of tender friendliness for my fellows and disgust at the squalid comforts and distractions we humans resort to in the face of pain.

Often – more than one or twice on every single shift I worked – I'd get what we nicknamed an 'M-call', usually from a man who wanted to chat to me while he masturbated. I wasn't alone: every single female volunteer would take multiple of these calls per shift. As early as 1958 Chad

The Parallel Path

Varah himself had written a training manual called *Telephone Masturbators and the Brenda System for Befriending Them*, which advised these specially trained female volunteers known as 'the Brendas' to allow the man to do what he needed to do and, as he was doing it, to offer him warmth and friendliness. The hope was that he'd eventually start speaking about what was really on his mind. In the training manual Varah talks about the 'horrid private universe' these Brendas were willing to enter, reminding me a little of Woolf's 'virgin forest' – that inner unmapped geography of misery. On the front of the manual there's a photograph of a young dark-haired woman. She's pretty, kind-faced and curious, her eyes open wide, her face turned up thoughtfully and ready to listen. This woman is two things at once. First, she is Chad Varah's secretary, Suzan Cameron. Cameron was a significant trainer and administrator in the early days of the Brenda programme. Secondly, she is Brenda, who isn't a woman at all, but, like Glinda the Good Witch, an amalgam of lots of women playing a specific role, and beyond that, merely a cup into which we can deposit our mixed-up ideas about what kind of help a good friend should give.

The Brenda system was ended in 1987. In 2003 – my last year as a Samaritan – Chad Varah, who had retired from the Samaritans in 1986, was trying to get the Charities Commission to strip it of its charitable status, in part because he felt so strongly about the loss of the Brenda system. Such was her fame that twenty-odd years after she'd been retired, men were still calling and asking to speak to her (and they still do). I'd been trained to tell them, with warmth and no judgement, that we 'didn't do that anymore'. Sometimes the caller would launch into the sex talk anyway, a tirade of rehearsed smuttiness belonging to the old-fashioned world of seaside postcards and *Carry On* films, full of frilly knickers and bouncing breasts. It was almost impossible to interrupt this, but you were allowed to, and if he persisted, to end the call.

Some of the men were more subtle and used to treat duping a female volunteer into staying on the call while he masturbated as if it was a game. Because these callers were less obvious, you had to be very careful. It would be terrible to accuse the innocent asthmatic or to silently suspect (as I once did) someone panting through an oxygen mask from their sickbed in a hospice. If you weren't sure, then you listened. More than ten or twenty or thirty times I'd listen to the caller tell me about his grief only for him to confess at the end of the call that he'd 'tweaked one out' as we were talking. The post-wank confession seemed to be part of the thrill for some of these callers: the pleasure caused by duping me greater even than their orgasm. I remember that phrase specifically – 'tweaked one out' – not disgusting or frightening, but merely teenage.

'That isn't what we're here for,' I'd tried to say, but the man laughed.

'Are you on this night every week?' he asked and hung up before I could answer.

It felt horrible. Humiliating. It wasn't that I felt damaged by it, only erased. I'd been on the phone to him for ages. My back hurt because I was pregnant with the baby who would turn out to be my daughter, but up until then I had been happy, warm in the glow of my own befriending. Once I realised there would be an endless supply of men who would treat me as if I was Brenda and I could either hang up on them or make myself available to them and both of these options felt horrible, I gave it up. My baby was due to be born soon, and Ben and I were moving home to Preston. There was ordinary selfishness in my decision: it felt nice to offer befriending, but not nice to be an unwitting prop for someone else's self-soothing strategy. But underneath that, and bigger, was the shame I felt at knowing I was unable to shelter everything. I still believed that everyone in the world deserved some friendliness and saw clearly that I was unequal to the task of providing it. Later that year Chad Varah broke with the Samaritans because, in his version of befriending, a good Samaritan never, ever hung up on anyone. Ever. I didn't know then what had become obvious to me on the walk that day, which is that we don't all have to be able to listen all of the time, but that we can take turns helping each other.

The moor's crossing was a strange route for Richard of Teesside to choose as a reminder of 'walking's potential to alleviate despair'. So strange it might feel a little like the darkest of practical jokes. Wainwright describes these high moors as 'eerily lunar', bringing to mind the loneliest walk in human history – one man alone on the moon, a planet's worth of space and freedom, all to himself. Across these same moors on a parallel route runs the Lyke Wake Walk – a forty-mile stretch named to remember the old coffin paths. 'Lyke' is the old word for corpse, cropping up in Icelandic, German and old Norse. 'Lyke wake' means, literally, 'corpse watch', and while this all makes the walk sound like an ancient rural tradition, the route was actually devised in the early 1950s by Bill Cowley, who, when challenged on his claim that you could cross the entire North York Moors without taking your feet off the heather, devised a route from Osmotherley to Ravenscar that did just that. If you complete the walk within twenty-four hours, which always means a stretch walking through the dead of night, you can apply to the Lyke Wake Club for a badge shaped like a coffin decorated with the tumulus (the Ordnance Survey symbol for a burial mound) and this would, for a small fee, arrive in the post along with a certificate of completion presented inside a condolence card.

This was such a clever bit of marketing that in its heyday in the 1960s and '70s the walk became so popular that the club had to produce guides for its walkers asking them not to make too much noise going through the villages at night and urging them not to wander off across the heather and damage the fragile moorland ecology. The club collaborated with the national park and various landowners to have waymarkers put in, and though the walk's popularity has declined in recent years, those markers still remain and now and again you can see groups of wake walkers making their crossing wearing black and carrying empty cardboard coffins as if they are time-travelling actors from a medieval mystery play.

Cowley, aware of the old coffin paths, if not strictly following them, named his walk after a traditional folk song, a fourteenth-century Yorkshire funeral chant called the 'Lyke Wake Dirge'. The song is raw, cold, bleak: it is addressed to both the corpse and to those who mourn it and narrates the soul's journey from home to purgatory and judgement, figuring this as a lonely stride across the exposed moors. The song is instructive and harsh. Those who gave care to others in life can expect to receive it after death, in the form of shoes to protect their feet from the rough terrain. The less generous can expect an entirely different sort of walk:

> But if hosen or shoen thou ne'er gavest nane,
> Every neet and all,
> The whinny will prick thee to thy bare bane,
> And Christ receive thy saul.
> From Whinny Moor when thou mayst pass,
> Every neet and all,
> To Brig o' Dread thou comest at last,
> And Christ receive thy saul.

In 1898, Richard Blakeborough, in *Wit, Character, Folklore & Customs of the North Riding of Yorkshire*, wrote about Whinny Moor, the place named in the poem.

> Old people will tell you that after death the soul passes over Whinny-moore, a place full of whins and brambles, and ... would be met by an old man carrying a huge bundle of boots; and if amongst these could be found a pair which the bare-footed soul had given away during life, the old man gave them to the soul to protect its feet whilst crossing the thorny moor.

The threat of hiking blisters in the afterlife might be enough to inspire friendliness towards your fellow man in this one, though the grudging transaction of this – charity extracted by threat – feels inadequate. I can't imagine wearing shoes given under such circumstances would feel that great either.

Every Home a Hospital

I think of Glinda again, instructing Dorothy to steal the dead witch's ruby slippers, knowing when the time is right, they'll take her home. The club awards those who complete the walk a title: men become Dirgers, women, Witches.

I was walking my one-hundred-and-fiftieth mile, more or less. Each step took me both a little further from home, and nearer to the day I'd turn around and go back to it. I was eager, ambivalent – as stop-start in my thinking as I was in my physical progress. This gloomy terrain is home-from-home because back in Lancaster I walk on moorland too. Clive and I take most of our walks in a specifically haunted part of our city, with as bleak an ancient and recent history as the allegorical Whinny Moor of the 'Lyke Wake Dirge'.

Nearest to us is Williamson's Park, with its heated butterfly house and duck pond and outdoor theatre and summer music festivals. It's built on the site of an old moorland quarry; those neat paths and the elegantly curved pond with its nicely cobbled edging were landscaped out of the naked rock by unemployed mill workers during the Lancashire Cotton Famine, the project organised and paid for by the Poor Act in the 1860s. This project was a civic good, sold to the general population by pointing out what a nuisance a big group of labourers with idle hands might wreak domestically and to the city at large, and what a benefit to the health of the populace a park to walk in would be. The park is across the road from the cemetery where I practise kinhin sometimes, attending to what I can see of the North West's energy coast; the nuclear power station out at Heysham, the wind farms along the Furness peninsula and, at night, the twinkling lights of Barrow and its twenty-four-hour war industry: we still call the hangars built in the 1980s 'Maggie's Sheds'.

A stone's throw from here, on the old road out of Lancaster and up on to the moors, is the slaughterhouse. Clive and I have both poked around here, fascinated by the noises of its machinery, the sad bleating death-traffic trundling through its gates, the '24-hour operation' signs, its views of the western Bowland fells. This is the road where Clive had found the suitcases containing the old skin mags and Charles Atlas course. By here too are the former Ridge Lea and Lancaster Moor psychiatric hospitals, built on the moor-covered hills to the south of the city.

Lancaster Moor Hospital closed in the 1990s and has been converted into apartments – some of which have a view of Lancaster Farms Prison, where the prisoners from the castle in the city centre were decanted to when they moved the criminals out and the tourists in. The multi-million-pound conversion – hospital to flats – happened well before I came to Lancaster, though while it was a hospital the place was renowned for what was believed to be a pioneering treatment for depression; Alan Bennett's mother received her electroconvulsive therapy here and, for a while, one of Clive's relatives stayed there. The relative had been taught to knit, either as part of his treatment, or to entertain and distract him while the treatment took place, and Clive told me once, with a Northern mirth elastic enough to hold both sadness and rage, about the two of them sitting in the high-backed vinyl-covered hospital chairs, struggling with their needles and yarn.

Ridge Lea, the smaller sister hospital, still stands, though it is on its way to dereliction now, left to the deer and the urban explorers. It can't be demolished or restored as nature has reclaimed it and there's a breeding population of rare bats here. I walked around the grounds once during the first spring lockdown, knowing trespass isn't so risky if you're a small white woman and have a poodle-cross dog with you. There are steel panels screwed over most of the windows, the slates and lead are gone from the roof and the bones of the joists and rafters are exposed to the air. There are buddleia bushes and nettles and fox shit everywhere; the marked car parking spaces for the doctors remain but the tarmac is cracked and swollen with dandelions. The formal flower beds are overgrown with brambles and still glow with throttled rows of daffodils. This is a sad place, and I'm glad the teenagers have got into it: the rooms you can walk through are full of bottles and cans. Someone has lit a fire at some point, the hospital bed frames have been upended and laid against the walls, and an old table football set takes centre stage – a little weather-blown with damp, but still functional.

Where I walk most often, mainly alone but sometimes with Clive, is a strange, scruffy little loop between the park and the slaughterhouse and the hospitals and the prison and the cemetery. The locals have always called it Fenham Carr: a sixteen-acre piece of woodland surrounded by a low wall and accessed via a gate from Williamson's Park. This managed, tamed piece of the moorland was walled in and added to the park in the 1990s, but before that, it was part of the Lancaster Moor Hospital estate and used for the recreation and exercise of people compelled to live within the hospital – an extension to the more formal 'airing courts' nearer to the hospital and beyond the wall.

The Parallel Path

The airing courts and the walled woodland and reservoir just beyond it, where the patients were taken to tramp the same loop as Clive and I sometimes tread today, are evidence of a belief that persists now and shows up in the existence of the Samaritan Way: fresh air and time outdoors is good for the mind. But I also see – in this set of buildings and the tracks that run between them – what happens to people whose sorrows we are unable to shelter through relationship and the kinds of buildings we create as a substitute shelter, more rubbish bins than refuges. Before the park and the quarry, before the prison and the hospitals and the slaughterhouse, before the old road up to the execution place – for thieves and traitors and clever or eccentric or annoying women who in the language of their time they called witches – it was just moorland and beneath the gorse and bracken there were mounds stuffed with bones and urns. The village nearest is named Golgotha – place of skulls – then and now. This is the place my lockdown walking knitted me into and the place to which I have become tethered: home. As my walk approached its ending, I started to miss it.

I sat by the path with the heather crunching beneath me, tearing open the reinforced cardboard envelope that I'd picked up at Ingleby Cross that morning. The friendly hosts had asked me about it, and I'd explained my friend was writing to me every single day as I went along. They'd been charmed by this.

'A nice bit of encouragement for you,' she said, reassured that this odd, possibly thick person they'd hosted for the night did have proper company and supervision after all.

Clive's letters *were* encouraging; the opening of them, the carrying them around, the picking them up at the end of each day had become part of a routine that I started to enjoy and feel comfortable in. Each unfamiliar resting place became an instant kind of home because the letter from my friend always arrived there before me.

Clive had written his letter on the back of a large black and white photograph of some woodland. The woodland is deep and cramped, but not untouched. One of the trees has been used as a support for a lean-to wigwam made of fallen branches. Clive had overpainted this photograph before printing it with some figure, part skeleton, part ghost. I looked closer. The creepy folkloric figure could have horns, or those could be branches growing from his skull. That outgrowth might be painful or joyful. It isn't clear if the man is emerging from the woodland or being swallowed by it and if this is a picture about confinement or freedom. Later, Clive will tell me I'm looking at an image he's collaged from an old engraving of the circulatory system; the private inner threads of life exposed, the man part-wood, or the wood part-man.

Clive has dispensed with any kind of greeting: it's been a little while since I've seen 'Dear Jenn' and the letters feel less like messages addressed to me and more like access to an ongoing private conversation he is having with himself. It is rare that we are allowed to know our friends like this. Clive tells me about walking, the way he breaks into a run sometimes, the speed 'a delusion that makes me think I might live longer'. He's been at the hospital again. 'They tell me that my bones are shot-at but this cancer of mine, although they don't use the word metastasised, that's exactly what's happened . . . that lovely old spine of mine is a highway for what they call euphemistically "lucencies" or "geographic lesions".'

As happens so often in these letters, I'm presented with two locations and two Clives; there's the man in hospital who is both measured and confined, obediently turning up at the time allotted to receive information about the secret inner worlds of his bones expressed in language that obscures more than it reveals. The other Clive, the one who pokes around in the undergrowth, has been run-walking 'like a clown', unfettered from what is happening to him and from fear. He feels it too, this doubleness, and it is being out in the woods that helps him feel it: 'Now I wonder if there is another me – twigs and branches – veins and nerves set loose in the thickets, wild and free.' Clive asks if it is the same for me, if the peaceful freedoms I have described finding in my own walking feel the same for me as they do for him: 'is it possible that your mind leaves your body and bits of it (invisible to an MRI) float off and snag on branches and clouds?' The image of a man both lying still in a tube and clowning around in the woods is affecting. Though I don't really believe in a soul that can detach itself from the body and live on after death, sometimes when I speak to Clive, I think that a person is more than a body can hold, the body itself a leaky and derelict site of confinement. We've both had the feeling that we can escape from ourselves, that walking turns us into a kind of living ghost, allowing us to seep into the places that have formed us and leave some kind of mark – a smear, a sign of passing through.

* * *

Every Home a Hospital

From Lordstones, it's only three or four miles along Kirkby Bank to Clay Bank Top, but, eager as I was to complete them, they were hard miles across Cringle Moor, the temperature climbing through the early afternoon, and despite the hat I'd been given and the relief of the wind, the back of my neck got sunburned. I drank all my water and headed onwards for the Wainstones.

The stones are, collectively, a dramatic outcrop of dark sandstone right across the path and popular with rock climbers. I saw a couple, scrambling about up high: they were all knees and elbows, like spiders. The feature's name is a shortened form of 'Swain Stones' because they used to be, as legend goes, a meeting place for courting couples; there are plenty of crevices and gaps to tuck yourself away between the boulders. Wainwright is very clear: you go *through* the stones rather than around them, though all I can say in my defence is that I thought I *was* going through them, and it wasn't clear I was going around until I found myself needing to scramble upwards, hauling myself up an almost sheer slope and relying on the rootedness of the heather I was hanging on to to stop me falling.

For a while, Clive was confined to his room at Blackpool Victoria Hospital. He'd enjoyed making a nuisance out of himself again: wearing his day clothes, insisting the doctors looked at him eye to eye and spoke to him as an equal, getting up to no good with the room's fixtures and fittings in a way that looked very like vandalism but which he insisted – gleefully – was more properly called 'curation'. Clive had told me that on one of those locked-in nights he heard strange cries and groans, echoing in through his

The Parallel Path

window from a direction he couldn't quite place. At first he thought he might have been hearing patients in another part of the hospital. We were in a café in Morecambe: every inch the seaside entertainer, Clive enjoyed telling me this story and I enjoyed hearing it. Was it the maternity ward, I speculated? Or psychiatry? The noise someone who awakes from one nightmare into another might make? Maybe it was a dream or hallucination – a surprising effect of the drugs they were giving him. Should he call a nurse?

'It was the animals,' Clive said, reminding me that the hospital is more or less across the road from Blackpool Zoo. We snorted at the image: two sets of confined creatures calling to each other in the dark.

During one of the coldest, whitest winters his part of New England had seen in many years, Thoreau, a fan of walking in all conditions, wrote: 'We must go out and re-ally ourselves to Nature every day. We must make root, send out some little fibre at least, even every winter day. I am sensible that I am imbibing health when I open my mouth to the wind. Staying in the house breeds a sort of insanity always. Every house is in this sense a hospital.' He was writing this a few days after Christmas – the world was frozen, the conditions poor. And yet, 'A night and a forenoon is as much confinement to these wards as I can stand.'

The strangeness of these few sentences bothered me on my first reading, and I wrote them down in a notebook I keep for fragments of writing that have puzzled or irritated me, sentences I want to go back to and fiddle with, like tangles in a skein of yarn I am knitting. That word 're-ally' snagged me – *ally* – to connect with, relate to, to accompany. Every single day we needed to go outside and befriend the world again? The word 'root' too – which suggested a kind of domesticity to me – a sheltering in place, a keeping close to the kitchen that fed you, the bed that held you. But Thoreau is talking about making rootedness by going outside. And hospitals are places of infection and contagion, not places of cure or rest. It reminded me of Clive, the way hospitals always felt like prison to him. When he's in, I text him and pretend he's been kidnapped, that he's a heroic hostage and should stop at nothing to win his freedom. 'Fight them! Bite them if you have to!' I tell him, and he sends me back pictures of all the phials of blood they stole from him that day and I tell him how disgusting and filthy doctors are, and what a nasty habit it is they indulge when they do such horrible things to people.

I slowly followed a steep and stony track that zigzagged downwards on the eastern edge of Hasty Bank through ferns and bracken towards the road and Clay Bank Top car park, where I'd been instructed to wait and phone the hotel for my lift. The hotel I was booked into was in Great Broughton, a village just a couple of miles away, and was well used to providing a shuttle for coast-to-coasters on their hike's final stretch. I fell a couple of times as I descended, palms outstretched, into the dry bilberry bushes, which both cushioned and stung. The damp coolness of the woods or the dry windiness up high on the moors was gone now; the sun had burned my neck and the backs of my knees where the sunscreen had rubbed off. Every movement seemed to stretch my skin and set off a fresh burning sensation.
    What had propelled me into speed that morning – my haste to get a glimpse of the sea – was now slowing me

down. I was nearly done and whatever sense of achievement I might enjoy from anticipating the completion of the walk was coupled with anticipatory sadness. I was coming to the end of the trail and, beyond the North Sea, home was waiting. As Glinda would remind us all: there was no place like it. I couldn't find a way through this – the grief I felt at how little and limited what a person can offer really is. The way the buildings we construct to deliver care – hospitals and houses, classrooms and churches, all of them – can so easily become prisons and make us sick with their infected air. But despite what Wainwright had said about the moorland's eerie, lonely quality, the place seemed to have space to hold my troubles while I wandered; these moors were remarkable to me not for their bleak emptiness, but for their sheltering fullness. And the 'Lyke Wake Dirge' had its own dark comfort – something as small as the gift of a pair of shoes could be enough, and that those who give are comforted by it.

When my lift arrived at Clay Bank Top, the car came from a different direction than the one I was expecting. I was disoriented again, as I had been the night before. The woman driving the car had brought a bottle of water and I was too loud and effusive with my gratitude, like a drunk set to broadcast only. I didn't worry too much about it; I was familiar with what I thought were signs of dehydration now: a left-sided headache, wobbliness in my knees and ankles, a rushing sound in my left ear. In a couple of miles, I'd be home-from-home for the night and food, water and sleep would cure everything that was wrong with me.

DAYS FOURTEEN and FIFTEEN

The World's Greatest Moaner

(In the Bag Van)

I woke just after four the next morning. I'd slept with the windows open but during the night the heat had gathered and the room was airless. I drank a bottle of water, refilled it and drank again as I scrolled the BBC website. The heatwave that had been promised all week had arrived: by six a.m. it was 24 degrees Celsius outside and rising. In a WhatsApp group that had started during the lockdown and persisted after it, two of my closest friends began arguing with each other. A friend from Yorkshire, familiar with the moors, reminded me about the fires that can ignite so easily up there, about how remote my twenty-mile route would be, about how hard it would be to carry enough water to make it through the whole day. Setting out this morning, he said, would be foolish and, if the weather got hotter, it could even be dangerous. And it was definitely, definitely going to get hotter. He was right, and these were things I already knew.

My other friend wanted me to achieve what I'd set out to do and knew how sad I would be to stop. She reminded me of what I'd managed on the very long and hot day across the Vale of Mowbray when I'd decided every ten steps during those last seven miles that I was going to give up. She reminded me that I am a person who can take my mind away from pain when I need to. That my desire could carry me through my miles. She was right and these were things I already knew too. The row they were having with each other was exactly the same as the conversation I was having with myself. Different parts of my inner chorus presented their rational points of view and edged their way towards a barney. When parts of me go to bat with each other, taking sides does not help. I got up and went in search of my three-course walker's breakfast.

In the dining room of the hotel, it was already busy. There were lots of other walkers with their phones and tablets out trying to plan alternate routes or looking for places to stay where they might break their day's hike early. I went through some possibilities: the Lion Inn on Blakey Ridge was only nine miles away. I could take an umbrella from the hotel's lost property, load up on water and, if I set off right this second, get there before lunch, using the umbrella as shade. Then I could stay there and try to rearrange the rest of my onward journey. I was so desperate that the thought of proceeding through forty miles of combustible heather protected by an umbrella like a sweaty Mary Poppins struck me as a reasonable plan. I phoned the Lion but all the walkers in the hotel had had the same idea and there was no room at the inn. I pictured all of us coast-to-coasters like a trail of ants marching slowly across well-worn paths, clogging up the hotels and pubs, leaving water bottles and wet wipes in the hedges, summoning taxis, getting sunburn, wandering across the moors with heatstroke and delirium. There was no alternative route to take. The North York Moors must be got through, one way or another, and after working with the receptionist at the hotel to patch

The World's Greatest Moaner

something together via public transport – impossible as the train services closed down entirely, the rails buckling with the heat – I admitted defeat.

All the parts of me that suspected everything I'd discovered on this walk about surrender and gentleness and gratitude were just nice-sounding excuses for laziness and incompetence reared their heads. Patricia would still be on the Pennine Way, I told myself. She wouldn't even be *considering* packing it in, and she's a *medical doctor*. These inner voices are ferocious, and they are there to protect me from the way I feel when I fail. Their intention is kind – nobody enjoys failure, do they? – but they set about their work so brutally that I packed up my clothes and carried my bag to reception feeling like I'd been beaten up. I tried to make it easier by remembering what I'd learned on the mountain navigation course: being responsible for yourself is a way of caring for others. If I got into trouble out on the moors, it would mean the expense and drama of an ambulance or a helicopter. Refusing to put myself into unnecessary danger is a service offered to everyone else too. These harsher parts of who I am did not buy the cover story for a second.

Finally, it was all arranged: the van that came every day to pick up everyone's luggage and deliver it to the next set of hotels and bed and breakfasts would take me as a passenger. I was *only* twenty-one miles away from my next stop at Egton Bridge, but the driver warned me that he'd be taking a long route, going right up to Saltburn-on-Sea and back again. When I realised that meant I'd get to the east coast a day early, it felt like cheating. I cried, and one of the women who'd got a room at the Lion Inn hugged me. In the dining room, where we stymied walkers milled around, making arrangements, weeping, geeing each other along, a little sign near the bar caught my eye. *The World's Greatest Moaner.* The appropriateness of the sardonic Yorkshire wit was somehow comforting. If a person is going to flake out and spend a day *gittering* about it (the word is a gift from my Scottish mother: it means to complain or whinge at length), she may as well be good at *that*.

In the van on the way to Saltburn, the radio broadcast regular news bulletins. Network Rail issued a 'do not travel' warning. The local bus services had been cancelled. Someone phoned in to remind everyone to look after their dogs: the pavements would be far too hot for them to walk on and they should be exercised after dark. The UK Health Security Agency issued a Level 4 alert for the first time, and by late morning, the government had declared a national emergency. Some parts of Yorkshire experienced power cuts, and in a moment that felt almost apocalyptic, the Aysgarth Falls in the Yorkshire Dales National Park ran dry. Every pub we drove past had a beer garden full to overflowing, the smell of barbecues filled the air and the sunworshippers celebrated. A lot of the schools let the kids go home early. The atmosphere on the moors, especially for those who lived and worked by the heather and knew how easily it could combust, was doomy and watchful. At home, Duncan was doing laundry, filling the line in our sunny garden with bedsheets that would dry in less than half an hour.

A couple of months later, the Met Office National Climate Information Centre published a report on the heatwave, which they said 'marked a milestone in UK climate history'. The report placed these strange few days into context: while much of the UK was affected as hot air moved upwards from mainland Europe, the effects were most pronounced in the North of England. The highest temperature recorded that day – 40 degrees Celsius – occurred in Topcliffe, North Yorkshire. But this Northern heatwave was no one-off and instead seemed to be part of a trend: in an area-average graph of the daily maximum temperatures in the North of England, fourteen of the thirty hottest days ever recorded have occurred since 2003 – in the lifetime of my daughter. I sat in the van, scrolling on my phone, watching the temperature rise on the LED display on the dashboard. When we arrived at Saltburn I refused to get out even though there would have been time to go down to the sea's edge and get my boots wet as the driver did the bag exchange. I took a photograph out of the van window: the sea bright and sparkling, a row of stripy deckchairs, a beach so full you could hardly see the sand. *I should message Clive and show him I got to the other side after all*, I thought. But not knowing what to say and how to say it, I didn't.

A couple of months before I set out on the Coast to Coast Walk, I had taken another long walk across London as part of the April 2022 Extinction Rebellion action. These walks follow the long tradition of walks as acts of protest and embodied complaint. This tradition includes events as various as the 1932 mass trespass at Kinder Scout in Derbyshire, where co-ordinated groups of walkers protested the enclosure of open countryside by wealthy landowners, to the 1972 Reclaim the Night protest in Leeds, where Yorkshire women organised a city walk after dark to protest against the police's attempts to curfew them during the ineffectual, hampered-by-misogyny hunt for the Yorkshire Ripper. When walking stops traffic and commerce or puts too many bodies to arrest in places where they should not be, it becomes a complaint that cannot be ignored. This type of complaining is a kind of love, and because it happens in groups – very large groups, sometimes – it creates a community of care. It is also, as Rebecca Solnit points out in her book *Wanderlust: A History of Walking*, a 'mutant form of the pilgrimage' because the complaining, protesting walker uses their walking to both ask for and imagine change.

Back in April we'd met at Hyde Park in our thousands, formed a straggling line twenty abreast, and walked together. I took my place in a shuffling, noisy crowd, just one pair of feet in a snake of people miles long. I was pressed in with other people's rucksacks and elbows, bumping gently when we moved around corners or waited together, blocking traffic. The slow, stop-start ambling punctuated by sitting on hard pavements felt almost aimless: I didn't really know where we were going or how we would get there, I only followed awkwardly, almost blindly, submitting to the movement of the crowd. I was here for a reason, and I had a purpose, though as just one person, it didn't really matter whether I was there or not.

On Oxford Street, we stopped for a while. The usual London noise layered up with the loudspeakers of the stewards who were directing the march, the intermittent sound of police sirens and the walkers around me singing and talking and playing musical instruments. The buildings there are tall, lit up with brightly coloured shopfronts, each window filled with things to buy. The sky had been reduced to a white strip over my head. I was walking with a group of Buddhists from different traditions and during this stop – which was intended to hold up the traffic and draw attention to the protest in the busiest shopping street in the city – we kneeled or crossed our legs or propped ourselves up on folding camping chairs or zafus and either closed our eyes or left them open, depending on our tradition. Walking became sitting, and we waited, holding still in the whirl of the city and the din of the protest.

I sit like this almost every day, and when I do the landscape I find inside is like the bay I walk in at Morecambe: cool and flat and numb, gentle colours flowing into each other, not quite silence, not quite stillness; a soft soup of sand and water, silt and mud. There's no distinct line between the land and the horizon's edge, even on clear days. There is space but not emptiness. It is beautiful but not safe. This is home, but it is also an unmappable, haunted kind of place. In her memoir *A Flat Place*, Noreen Masud describes Morecambe Bay as 'a dreamy amphibian' and it is not only because I can see it from my bedroom window and I have walked across its shining mudflats that I feel like it belongs to me, or me to it (or that these two types of belonging are not different things *at all* and only sentences make them so), but because when I settle into stillness and look inside myself, 'a dreamy amphibian' is what I find: something that shimmers, is neither one thing or another, is both there and not there.

* * *

The Parallel Path

The day before I'd gone to London for the protest, I'd walked at Bardsea; a coastal village south of Ulverston that overlooks Morecambe Bay from the eastern edge of the Furness peninsula. I was with Duncan. I'd asked for the day out because we'd been having a fractious time, the competing post-lockdown forces of work and children buffeting us both. We took our van and things for making coffee. There are lots of places to park at the sea's marshy edge, and an interesting walk inland across Birkrigg Common, which is a wide and hilly expanse of moorland and exposed limestone covered in a network of paths that looks out over the bay.

It was one of those bright, cold spring days and we could see a long way. Sometimes the sands shone like water, and it's always tempting to go out on them. People drown out there or get sucked into the quicksand channels, and if you walk out far enough, you'll find the skeletons of old tractors and the horses that rode out to rescue the people who drove them. Just a few months before moving home to Preston and while I was pregnant with our daughter, Ben and I had watched the news coverage about the twenty-one cockle pickers who had drowned in the incoming tide on Morecambe Bay, and we never forgot it. Always better to go with a guide. That day, Duncan and I turned away from the sandflats and saltmarsh and went inland, upwards and over the common. I'd promised Duncan that I'd use my new map and compass and take him up to Birkrigg Stone Circle, which is a Bronze Age circle of small standing stones and cobbles that is sometimes called the Druid's Temple and, placed high up on the common, is the best place to wait and watch the night come in over the water.

The World's Greatest Moaner

I thought I'd be able to find the way easily, because my friend Hilary and I had come together a couple of weeks earlier. We'd parked up at Bardsea and she had guided me along a narrow lane and towards the old Quaker burial ground just past High Sunbrick Farm, which lies on the edge of Birkrigg Common. Hilary has written a book about early Quaker history and studied the travel journals of George Fox, the founder of the Society of Friends. He'd started life as a shoemaker's apprentice in the Midlands, though after climbing Pendle Hill in Lancashire and receiving a vision, began a wandering ministry in the Northwest of England.

I learned from Hilary that to wander, as Fox did across Westmorland (as it was called then), Lancashire and Yorkshire during the 1650s, became one of the things Quakers did; they were a restless, itinerant group of people. The early Friends criss-crossed the country from the Midlands to the North, then into London, Scotland and Wales. This paradoxical restlessness seemed to be at odds with the Quaker belief in the Indwelling Light; surely there was no need for a pilgrimage to find God if everyone was already intimately accompanied? But George Fox understood the double-sidedness of walking. It could be a kind of embodied complaint about the prevailing religious and social cultures of the time, a way of drawing attention to himself and his message, and also the means by which he experienced dependence, emptied himself out and submitted to where he'd been led. There's no real paradox in this: a walk can hold most things, not least a protest against human institutions and a submission to a higher leading. Fox had ended up at Lancaster Castle a couple of times too, imprisoned for causing a disturbance.

The Parallel Path

Hilary and I had followed a lane between some old farm buildings and reached the burial ground: a field surrounded by dry-stone walls, empty save for a few limestone boulders and some young trees growing between them. There was nothing to see here: the only marker is a later-added plaque reminding us that there were 277 people buried in this place, among them George Fox's wife, Margaret Fell. The unmarked resting place is a Quaker tradition: they consider all humans to be equal to each other, each one of us a 'Friend', and if all a headstone does is mark one person out as different from the other, a dead Quaker has no need for one. The sun was falling, looking like a weak lightbulb shone through a faded blue sheet. Though it was spring, the air was cool and the wind came at us hard across the limestone rise and the full and empty field on Sunbrick Lane.

Our visit to Bardsea had come at the end of a long day; we'd spent most of it on the southern tip of the Furness peninsula, exploring Barrow and chasing the traces of Nella Last, who had lived and written there. Nella was an ordinary woman: not poor (she lived in a 1930s semi-detached house, had a car and a garage and a woman to help her with the cleaning) but not remarkable. Her diaries, begun in 1939 as part of the Mass-Observation project, are thick with detail of everyday life; she describes the cooking, the sewing, the worrying about her sons, one of whom was called up almost as soon as the Second World War began. Hilary had lent me a set of the published, abridged versions of her diaries, and I'd read them during the spring lockdown and found solace in them.

Nella was stuck at home too but her work became a way of attending to the enormity of war. She was not a religious woman and did not 'find comfort and faith in bombarding god with requests and demands' but her care work became a way of requesting and demanding both from herself and her community. She was active in the Women's Voluntary Service and the Red Cross. She was the woman the local doctor relied on to take care of a motherless baby. She led her group of volunteers in their grief after the sudden suicide of a friend who despaired as the war began. She sewed chintz bags to raise money for injured soldiers and their families and she worked out how to make a birthday cake for a husband she felt ambivalent about, using only rationed goods. Her work both drew attention to lack, and enacted the way she thought things should be.

I think it was Nella who'd put the idea of the walk into my head, or, at least, first put into words what I'd felt as I stayed at home and mopped the kitchen floor as the world fell apart. Though described only as a middle-aged housewife she also knew herself to be a wanderer. 'I used to be nearly wild with longing to be off and away,' she wrote, remembering her pre-war self. That wildness had never left her; 'Even now, when wood smoke begins to hang around the chimneys at Spark Bridge or when the thin sweet wind coaxes the primroses out, I have my wild fits.' Though the war transformed her domestic work, politicised it and brought her into community with other women, she credits the place she'd worked to care for, not the war that had threatened it, with reminding her of her inborn wildness. 'The sound of a ship's siren as she moved down Walney Channel has, at times, changed a busy capable housewife into a wild, caged thing who could have set off without a backward glance.'

The Parallel Path

Hilary and I had gone to Barrow that day in search of her, and eaten our packed lunch parked up in front of her house, which had no blue plaque to say she had lived and worked and written there. Although Nella is one of the most prolific and sensitive writers the Northwest of England has ever produced, the people we asked at the Dock Museum in Barrow had not heard of her. The ordinariness of her work had conferred its own kind of anonymity; proof that even a richly recorded life can easily be forgotten. Despite all that writing, she'd disappeared as easily as the unnamed Quakers in the burial ground above Bardsea.

The lockdown time I'd spent with Nella had been one of the few things to comfort me, and Hilary and I had been talking about her a lot as we walked over Birkrigg Common. I'd been a passenger, allowing her to guide me upwards through the paths and narrow farm tracks. I think that's why, during that second trip up to Bardsea when it had been my turn to be the guide and lead the way, I'd found myself unable to remember the route across the common and I'd got myself and Duncan lost.

There were so many paths through the rough grass, none of which quite seemed to correspond to the green dotted lines on my map. Duncan waited. Across some dips and rises was the Bardsea Monument – an old folly built by the rich families who'd bought and sold the Conishead Priory which had once been a home to monks, then after the dissolution of the 1530s a private house, and since the 1970s, home to a Buddhist community. The monument had once held urns remembering the lives and deaths of the people who'd owned the priory in the eighteenth and nineteenth centuries and it was visible for miles around. I thought I could use it to take a compass bearing and find our path, but I couldn't remember what I'd been taught so I had us walking around for a while, frustrated and aimless. The reward I'd promised us – a visit to a walled-in piece of grass remarkable only for what was not there – did not materialise and when we finally did blunder into the circle (the stones it is made of are short and squat, the smallest almost buried in the sheep-nibbled turf) Duncan was less impressed by it than I wanted him to be.

These little disappointments about being lost, being unable to remember, of nobody remembering Nella and her wild ordinariness, were part of what I sat with on the tarmac of Oxford Street a few days later. My patience had run out and a small sadness about what the pandemic had done to my family connected to some bigger hurt I could only feel but did not then understand, and all of it shaded by a noisier layer of guilt at the fact of my self-pity. It was shameful, really, to attend to these petty gripes when I was supposed to be thinking about the effects of climate change in the global south, the collapse of biodiversity, the way the end was coming, coming soon, might not be preventable. I tried to get away from myself, to consider the suffering that would come before the world's lights finally went out.

I have never really been sure if the care-led activism of refusal and obstruction, of stickering cars and throwing paint at buildings is likely to change anything. Sitting in the street that day, I doubted it. But I hoped that complaint could be a shelter big enough for contrition. I hoped that walking, especially walking together, could make space for the full-and-empty experience of grief and for the mourning of what had been and what will be lost. The encounter with all of this gathered inside me like a tidal bore of brine and sand and I wept a little, with the thwock-thwock of a news helicopter circling overhead, the horns from delayed traffic tearing at the air. Someone on the pavement who wanted to cross the road started shouting at us, and the man sitting next to me was breathing so softly it felt both obtrusive and necessary to listen to the sound of it, to cling to it.

The bag van deposited me at Egton Bridge. In the bathroom I sat on the edge of the bath and sent a voice note to Clive. I'd tested the water with a few complaints on my walk across the Vale of Mowbray, but that afternoon, I did something I hadn't done before – not in years – and told a friend what was wrong with me. It started with the heat, with the failure of the walk, but moved on to all my other sadnesses too, as I tried to tell him what I'd come to understand about why this walk was so important to me. I told him how sad I was about letting him down, about being a bad friend who'd only sent one postcard and hadn't even managed to finish the walk. I told him about Alice and what I'd done with her picture inside the medicine bottle, and about Patricia in Keld, and the mix of dislike and recognition I'd felt while listening to her. I told him about the woman with the sick daughter I'd met on the moors, about her despair and anger and relief at being away, and about the gnawing, relentless worry I'd felt for my own daughter too – that sense I had of not being able to help, and how angry that had made me. I remember I was crying, and that the plumbing in the bathroom was making gurgling sounds as I tried to talk and made me feel ridiculous. When I was done, I waited on the edge of the bath and worried about committing all of this to a recorded message. It was an old, familiar fear: what if I had just handed someone the means to harm me? Clive replied almost right away: full of warmth and kindness. There was a smile in his voice: not that he was entertained by my sorrows, but only that he'd been pleased, finally, to meet me and see what I'd been carrying.

I slept, then caught the early train the next morning to Whitby, then a slow and sweltering bus to Robin Hood's Bay. There, I skulked about on the beach, sat on the sand, tried to cheer myself up with ice cream, with chocolate, with a bag of chips. I sat in a hotel bar and opened my last letter, which Clive had written before hearing the news of my failure. The envelope was big and padded and there was unearned ceremony in the way I opened it, as if I really had just achieved something.

Clive had sent the last Charles Atlas lesson. Charles praises his student on a job well done so far and urges him towards clean living and regular stretching. He says he'd be very happy to receive before and after photographs, if anyone felt like sending them. And, at the end of their time together, he introduces the idea of the 'perpetual lesson', which is intended to move the student on from learning a set of remedial exercises to understanding Atlas's great unified theory of healthy living. 'This compelling power of radiant health,' Atlas claims, 'is the result of obedience to the simple laws of nature, performed in the spirit of HOPEFULNESS combined with the DIRECTED WILL.'

There was a photograph in the envelope too. It's a big, black and white copy of the picture Clive asked the waiter to take of the two of us as we had coffee together at Lancaster Castle before I set off on the train to St Bees. Just over a fortnight ago, and another life entirely. Clive, always a dab hand with a box of paints and a scanner, has doctored the image and reduced himself to a headless shadow. This was our 'before', and he has turned it into a premature glimpse of his 'after'. Now, he is asking me in a way less gentle than before to meet him.

It is a horrible picture. I'm grinning and excited to be off, oblivious to the fact that I'm drinking coffee with a shade, a headless spectre, a dead man. This photograph illuminated a painful and unmarked place that Clive and I had never visited before. I thought about the scrap of paper with Clive's name on that I'd pushed on to the branches of the tree at St Bees. I hadn't dared make a wish or say a prayer. But now as I looked at the photograph Clive had sent me I realised that if I had been brave enough to dare, my wish would have been for a sudden and magical transformation. In Clive, of course: he'd get better, overnight. And I'd wanted to be different too: in overcoming all obstacles and completing this walk I would surely become some better, sleeker, more generous and happier version of myself. This is one version of prayer: an articulated desire for the 'simple laws of nature' to bend a little, for the world to make me and the people that are important to me special exceptions to the way things are. And if I did articulate – in the spirit of HOPEFULNESS – that kind of wish, would it still 'take' – seeing as I hadn't been able to master my DIRECTED WILL and finish the walk?

I am not the only walker to ask herself this question. In November 1974, Werner Herzog was told that his friend and mentor, the filmmaker and critic Lotte Eisner, was dying at her home in Paris. He decided on impulse that he would go and see her, arriving on foot from Munich. He wasn't going to say goodbye nor to comfort her, he was walking to prevent her death. 'This must not be, not at this time,' he'd decided – as if Herzog was the best judge and arbiter of such things. He made his protest and his pilgrimage 'in full faith, believing that she would stay alive if I came on foot'. I wonder about what Herzog placed his faith in. Himself, mainly, and the power of his will, expressed through a walk of over five hundred miles through the ice and snow. 'We would not permit her death,' he vowed, imperiously.

He wrote an eerie, short account of his journey and published it a few years later as *Of Walking in Ice*. *In* ice – not *on* it. This is a story of endurance, not precarity. Because I already knew that Eisner had lived, I'd imagined a triumphant arrival. Herzog would kick open the doors of the sickroom with his worn-in boots and declare he had finished his hike and thus found a cure for mortality. Lotte could be a good girl and get up from her sickbed and walk now. But the man who arrived in Paris is not the man who set off from Munich. He went to see his Madame Eisner quietly and did not tell her how he'd arrived there. He's not proud of his walking injuries but embarrassed by them, and has to be guided by his unwell friend to put his tired and aching legs up on her armchair. Herzog is no hero, but a man in tatters. His walking has helped him to remember his vulnerability, and Eisner, no longer in need of saving, recognises it too; 'she knew that I was someone on foot and therefore unprotected'.

I too was unprotected when I opened Clive's last letter, undone by my own bad weather. The truthful horror of that photograph was almost too much to bear and the image made a wound in me. This is what happens when you make a friend who is dying. Or when you make a friend. Or when you care about anything at all. How do we dare? There was a letter in Clive's last package too, though it took me a while before I was fit to read it.

'I do feel out of joint knowing I won't exist in the long term,' he writes, and I know that photograph of us at my journey's beginning was one way of him imagining what it would be like to have his friends walk on without him. He thinks about what being-towards his death means he must now start grieving. First, his family and the way the threads of their lives will unspool without him: 'the twists and changes in the lives of those I love the most: that is my living disappointment'. There is pain in this, though he knows he will 'live on for a little while, a figment of a life flickering in my children's minds, my partner's mind'. He also writes about the way the doctors look at him – those professionals who despite their respect and courtesy have left him cold, 'a piece of infected meat'. He wonders what it will be to 'pass in front of a writer' and imagines how I – not doctor, not family – might attend to this strange conversation we have been having. What will I make of this 'failing flesh and blood person'? This is another kind of afterwardness: Clive

The World's Greatest Moaner

imagines himself as 'a fading ghost on the internet and maybe in the margins of your mind too, on a sheaf of paper, an experience of finite living'.

On one of our trips out Clive and I went back to Morecambe and had tea in a café on the old stone jetty. The café started life as a lighthouse keeper's cottage but for most of the 1960s and '70s it had been run as a tiny zoo, stuffed with depressed, cage-rattling and masturbating primates. There was a parrot you could feed with apple slices for sale on the way in, a sun bear that lived in a cage too small for it to turn around, and a slouching porcupine that never saw daylight. Things were different then – that's what people who remember the little zoo say. The monkey would piss on you as you walked past its cage and one day BooBoo the sun bear escaped. Local legend has it that he was heading swiftly down the jetty in the direction of the seafront arcades and ice cream parlours when the vet and the police caught up with him and shot him.

Clive had been walking me around the West End of his childhood, showing me the place that used to be a barber, the shop where his mother would pick up their bread and milk, telling me stories about the old friends he knew who used to live here. We'd eaten teacakes at the café the zoo had become and I'd been telling him, again, how worried I was about my daughter. I'd walked this promenade many times before, right the way along from the great white boat of the famous Midland Hotel, past the Eric Morecambe statue where he eternally poses on one leg, grinning in all weathers, as far as the Old Pier Bookshop, a place famous for both its unexpected taxidermy (misshapen squirrels peep at you from between the shelves) and an owner who can locate anything. But I'd never seen the Time and Tide Bell before, and after our coffee, Clive took me to see it and we stopped to listen for a while.

The bell is affixed to the seaward edge of the stone jetty, positioned so the motion of the incoming tide rings it. It was designed by the musician and sculptor Marcus Vergette, and his attention to space, to shape, to sound is clear. The finely tuned harmonic sound is haunting and persistent. The bell asks the listener to consider the vulnerability of an already precarious coastal community to climate change and to listen for the connectedness of human life to the rhythms of the sea. Clive and I had listened to the tide coming in, counting each wave as it gently dinged the bell's clapper and set the chime going softly over the water. There's an information board close by that explains the project and displays a graph demonstrating the rise in sea temperatures in the area since the 1990s. This bell shows me a bit of what Thoreau might have meant when in his journal, he talked about 'opening my mouth to the wind'. This is not passivity, exactly, but a practice of standing 'unprotected', an instrument entirely available to the world. I've come back to this place many times since, especially when I need to spend some time nursing my fear, to remind myself that some days, the song happens when you let the world move you, and that when I am too small or fearful to shelter everything, the world – ailing though it is – is still big enough. One day all of this will be underwater, the bell says, and *this* is how we dare.

I put Clive's letters back in the envelope. The bar in Robin Hood's Bay was full of walkers who had done what I could not do and found a way, through hope and will, to brave the heat. They were rowdy and cheerful. I was jealous. A man by the bar swayed on his stool. At first, I'd taken him to be very drunk, but he was actually suffering from heatstroke; the manager begged him to go to the hospital and rolled his eyes when he refused. Every time he toppled a cheer went around the bar. He was delirious with success, swapping war stories and pooling money for a drinks kitty with a pair who had just arrived by taxi.

Walkers' bars are often like this: the carpets a shocking state, the floors muddy and the chat ribald, the stink of the living something to acclimatise to. Through the window I could see yet more hikers coming in off the cliff path from Whitby. They passed around mobile phones and took turns posing for their photographs outside, pints held aloft, the blooming headland and bright water stretched out behind them like a gaudy boast. The steep road down through the village to the beach was clogged with tourists, the late-afternoon sand full of kids building sandcastles and dogs chasing after balls, everyone enjoying the strange offering of this deadly summer.

The next day Duncan brought our son and my dog and drove out to meet me on the east coast. Home rushed in through the door of the little apartment we'd rented for the weekend barking and laughing and carrying too many bags of shopping from the Co-op around the corner. I'd missed them, was glad to see them. This was the longest we'd been apart from each other in many years, and I was alert to any little difference. My son, when we went out for a bag of chips, told me I was walking too fast: I'd forgotten how to amble, how to saunter, and was striding along as if the promenade was a fell. He'd picked up a suntan during the heatwave and bounced around, delighted by the end of school and the start of the long holiday. I looked different too: my hair streaked by the sun, my legs stronger, and my feet in dire need of some plasters and antiseptic cream. I woke early each morning, ravenously hungry, my body demanding big meals because it didn't yet know I wasn't hiking the days away anymore. Everything seemed so noisy, and I was out of the habit of joining in: I had to keep reminding myself to talk, to ask questions, to pay attention when someone was speaking.

We spent the weekend in Whitby eating ice cream, visiting the Dracula Experience and taking a boat trip. I'd treated every place I'd stopped over the past couple of weeks as if it existed for my comfort alone, with little interest in anything other than how quickly I could get food and how powerful the shower was. I hadn't been resting or recuperating in Grasmere or Reeth or Great Broughton, I merely *refuelled*. In Whitby, there was time to linger a while and play the tourist, no need to worry about what a late night would do to my ability to walk twenty miles the next day. We indulged all our childish pleasures. I fed coins into the penny arcade machines and we went to all the little shops on the seafront, browsing vampire-themed souvenirs and looking at an exhibition that explained where Whitby jet came from. We bought rock and ate it wandering around the harbour looking for seals. We stood under the big whalebone arch on West Cliff and asked a passer-by to take a photograph of the three of us together in front of the statue of Captain Cook. We got in the car and headed up the coast to Robin Hood's Bay. I became reluctant then and had to be reminded about the nice second-hand bookshop that had old knitting patterns and maps for sale. The beach would be quieter there, and we could look for fossils. I let myself be convinced but I wasn't sure I wanted to go back down to the water. Better, really, to forget all about it and just enjoy a weekend in Whitby.

At the top of the steep hill that leads down to the beach there is a gift shop that sells badges and certificates to successful coast-to-coasters and a pub where hikers can sign their name in the finishers' book. Duncan was of the same mind as Clive: I *had* finished the walk. He took me to the gift shop and I followed, sulkily.

'Go on, go and choose a badge to sew on your bag. I'll buy it for you,' he said.

When I am in a fit like this I do usually allow myself to be cajoled, to be taken in hand, to be teased and firmly nudged out of my nonsense. But this time I would not budge. I wouldn't even have my photograph taken in front of the famous end-of-the-walk sign in front of Wainwright's Bar, which is something all coast-to-coasters do. I was not one of them and did not deserve it.

The drive back to Lancaster on Sunday evening took less than three hours. The place names that had become familiar during my slow walk from village to village slid past the passenger side window too quickly to read as the car headed home.

PART THREE

An Autumn Weekend on the North York Moors

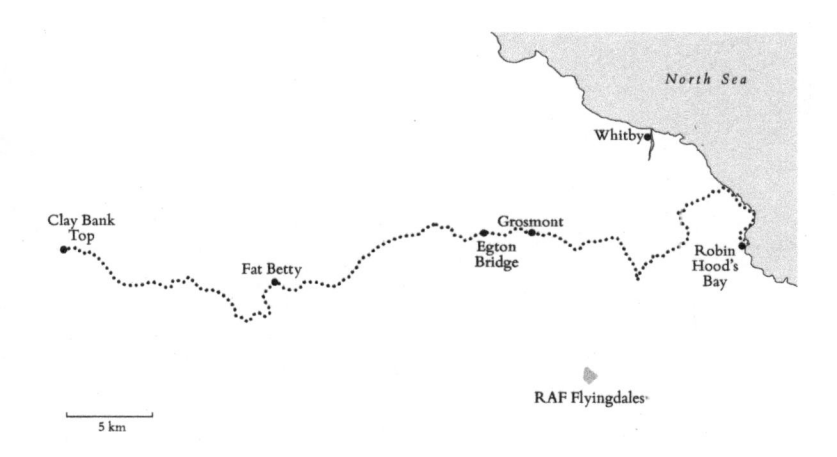

The Return

Clay Bank Top to Egton Bridge (19 miles)

The journey, and the story, was not quite over. Back home, I brooded over the walk's failure, not knowing whether to give up on whatever inner transformations I'd wanted to achieve, or whether I owed it to Clive – who would have thought the idea nonsensical – and myself – to make up for it in some way. The end of the walk had brought me towards an uncomfortable kind of knowing: my body is more fragile and vulnerable than I wanted it to be, that willpower melts in the face of the world's reality, that there will always be a gap between what I want and what is possible. How to befriend those truths? The ones Clive had long ago accepted for himself?

There had been one other slip of paper in that last envelope from Clive, placed there to remind me of the day he'd gone back and found my lost compass on a hill above a beck just south of Littledale. It was a photograph of a homemade plaque he had created both as 'a memorial to commemorate' the mishap where the compass had slipped out of my hand and to 'celebrate the heroic efforts of her fellow walker' who had 'retrieved the instrument and reunited her with it prior to her solo walk'. The joke memorial, placed at the point where the compass had been both lost and found, looked just like a headstone; there was a bluebottle crawling around on the plaque and, back on the east coast at the failed end of my walk, its naked deathliness had upset me. But at home in Lancaster, my hiking kit unpacked, and my boots cleaned and put away, I looked at Clive's letters again and realised I'd missed the most important thing. I wasn't the healthy person striding across the countryside to witness the world for my ailing friend: I was hapless, forgetful, liable to let the important things fall from my grasp, and my friend was sick, yes, but sometimes heroic too, and he had retraced my steps for me and found what I had lost.

Hilary had offered to drive me back to Clay Bank Top and the Wainstones Hotel: I could take two days to walk from the very spot I'd had to ditch the walk right out to the coast. It felt like a favour too big to accept but she patiently persisted with me: all I needed to do was pick my weekend. Eventually, I got over myself, dug out my boots and found my copy of Wainwright's *A Coast to Coast Walk*. The first part of the book was muddy and tattered, the last twenty pages neat and clean. I packed my bag, ready to complete my unfinished business with the North York Moors.

Saturday's walking took me back over the moors on a long, straight, easy path. I started with a steady climb up from the car park where I'd been picked up in the summer, up the edge of Carr Ridge and on to Urra Moor, the highest moorland in North Yorkshire. I got a sense of what I'd missed when I'd driven through here in the summer in the comfort of the air-conditioned bag van. I'd watched the birds of prey waiting on fence posts for the van to pass so they could return to stripping the carcass of a piece of roadkill. From behind a windscreen, I'd felt some small sense of vastness of the moor and of how strange and vulnerable a long path might feel when there's nothing in sight but more of the same, and not a single tree for shelter. But the comfort of the van had hidden the bleakness of the place, the chat with the driver obliterating loneliness.

The heather had shrunk since I'd been here last: in June it was purple and white, springing up from the ground high and loose and interrupted by large, singed areas. These burned parts were the remnants of the spring muirburn, where the tough older growth is burned off in a series of carefully managed fires to stimulate new shoots; the kind that deer and grouse like to feed on. Curlews and plover like the muirburn, apparently, and the larger birds of prey don't. I guess the people who like it most of all are those who shoot the grouse. But unmanaged, the heather would die off, the moorland turn to scrub, and, eventually, to woodland. The burning holds the landscape in a kind of unnaturally youthful stasis.

By the time I'd gone back, the heather was brown and damp, the shoots bare and stiff and woody. There were no waymarkers, and though the path soon joined the track of the old Rosedale ironstone railway and cut clearly through the heath, I saw no other walkers. Nobody would ask anything from me today, and unwanted, I felt myself dissolve into the wide bowl of space. Urra Moor became Farndale Moor, at some point. Whole half hours passed where I thought, more or less, about nothing – stray ideas or fantasies or desires slowly scudding across my consciousness then evaporating, like the clouds in the crisp bright sky. Empty-headed, I was something close to happy. I was not alone: there were fat sheep with loose, tatty fleeces trotting along the track. The gorse they moved through must have been wet because although it hadn't rained that day, they all had water beading in their greasy yellow wool. When I moved off the path to take a wee behind a wall, a pair of grouse exploded from the heather. The sudden beating of their wings sounded like dropped library books.

I stopped, nine or so miles in, at the Lion's Inn on Blakey Ridge for a hot chocolate. The car park was full and inside a huge fire filled the room with a fierce heat. The autumn wind had made my fingers so stiff and cold I couldn't undo my shoelaces to get my muddy boots off at the door. A seat in the inglenook was free, I had a paperback and a half-knitted Whitby gansey in my rucksack, and I stayed an hour. It was an effort to force myself out of my chair and back on the road for the other half of the day's miles, which would take me down off the moors and into the Esk Valley.

On the road after the Lion's Inn, just as the walker turns east from the road to the more obscure paths crossing Danby High Moor, there is a squat stone marker that might look, in poor light, like a bulky person crouching by the path's edge. This is Fat Betty, named after a nun who got lost in the fog on her way to Rosedale Abbey. People like to name the waymarkers around here: there are a couple of smaller stone crosses, Old Ralph and Young Ralph, and some ribald tales circulating about what the Ralphs junior and senior and Fat Betty might get up to after dark.

Betty is especially beloved by walkers; the Dawnay Estates, which maintains all the land around here for grouse shooting, keeps her whitewashed so she's easy to spot. As you pass her, you're supposed to leave a treat behind and pick one up from her broad shoulders. In the summer, the walking traffic is such that your chocolate bar or apple is likely to be only an hour old: a present from the walker just ahead of you on the path. By October I found nothing but a big puddle filling the depression a summer's worth of hiking boots had made around the marker. The puddle was almost a pond, deep enough to be growing its own foamy lime-green scum and bathing the brown and greasy ribcage of some large mammal, probably a sheep, that had died in it. I gingerly skirted its edge and left a packet of Haribo.

The afternoon's miles passed quickly, my mind elsewhere. I spent most of them along a blustery Blakey Ridge, Roseberry Topping just about visible to the northwest. I walked fast, out of puff even on the flat, my shoelaces pulled tight. I hadn't booked the bag van this time but even carrying my loaded rucksack didn't slow me down. After Glaisdale Moor, the bleakness gave way to green and there was a sudden downpour. The rain started and stopped quickly, making me even colder and ensuring I reached Egton Bridge bedraggled, and with my teeth chattering. The little village clings to the riverbank and is held tight by woodland and pastures. The chocolate-box cosiness of it made it hard to imagine I was still so close to the moors. I stayed that night in an old mill house, the Esk running gently through the back garden. *One more day to go*, I thought, in the spirit of getting something over with.

The encroaching turn of the year had forced the giddiness and euphoria I'd found in my summer walking right out of me. Some of this was down to the sense of failure that had

The Parallel Path

persisted however much Clive had tried to talk me out of it. I had let him down. And something else was happening too: I had started to realise that I was unwell. I was frightened, and ignoring the fact I was frightened: not fully at home to myself, my body announcing that something was wrong in a way that became too persistent to ignore. My future hunched like an animal behind a dry-stone wall.

From time to time, I'd started to get mild fevers and night sweats. Sometimes I'd experience tinnitus so badly I could actually *feel* the vibrations of a noise that was, in actual fact, not there. I lay awake at night and followed the thrumming buzz the bees inside my head made as they rattled along the left side of my jawbone, along my teeth and through the papery catacombs of my sinuses. Something had happened to my hearing; it was almost impossible to keep up with conversation when there was any kind of background noise. In groups of friends, I'd either interrupt awkwardly or give up and watch them talk to each other, their voices bubbling away as if they came to me from underwater. The dizziness I'd first noticed on the way into Richmond came back sometimes, and often, when we walked together, my daughter would complain I was blundering into her, unable to follow a straight line and keep to my own side of the path. It felt like a meaningful complaint: we jostled for space against each other in other ways too.

I am generally lazy about going to the doctor, but the week before I went back to the moors, my GP had taken my assortment of minor ailments seriously, sent me for some hearing tests and referred me to the hospital for some further examinations. I might, she'd said gently, have to go and have an MRI. Just to rule out a few things. Duncan is a radiographer: he works the MRI machines sometimes. I told the GP this and she'd told me that when patients have a family member who works in the imaging department of the hospital, they can ask to be telephoned at home and invited in at short notice if there happens to be a last-minute cancellation. She was so delicate about this that I convinced myself I didn't understand she was hinting at the need for the scan to be done as quickly as possible. Clive has had loads of MRIs and had given me tips about lying still and managing the claustrophobia I might feel as they fed me into the tube. I'd only half listened. *It won't come to that*, I thought.

As the summer bled into autumn, a late and bright one, I'd taken my daughter to a university open day. She had been excited, nervous, guarded. I watched her as if she was a finely balanced scale, teetering in that tight place where her urge to leave home weighed the same as her anxiety at what the wider world might have to offer. Soon, the scales were going to tip: until they did, we struggled with each other. That day, we ordered hotdogs in a busy forecourt in a big glass atrium. The jaunty piped music, hissing coffee machines and clattering cups combined to drown out the voice of the woman serving us. My hearing was getting too bad to ignore. The woman leaned over the counter, tried shouting, then turned to my daughter to carry the message. I've seen the same happen to the children of parents who don't speak English fluently or to children whose parents use wheelchairs. It is just as annoying as I'd always imagined it would be.

'She wants to know if you want red or brown sauce,' my daughter had said.

It was the first time our roles had been so obviously reversed and I sensed in my daughter those jostling states – of love and tenderness and irritation and embarrassment and resentment – that being her mother had first invited me into. The attentiveness that care both requires and instils is not new to her: she is an excellent older sister. When her friend died, her teacher had phoned to tell me my daughter had been looking after her friends, guiding them into the new territories of grief they'd all found themselves lost in, a place she had already started the lifelong process of mapping. Care was not new to her, but between us, it had only flowed towards her, and now she was an adult and I was struggling to manage, she leapt quickly into the space, translating what I could not hear.

Once we had our food, we found a quiet, out-of-the-way spot on a sofa in a corridor where, in a room opposite, the student paramedics were demonstrating how to perform emergency CPR. My mobile phone rang, and it was Louise, phoning to tell me that Ben's mother had died. She had been unwell, but we had not expected this. I turned away from my daughter to watch a woman in a green boilersuit who still looked like a kid kneel over a plastic torso. She was demonstrating how to tilt the chin and use a hooked finger to sweep the mouth for foreign objects. *They're too young to learn about that*, I caught myself thinking.

There was a relentlessness to it all. More death; the world was full of it. But not for my daughter. I tried to get between my daughter and the window of the room where the CPR demonstration was happening. I turned my back as the

The Return

phone call continued, listening and not saying much because I was trying to get between my daughter and the news too. Between my daughter and the entire world. I knew one of the things the MRI would be looking for was a tumour in my brain. I wanted to get between my daughter and that too. How to turn myself into a locked door against the world's bad news when my body was delivering it to her personally? We left the open day early and went to be with Louise and the younger girls. The preview of what my daughter's future might hold was prematurely cut short as she was hauled back to the facts of her life, with nothing a person who cared for her could do about it. She was going to leave home soon and I felt such a terrible and selfish dread about that: there had not been time yet to make her happy. I didn't want to let her go until I was sure she was happy.

Muscling Through

Egton Bridge to Robin Hood's Bay (21 miles)

I have heard that before a person gives something up for good – a substance, a relationship, a way of being in the world – they have one last intense bout of indulgence; the alcoholic's final weekend bender before rehab. On this, my last day, I woke with aching shins and knew I was not quite done with my habit of gritting my teeth and getting on with things.

My plan was to leave Egton Bridge early and arrive in Robin Hood's Bay, twenty-one miles away, with plenty of time for a leisurely pub tea. I limped, instead, into a hot bath and soaked my legs, delaying my start. I am no stranger to the delayed muscle soreness a strenuous hike can cause, but this was a pain I'd never felt before. I guessed what it was – shin splints – because Ben used to get them sometimes after running his marathons and he'd described to me how they'd felt. Putting my heels down made me feel like the muscles were peeling away from my bones. Whenever Ben had mentioned them, I'd tease him for his self-inflicted sufferings. Walking hard in the cold carrying a backpack loaded with fancy pyjamas, books and knitting had given me a dose of my own. I'd overdone it on the moors. Failed to pace myself. Was so distracted by the task of ignoring what was coming from the doctor that I had also ignored the twinges I should have felt as I'd pounded out those few

Muscling Through

miles on the unyielding road surface. On my last day, I would pay for that lack of attention with every step.

The hard miles out of Egton Bridge and a famously steep climb through the village of Grosmont had me whimpering under my breath. There's a sweetshop halfway up the hill and at the top of it I'd be able to see the sea, and, if it was clear enough, the famous silhouette of Whitby Abbey. There's a train station at Grosmont and an old-fashioned steam train that keeps the relic of George Stephenson's work in these parts alive: if you time it right, you can jump on and it will take you all the way to the coast. The idea of a train was as tempting as the sweetshop, but I turned my face away from the station, passed over the train tracks and crossed the River Esk. At the top of the hill, the path straightened as it emerged on to higher land and cut eastward across Sleights Moor. It was clear enough: the cold had rinsed the haze from the air and I could see the abbey. I could see the sea too.

At this point in *A Coast to Coast Walk*, Wainwright is so pleased that he figures himself, in the most self-congratulatory terms possible, as a kind of Old Testament prophet. The view goes to his head as he describes it; 'indisputably (= without doubt) the Promised Land (and Sea), just like the man said. (Smart fella, this Wainwright.)' The abbey's skeleton was scraped into the slate grey blueness of the North Sea like a sketch in chalk on dark paper. The horizon and my destination were ten miles off, at least, but there were seagulls overhead. My ankles swelled. I slowed down. I limped. I squared my shoulders and listened to an audiobook, trying not to be in this place, with this hurting body. I thought of Herzog again, getting out on his own walk 'in full faith' in his own power to cure death: he'd got what he wanted, his friend ready to care for him as he arrived in her sickroom a softer, gentler man. My summer walk had helped me to understand that and to begin to approach myself with a new kind of gentleness, to be more available for the care of my friends that had always been there and to let them see me beyond my toughness a little more clearly. But the prospect of being ill, *seriously* ill, presented a new challenge. I was right back up to my old tricks again. *Don't be ridiculous*, I'd said to Duncan, nearly offended by his obvious worry, by the way he'd tried to prepare me for what it might mean if they asked me to come back for a second MRI scan, *I won't have a brain tumour.*

Nearer to hand was the RAF Fylingdales ballistic missile early warning and space surveillance system; big white golf balls perched on Snod Hill. The technology here was first developed as part of the four-minute warning system devised during the Cold War. At home, I live within sight of Heysham Power Station, just outside the radius where homes are issued with iodine tablets in case of emergency. I can hear the test alarms going off sometimes if the wind is blowing in the right direction. The path took me down off the moor and towards the woods. I followed it and wondered what I'd do if the doctors gave me my own four-minute warning. Would I really want one?

I didn't message Clive much that day. My insistence on mind-over-matter for the walk and for my own health was an idea too foolish to report back to him. Where four-minute warnings are concerned, the trick was to live, as far as you could, so that you were already doing what you'd most want to be doing when death came for you. Hadn't Clive tried to tell me that over and over again – to treat all my days as time lived after the siren had sounded? I had imagined myself cutting across the country on Clive's behalf, showing him everything I saw and listening to everything he wanted to say. I'd imagined myself bringing my friend news of my feat. My anger at being small, at being fragile, at being subject to heatwaves and shin splints and whatever else the doctor was going to tell me was wrong with me came along the moors with me, tugging at my hand like a toddler as I waded through the dead heather.

The last ten miles involved a bit of up and down through the gentler, more sheltered parts of Eskdale: I came off the moors and endured a long trudge through woodland towards Falling Foss. The word comes from 'force'; it means waterfall and there is one, glimpsed between trees, its rushing sounding like the patter of static; a radio between stations. It drove out my tinnitus for a while and this part of the walk felt like rest because of it. There were families here, out on a day trip – the weather was brighter than the day before, the wind less cold. I stopped for a coffee at a café in the woods where the toilets were in wooden huts wreathed in fairy lights. My limp was worse – almost a shuffle – as I reached Hawsker, which is an old Scandinavian upland settlement and the last village before Robin Hood's Bay. There was a bench there, and I rested a while. The urge to stop, to give up, to admit these last twenty-odd miles had been too much for my little legs, came gift wrapped in boredom, itself wearing a mask of mischief. *Imagine*, something inside me said, *if you just didn't bother.* It would be like playing truant from your final exams or jilting someone you loved at the altar. The possibility of it – *nobody would ever know* – made me laugh, and laughing, I got up and carried on.

The final miles join the part of the Cleveland Way that hugs the coast between Whitby and Robin Hood's Bay, heading southwards. The clifftop path follows the route of the old Whitby to Scarborough railway line, disused now and hidden by great shaggy tides of gorse and brambles. The thorny branches hook around the edges of fences, clogging up the stiles and springing into the kissing gates. The sea was dark and choppy, and I, underwhelmed, wondered how I'd have met this sight if I'd have walked all the way here like I was supposed to. You're actually at the land's edge, more or less, a little while before you're at the walk's finish. This slightly circuitous route, longer than it strictly needs to be, has been designed to give the walker the most dramatic entry into Robin Hood's Bay possible. It reminded me of that idiosyncratic march north over the headland at St Bees, accompanying the sea for a few miles before abandoning it for West Cumbria.

The main route that descends to the beach through the village is a steep incline lined by fishermen's cottages and fishing boats loaded with knotted rope and bright orange buoys. I walked down that hill as if I was tiptoeing across broken glass and didn't let myself think about how my legs would manage when I had to turn around and haul myself back up to my hotel. This was the end of the season as well as the end of the day: most of the day-trippers had already packed up and gone home. Not many people live here; most of the red-tiled houses have been given over to holiday lets

Muscling Through

and, out of season, the place is a ghost town. The café and the little bookshop that had been so lively when I'd passed them in the summer were closed and the tiny newsagent's had already brought in the rack of postcards and put down its shutters.

I got to where I was supposed to be. At the opening of his book, as Wainwright tries to explain the appeal of a long-distance walk, he makes much of its ending. Robin Hood's Bay is 'a definite full stop' and 'a terminus absolute'. Even if you had more miles in your legs, you'd have no choice but to take a seat and look at the horizon because, as he reminds us, 'you can't walk on water'.

That 'can't' intrigued me. I'd first met Wainwright as a Charles Atlas sort of being, powered by purpose, as tough as the Northern landscapes that formed him. But he was a man who knew when to let a rainy day keep him at home and who understood that the walk would find its ending in a surrender to the edge of the land. He had faced the fact – however grumpily – that the last time he'd get up the high Lakeland fells he loved he'd be in an urn, carried by those that loved him. And perhaps I'd had the wrong idea about Atlas too: I thought Charles had named himself after Greek myth's strongest man, the muscle-bound being responsible for bearing the weight of the world on his shoulders. But Atlas was no Zeus, he was just a man given an unreasonable load, presented with a god's labour as a live-action lesson to prompt him towards humility: a man could no more bear the weight of the world than he could walk on water.

The sea glittered. It was colder and windier than the last time I'd been here, the headland brown and not green. I

The Parallel Path

lingered, glad of my jumper. Sore shins had meant slow time and the light was starting to dim. Autumn had arrived earlier to the east coast than to the west and I imagined it streaking across the country in a yellow and orange haze, following the path of the sun. The sand under my boots was grey, rippled with tidemarks and studded with seaweed-covered rocks. I went out as far as I needed to get my boots wet, turning back to admire the rust-stained metal flood defences, the way the houses were so crowded together on the clifftop they looked like they were about to topple over. The tide licked at my ankles and wet my shoelaces. There were a few hikers wandering around the sands in their walking kit, striding out, as I had, to inspect the beached and empty fishing boats, find the distant sea's edge at their journey's end and throw in their pebbles. I didn't have mine anymore: I'd chucked them into a rockpool in a huff while I was here during the heatwave in July. Stripped of an excuse for triumph, I rested unsteadily at the tide's edge. The seawater lapped at my boots on its way in and dragged the sand from under my heels on its way out.

PART FOUR

*Salford Neuro Ward via the
Preston Guild Wheel*

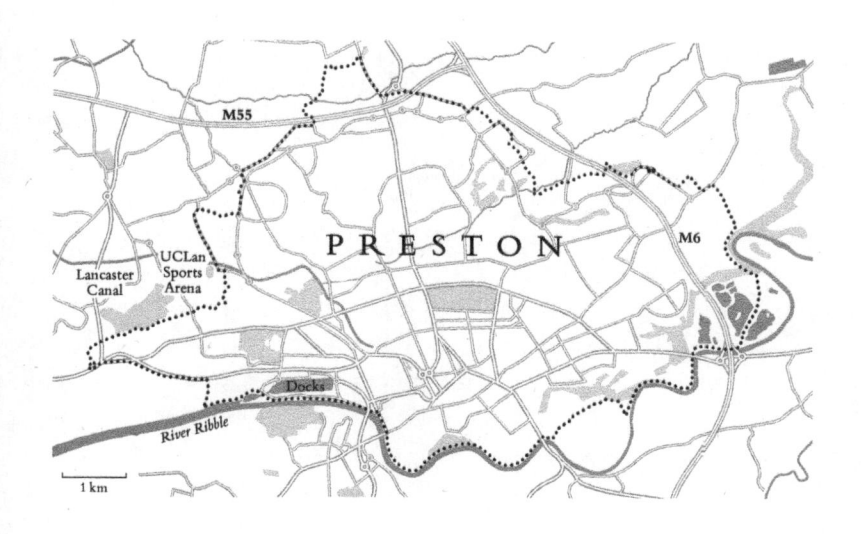

Walking Widdershins
The Guild Wheel (21 miles)

A few weeks after returning home from Robin Hood's Bay, I'd sat in a nondescript room and listened to a doctor tell me that, despite all my objections, I really did have a brain tumour. The consultant showed me the image from the MRI scan on his monitor. The brain tissue looked vaguely insubstantial, like mushroom clouds, fog, or the ice patterns on car windows. It reminded me of Clive's cyanotypes: beautiful and shadowy. The tumour was bright and solid and (the doctor gestured with the tip of his biro) very obviously pressing into my brain stem. I pulled out my phone to take a picture of his computer screen.

'That's ridiculous,' I said. 'I don't feel *that* unwell. I'm very healthy.'

The doctor patted my hand and smiled.

'And you will be healthy again,' he said.

I thought about Clive and how unfair it was that I'd had the best news delivered alongside the worst. My tumour was not cancer, but the doctor said that 'they' would probably want to test it for cancer all the same, just to be sure, but that wasn't something I needed to worry about. That was how I realised I needed brain surgery: if they wanted to test it, they were going to have to get it out of my head first. I thought about saws and drills. The consultant told me I was going to be transferred for the rest of my treatment to

The Parallel Path

a hospital in a different trust: the Northern Care Alliance in Salford, north of Manchester. He said that if I woke up with either paralysis or a sudden increase in my hearing loss, I should present at Accident and Emergency, tell them the name of what I had wrong with me and ask for steroids. The balance problems I'd been having, he said, were probably going to get worse; I should be careful where and how I walk.

I pricked my ears up at this, meaning filtering in only slowly. He kept on talking about my hearing. I'd lose what was left of it on the side affected by the tumour. That was inevitable. But in that moment, I didn't care about that.

'I won't be able to walk?'

'The tumour grows along your balance nerve.' He pointed at the screen with his biro again. I wondered if he didn't want to use his finger to gesture towards my tumour in case something nasty leapt from its image on the screen and into his body. 'They sacrifice the nerve to remove the tumour. Some people have a lot of trouble walking afterwards,' he explained.

I laughed. He'd already told me that the tumour had been in my head a long time; I'd carried it in my skull through the pandemic and across the entire country, my secret passenger, softly growing a few millimetres a year. I wanted to know what he knew, which was how other people had responded when he'd given them this news. Did they laugh? I was sick, but was I strange too?

I left the hospital and walked home through town. All the shops were playing Christmas music and I tried to listen hard to every snatch of it and to feel my feet pattering along the wet pavement, wanting to savour these ordinary things as priceless pleasures. A fragment of one of Clive's letters came back to me: he'd described a visit to Sainsbury's shortly after his diagnosis, the ordinariness of his task and the enormity of the news and what it meant crashing into each other in a way that was nearly overwhelming. Sainsbury's was the other side of town, so I went to Boots and bought a bottle of shampoo because we'd run out. It helped.

As the date for my surgery grew closer I involved myself in the double task of preparing for it by filling the freezer with soups and casseroles and curries, and also convincing myself that the surgeons would probably cancel it at the last minute and it would all come to nothing. Living that double life was exhausting, but because I had already come to the conclusion that a walk is a room big enough to hold most things I laced up my boots and went out again. Clive's very first letter had been about Morecambe, the town where he'd grown up. He'd shown me how to belong to a place at the moment I'd been trying to shed it. So again, I allowed myself to be guided and went back to my hometown: Preston. I'd walk the Guild Wheel, I decided. A nice long walk – all twenty-one miles of it.

To get to the starting point I walked past the house where Ben used to live and approached the railway bridge over the River Ribble that still bears the red plaque painted with his name. The Ben Ashworth Way is the part of the Guild Wheel he used to run most often, the Wheel itself a loop around Preston. The circular walk has all kinds of meanings beyond the beetle-tied-to-a-thread miserable, confined crawling I'd experienced during the lockdown. I'd take this loop anti-clockwise, walking *widdershins*. According to the folklore, walking widdershins around an object – a church, or some other significant and sacred landmark – can bring bad luck, or it can transfer you from one place to another by opening a portal to another world. According to the old stories, a widdershins walk can also reverse the flow of time: pacing anti-clockwise can make the clock run backwards.

The first couple of miles hug the north bank of the Ribble and trace its brownly slopping waters eastwards, through Avenham and Miller Parks. When Ben and I brought our daughter here the day after she was born the track between the riverbank and the edge of the park was a kind of leafy green tunnel, the surface uneven and pitted with old roots, the exposed parts of them spotted with lichen and treacherous with moss. Later, they'd succumbed to a disease and been felled. The newly exposed edges of the walkway had since been replanted with younger specimens. I followed the new path and knew again the way a place can contain a time: the memory of the old trees was flanked by the presence of the new disease-proof ones. They'd freshly tarmacked the path too, and the walking was easy. During that earlier afternoon when we had wandered here shell-shocked and sleepless, Ben had been pushing the buggy over uneven ground, forcing it gently over the exposed tree roots. I'd taken a photograph. He still had long hair then and in the picture he looks tired and pale and happy: I remember the pair of us stunned and stupid at the ringside as our daughter's life began. The light still cast green shadows through the sycamore leaves and I felt again the precariousness of being the only person left who had been there as my daughter came into her world, this city, her home. In the weeks before, I'd been collecting all the family photographs from various cloud accounts and hard drives and arranging them into some kind of order: who would gather up these times and places for my daughter if I could not?

There are large parts of this walk that are almost wilfully unlovely, as Preston itself can be. The route misses out all of the most obviously interesting and photogenic parts of Preston and sticks to the outskirts, taking in what the environmental activist Marion Shoard taught us to call the 'edgelands' territory. She described these murky hinterland areas as 'a netherworld neither urban or rural . . . the hotchpotch collection of superstores, sewage works, golf courses and surprisingly wildlife-rich rough lands which sit between town and country in the urban fringe'. *Netherworlds* is right: I walked under a motorway bridge, my footsteps echoing and the ground littered with half-melted plastic bottles and shiny laughing-gas canisters, like drifts of metal owl pellets. I passed the Lower Brockholes sand and gravel quarry. Here, the Ribble is wide and shallow, there are exposed stony spits and, on them, men in plastic garden chairs with green cool bags and umbrellas sat fishing.

This edgelands route is full of the necessary but unappealing apparatus of cities. The path led me through the gardens of the city's crematorium, rows of shiny black plaques laid into the grass and trees planted for babies, their branches full of wind chimes and streamers. There was a queue of gleaming black cars down the main road in and I wasn't dressed right to be there. After the crematorium the path traced the edges of the city's main waste processing plant. There was a problem: two fire engines blocked the main gate and men in uniforms stood around, appraising a situation that seemed to be ongoing – inconvenient but not urgent. I took a selfie in front of the sign for the tip and the fire engine and sent it to my oldest friend. When we were teenagers, we used to call this place De-Preston and desperately filled out our UCAS forms, imagining that home was a skin that growing up meant shedding and the town that made you was a place that could one day be left.

Susan Sontag famously remarked that everyone who is born holds dual citizenship and that each of us will be called to use our passport and pass from the kingdom of the well to the other side – the land of the sick. I'd read this before, and imagined without knowing I imagined it that these two kingdoms were quite different countries, and that passing from one to the other would be something that you'd notice, like crossing a river, like moving house, like growing up and leaving home. Though we were neighbours, Clive lived in one country, and I lived in another, and across that line on the map he sent me letters. But now I know that there exists an unlovely edgelands territory where health is not entirely itself and illness can sidle up to you.

In the few months after my diagnosis my symptoms had either got worse, or, once I'd understood what was causing them, I had allowed myself to become more aware of them. Headaches, dizziness, a numbness in my face and mouth, a tendency to dribble a bit while drinking. The hearing on the left side faded out to such an extent that, accompanied by a more moderate loss on the right – probably the result of an ear infection in childhood – I was left struggling to keep up in noisy environments and with no sense of which direction the few sounds I could hear were coming from. Most speech, especially if there was any background noise at all, became indistinct – as if I was eavesdropping through a thick door or the conversation was just a radio left on low volume in the next room.

Stereo hearing informs our sense of space: I started bumping into things on my left, didn't leave myself enough room to get through doors, and a few weeks before my consultant recommended I stop driving, pranged the car on the deaf side. The world and the sense I had of myself moving through it flattened out. For parts of my brain, the space on my left doesn't quite exist anymore. I felt it all keenly on my walk that afternoon: every time I looked up too quickly (to check for traffic or admire a view) or down (to look at my map), the ground tilted: it felt as if I was going to fall over. Sometimes I did fall over. My walking had become tentative and uncertain: sometimes the ground itself felt soft.

I stopped for lunch in a Starbucks in the industrial park, drank black coffee and orange juice to perk me up, and refilled my water bottle in the toilet. I felt silly and conspicuous in my walking leggings and boots, couldn't hear the barista calling me to pick up my coffee, couldn't get my phone to log into the WiFi. I'd never been here before – not to this Starbucks, though it was more or less the same as all the others – and not to this industrial park. I must have driven through at some point in the years I'd lived in this city, but when I left, I needed the marks on the pavement that would guide me over the roundabouts and past the Northwest office of Girl Guiding UK to pick up the route again. I was home, apparently, but nothing about this place was familiar except as an example of its type: it was as all industrial parks are, grey and blocky, the steep grass verges studded with litter, a couple of newly discarded school ties woven into the railings on a footbridge, fluttering like prayer flags. I staggered across a main road at the pedestrian crossing looking, I am sure, like a daytime drunk. In an attempt to keep me upright and find a stable horizon, one of my eyes had started 'dancing'; as I waited on the central reservation for the traffic to clear, it flitted side to side in its socket, as if fruitlessly searching the landscape for the dotted lines that often appear on maps, desperate to organise these edgelands and mark one territory out from another.

On the northwest part of the route I navigated through a new housing estate and needed to bring up a map on my phone and squint at the screen in the bright sunlight. The houses were boxy and perfect, everyone had a matching hedge of neatly trimmed hebe and privet, all the cars were clean, the garage doors shiny. The pavements were spotless black tarmac, unpatched or repaired, with bright pale kerbs. My foot, the one Alice's grandmother had strapped up all those years ago, was hurting. It had hurt that morning when I woke up and I'd hoped it would relax into the day as I got moving, but the more miles I did, the worse it hurt. I told myself some stories about it. For example: I'd been walking on pavements and paved cycle paths: the impact was bad for the joints, which had been weak on that side since I'd injured it as a child. Or: I was out of condition after a lazy winter and spring: pushing myself a bit would do me good and I should pick up the pace. In three miles, if the foot was still troubling me, I'd relace my boot.

The truth is, I am a bad patient. A while before, I was throwing a ball for my dog in my back garden. There are three paved steps at the back door up to a patio and I was standing on them, twisting to throw the ball, when the ground softened, the earth tilted, and I fell. It was just like being drunk, except when I hit the ground, I felt it. The consultant at Salford had warned me to be careful *especially on stairs*. I had filed the advice away with other pieces of information that were theoretically interesting but definitely not relevant to me. Being careful on stairs was for other people – people who were feeble and frail because they have less control of their own bodies and minds. I broke a bone in my foot, refused to take any time off work, and was curtailed from any proper walking for several weeks.

I worried about what being sick would involve: housebound, locked down, being cooked for, having someone else put my clothes in the washing machine. Becoming the unwilling and ungrateful recipient of care. I'd made jokes about it to Clive (*well it's not cancer, unless it is*), who did not try to fix or improve or adjust what I felt. We took fewer walks together and made more frequent visits to Morecambe seafront or the café at Lancaster Castle and the change was to accommodate what I needed, not him. There might have been a part of him that enjoyed this version of our friendship – not a healthy person listening to and understanding a sick one – but two sick people muttering furiously to each other and cracking poor-taste jokes – a little better. Part of him might have felt more accompanied and less studied than he had. If it was like that for him, he didn't say so, and that was a kind of care too.

There was a rough simplicity in my walking that day that became a kind of comfort. My foot hurt, and I carried on walking, and it carried on hurting. I found my way through the new housing estate: a bit of my hometown I had never seen, making home into a place where I could still get lost. Someone walked a dog, someone else passed me pushing a pram. There was an *Edward Scissorhands* feel about the place – it was that kind of housing estate – and I got the feeling that I didn't belong here and was being eyed with suspicion from behind spotless curtains. Once I was through, the hedges got unruly again. Nettles, ivy, young beech saplings, brambles, fireweed – all the leaves grey and furry because on wet days the passing traffic sprays them with filthy water.

Next, the well-maintained grounds of the city university's sports grounds. The university advertises these facilities on buses and billboards, but I'd never been there before either. There are netball and tennis courts, nicely maintained surfaces behind chain link fences, white and yellow lines and circles painted on closely shorn turf. There are floodlights and neat little car parks. The path was obvious and there were signs telling me to stay on it: I was supposed to avoid loitering and get out of where I was only begrudgingly welcome and down to the canal as soon as possible.

I had no idea how much care is required of you when you're sick. Telling someone you have a brain tumour – even someone you don't know that well – hurts them. If they love you, it causes them worry and sadness and fear. If they're a more distant acquaintance, they might experience the embarrassment of knowing there's some kind of response to be made, and not knowing what it is. Either way, the sick person causes the wound by sharing the news. There's a lot of work involved in all of this. I had to find the right words to let the person I was telling know I was going to say something shocking before I actually said it, then tell that person how to help so they could be relieved of the embarrassment of not knowing what to do. Otherwise, they might accidentally say, *well, at least it's writing material*, hear the clumsiness of what they'd just said with a painful, belated horror, and need me to smooth that over for them too.

I learned a bit about this work too from the doctor I saw during the first couple of months of the year. Sometimes she turned her computer screen away from me so I didn't see the images from the MRI scans I kept having. It's possible to read this gesture as paternalistic but it felt protective to me. The care was also there in the way she asked me how much I wanted to know about the surgery I would need to have, the way she warned me in advance that she was going to have to talk about the risks now, and that might feel frightening, and did I have anyone outside in the waiting room that I'd like to come and sit with me right now, to be there while I hear this? The waiting room was another kind of edgelands place: the companions of the sick linger there, needing to be cared for because behind the closed door they wait outside, something frightening is happening that they cannot control.

I'd seen lots of cyclists on the route so far, from the kids in jeans showing off by riding with no hands to the serious guys in head-to-toe Lycra and aerodynamic helmets. I'd seen plenty of walkers too, doing the loop, or part of it, in both directions. But here, through the university sports facilities, the path was empty. It's unlikely anyone would walk there unless, like me, they'd committed to following the Guild Wheel right the way around. A small white van with the university logo on the side (I still think of the logo as 'new' even though it's not – nobody's called UCLan 'Preston Poly' for decades now) drove slowly past me.

The sense of being surveyed was vaguely threatening, though it was very likely the man driving the van had no interest in me at all. I was definitely not doing anything interesting. I wondered if I looked like someone who was about to have a thirteen-hour brain surgery, and what secrets he, in his cab, his eyes hidden under the peak of a university-branded cap – carried with him. I thought about Clive and the way he'd been so deliberately abrupt when we'd sat on the bench at Silverdale and he'd told me he was dying. I had stared, and he had stared back. The rest of the letters and all our conversations were about figuring out what each of us had seen in that moment and what it was like to watch another person look. I skirted the gaze of a few security cameras as the path finally left the university's jurisdiction and headed downwards, under a bridge and towards the canal. The surface was covered with duckweed, the clotted, greenish smell of the water alive and comforting.

For the last three miles or so I turned eastwards and walked along the edge of Preston's marina to meet the north bank of the Ribble again. The weather had brightened – it was almost hot – and there were people in office clothes sitting out on the benches eating sandwiches and chips, and seagulls perched on the railings angrily waiting for their share. The air smelled wet and warm and mouldy. I looked at the benches but did not dare sit: I'd never get up again, and I wanted this to be over with now. There's a part in every walk where I forget why I wanted to do it in the first place, am sick of the whole thing, embarrassed I ever mentioned it. On the water, there were rows of little pleasure boats nicely moored and the water itself was a foul unnatural green – nearly teal – on its surface a skin of half-decomposed twigs and leaf litter and plastic rubbish. The water gently slopped and scraped against the steep concrete edge under the railings. There was a burger van and the smell of frying onions.

In its heyday, this marina made Preston into a proper working port and the ships would come in here off the river, bringing mainly cotton and wood. It was easy enough for the ships to transfer their loads to canal traffic and though nobody was making much money, other kinds of transactions took place too. I had a hairdresser whose mum worked in a pub that the sailors would drink in. She knew the women who did sex work there, was matey with some of them, seeing as they all worked in the same place, and on hearing her teenaged daughter gossip about them with her friends, took her into the back yard of the pub and slapped her face for her.

'Those girls are putting food on the table for their kids, same as I am,' she'd said.

I can't remember what had prompted her to tell me this; the point of the story was the slap and not the sex work

The Parallel Path

– something about kids not being disciplined properly anymore and modern parents being too scared to teach their children right and wrong. My head was tilted back in the sink, the water sloshing around my ears. I was captive, and listening to her tell me about her mother was only like listening to the radio; no response from me was needed. I imagined this woman as a teenager in the 1960s, a back-combed Hitchcock blonde tottering back into the bar in her white boots, her hand against her mouth to hide the fat lip her mother had just given her: a strange lesson in kindness and respect; love's hard delivery.

There was once a big ship parked up on the docks (that's what we called it – what my dad called it, when he was 'off to the docks' with the dog: people only started calling it 'the marina' when the new apartments were built and the benches put in – 'the docks' was for work, 'the marina' for play). When I was a kid this one big ship was moored there and she never sailed anymore but was fixed to the edge with a permanent covered walkway and festooned with lights on ropes, like a Christmas tree. Her name was *The Manxman* and in her best times she'd gone back and forth between Liverpool and the Isle of Man. Then she'd got old and couldn't sail anymore, and after being delivered to Preston and beached here, she'd been converted into a floating nightclub. I was too young to go but had aspired to walk down the covered walkway and into its mysterious chambers.

I had no idea what happened in nightclubs but imagined it would be exactly like the fancy dining hall on *The Poseidon Adventure*, which was the only other boat I'd seen inside of. There would be blue drinks with crushed ice in them like Slush Puppies and glo-sticks and sparkling dresses and smoking. It never happened: by 1992 *The Manxman* had been towed back to Liverpool and scrapped, though not before she'd been featured on a show Richard Madeley and Judy Finnigan made before they got together, and as she waited in dry dock to be dismantled, as the backdrop for a music video for a Geordie indie band.

I have to strain to remember any of this. Mostly, I don't remember the Preston docklands being anything other than what they are now: no boats except little pleasure boats up at the far end of the marina, fancy apartments overlooking the water and the same old seagulls living on what they can get out of the chip wrappers and burger boxes. It's nice to park up here in the evening. If you put a chicken nugget on your bonnet, you can get the seagulls to land on your car. Every year there is a bright bloom of blue algae, dangerous and beautiful, like giant hogweed. At the bottom end there's a Morrisons and this is where Duncan and I would go for a Sunday morning fry-up, because the supermarket café was cheap. There's a cinema and a few fast-food places at the bottom end and nothing round here has changed in years and that's the point of places like McDonald's and KFC: they're no-places, almost magical: you could be anywhere, any time. Marion Shoard argued that we could be interested in these places because 'the living museum of our recent past is the powerhouse of the society of the present'. It felt like that to me – privately, personally – as I walked through the unremarkable, often ugly territory at the edge of my hometown and remembered the edgelands that powered me: that murky space between childhood and adulthood and the hinterland I existed in now between sick and well.

* * *

Duncan was at work that day, and had been texting me, worried that the walk was too much, that it was an unwise thing to do, that I was going to fall again or give myself heatstroke. Somewhere along the way an insect had bitten me on my elbow and the swelling had become painful. I took an antihistamine, then texted Duncan and told him that I thought the surgeons would probably cancel the operation because the pill I'd just taken would still be in my system. He encouraged me to carry on and finish the walk he was not sure he wanted me to do. I was contradictory like that too: practical and organised, taking books back to the library or checking emails or paying for something at the supermarket, then another part of me would interrupt, seize me with the urge to drop whatever was in my hands, head for the nearest door and run. Really run. Was this what Ben felt like? All those early mornings jogging around this Wheel, away from home and then back to it?

Bad news sinks in slowly, like gossip through a crowd. Years after Ben died, Louise and Duncan and I took all the children away together on a sunny beach holiday. After a day at the pool, going back to the hotel room in the lift, I noticed that our daughter had a patch of sunburn on her shoulder where I'd missed a spot: she has his skin – pale and freckled and prone to burning. He got sunburned through a white T-shirt once, when we were teenagers and walking along that difficult scree edge of Wast Water. She's just as fair as that. In the lift, I caught myself rooting through a bag for something for her to wear so that Ben wouldn't see the sunburned spot and moan at me for being careless. In that moment I met a part of me that had been protected from the news of his death and thought he was just sleeping in the hotel room. This part of me needed to be told and gently accompanied through the shock. Grief has taught me that there is no such thing as a delayed reaction. Each part of who a person is responds the second that they know, and people *are*, to repurpose Marion Shoard's words about the seeping edges of cities, multiple creatures, full of decay and stasis, both dynamic and mysterious. Care is an edgelands creature too: a layered, awkward, clumsy, collaborative thing. I know it better than I have ever known it as I go home to walk this loop and meet the things I care about, the ways I care about them, the ways in which I am careless and resent the burden that the inevitable interconnectedness of my being places on me.

I joined the riverbank again, walking along a gravelly path back towards the start of the loop in Avenham and Miller Parks. I knew this part of the route really well: time runs backwards so easily here. My dad would come exactly here in the early mornings to walk his dogs, crossing a main road between the warren of terraces where we lived and a building belonging to the sea cadets. There was a path between the sea cadet place and a railway line that led right on to the river – the path less well tended then, and before it became part of the Guild Wheel almost entirely overgrown by Himalayan balsam: in summer you'd have to fight your way through it. We kids would play here, rushing through the head-high stalks down towards the river and hearing the swollen seed pods crack. The seeds would patter down on us like rain. The syrupy smell of the pink flowers will always remind me of being somewhere I shouldn't, having crossed the main road on my own.

The Parallel Path

Part of the treatment I had during the spring involved a series of injections aimed at killing off the balance nerve on the left side of my head. The treatment was supposed to make the recovery from the surgery a little easier. The needle went through my eardrum. I got a week to heal, then I went back and the doctor did it again.

'I won't say *sharp scratch*,' she said, 'because actually, it really hurts.'

This is care.

Is it?

I change my mind about this every day.

When her father was sick I promised my daughter I'd always tell her the truth and never polish up the facts to make them easier to handle. No 'sharp scratch' because it really does hurt. I wanted her to be able to trust what I said, no matter what, forever – even if what I had to share with her was something we wished was not true.

Yes, he is going to die. Even if he does everything the doctors ask him to do. He will definitely die before you're grown up and it will be terrible.

Was that the right thing? There was something self-serving in it: a wish for the things I said to be taken unquestioningly as gospel truth, even if what I said was about as far away from Good News as it was possible to get. I wonder now if there was a place for comforting stories and for softness. For the addendum: *it will be terrible and you will be all right.*

Behind the sea cadets' headquarters, abandoned on the gently sloping and stony riverbank, there had always been a falling-apart rowing boat, the hull gradually disintegrating. Us kids had a rumour about this boat. A man lived in it, a bad man, who'd take an empty can of pop to the garage and buy 30p's worth of petrol and carry it away in the can, and he'd sit in this decrepit boat and drink it. If he saw you, he'd *get you*. Stories proliferated about him: he washed his face in milk stolen from doorsteps, he had a knife made of a sharpened chicken bone, he was rich and his coat lining crinkled because it was full of paper money he used to keep himself warm and never thought to spend. Wandering the streets after school, we'd see empty cans lying in the gutter and stamp them flat so this man couldn't get them. There used to be a warehouse belonging to a fruit distributor and the lorries would come in and out first thing and sometimes, on the way to school, we'd find not-quite-crushed bananas and oranges on the road. The gates of the warehouse would stand open during the day, and we'd dare each other to go in: in summer there'd be straw-berries. You could run away with a handful if you were brave, but Petrol-drinking man would be in there, waiting for us. We were sure of it.

What a deep well childhood is, full of the stories we told ourselves as we played together in places we should not have been: beneath railway bridges and round the back of industrial units and in tiny patches of woodland on the verges of busy roads. The netherworld of the places where we played during the edgelands years of our childhood spawned these half-made-up bogeymen. The stories, harmless and cruel, fearful and stupid, containing their own kind of magic, proliferated like an invasive species. That wooden boat was on its last legs when I was a kid, and on the day of the walk I looked forward to seeing it again: a private landmark before the path spat me back out in Broadgate and the railway bridge where I started. When I got to where it used to be I saw that it was gone, the riverside cleaned up, the balsam flowers finally under control.

I finished. At the end of the Guild Wheel, which was its beginning, I texted some friends and sent them pictures of Ben's plaque and the view over the Ribble, a man who some of them had never met strangely absent from every shot.

Many years before I moved away, I was driving home from work and saw a man in a red running vest jogging along the side of the road towards Penwortham Old Bridge. I thought it would be funny to brake slightly, roll down my window and shout helpful and encouraging abuse at him. It would have been funny too – Ben would have laughed – except it wasn't him, but some other poor guy minding his business while out jogging. A better person might have pulled over, apologised and explained herself. I accelerated, cravenly; in the back of the car the kids were laughing. I will carry on mistaking runners in red vests along this river for him for as long as I come here.

In Lancaster, I limped home from the train station, dragged myself up the big hill I live on and sent Clive a voice note. He'd been interested in the walk: both of us, prone to magical thinking and seeing portents in mere coincidence, pleased by the fact I'd done it on the anniversary of our hike across Bowland, the one where I'd lost my compass. I chattered into my phone as I made my way up the hill towards home. I'd done my marathon day across the Vale of Mowbray (*all of it*) faster than this and that had involved proper map reading and a bit of getting lost. This little loop around the city that had made me was *nothing* and it had taken *ages*. What was wrong with me? Clive sent a message back almost right away, his voice full of laughter, reminding me I'd had Covid, it had been a hot day, my worsening balance made all walks more difficult. I'd finished it, he said, and that was the main thing. I had come to my circle's end.

Tethered, Again
The Neuro Ward, Salford (0 miles)

I took my compass with me to the hospital, the cord grubby with sweat and suncream. It's in my suitcase as I am booked in, and it sits in my locker as I change into the surgical gown and elastic stockings I'm required to put on for the surgery. A nurse comes and draws an arrow on the side of my neck with a black marker; the tip of it points behind my ear.

The surgery itself is something my body will know, but I do not. I remember sitting up on a bed as the anaesthetist injected something into my canula. He told me I'd start to feel a little more relaxed, possibly a bit dizzy. I blinked, and someone was pulling something out of my throat, someone else shouting that the operation had gone well: all the tumour had come out. I was in recovery a long time, shivering and listening placidly to two nurses talk to each other about another nurse – trying to work out if he was single or not. An entire day had been lost, though Duncan had lived it, wandering around a park in Salford, coming home to sleep, driving back to meet me on the ward late at night. It was dark and I was high and giggling and I demanded that he take a book out of my suitcase and hold it in front of my face so I could test if I could still read, fearing what the surgery might have done to my brain. The rest of the week passed in a blur of pain, vomiting and sleep.

Tethered, Again

I came home but did not improve as I should have done. Most days I felt as if someone was hammering nails into the top of my head. A creeping paralysis spread over the left side of my face: I could no longer drink and needed a beaker with a spout. A few days later I went back to Salford to be fitted with a lumbar drain to ease the build-up of cerebrospinal fluid on my brain. The fitting of the drain was painful. A first-year student nurse with the same name as my daughter was instructed to observe. She held my hand but flinched and cried as the doctor performed the procedure (so did I). She came back later in the small hours to apologise, sat by my bed and looked at one of the books I'd brought with me. It was W. G. Sebald's *The Rings of Saturn* but in the dim light she misread the title as *The Rings of Satan* and told me that she liked horror novels too. Because she was having a hard day at work I didn't correct her and instead we had a whispered conversation about Stephen King, who we discovered we are both fans of.

I spent two weeks lying still and flat in that bed, my cerebrospinal fluid softly dripping into a bag. There were windows in the ward, but they were behind me so for a fortnight I didn't see natural light and my only sense of the weather came from watching visitors arrive with wet hair and listening to them complain about the summer rainstorms. The ward became a little world of its own, its regular routines taking small bites out of the endless days. Every now and again, someone came and asked me if I knew what day it was, took my blood pressure and measured how much fluid the bag had collected. Once a day, the tap on the drain was turned off and I was allowed out of bed, shuffling dizzily towards the shower, where I was allowed to wash while sitting so long as I didn't get my head or my back wet. Once, the afternoon tea trolley did not come and I was made anxious and furious by this: someone else's visitor gave me a packet of paper tissues and poured me a glass of water.

In a side-room, a man was dying. There was a little electric candle on a table and a sign telling the rest of us so that we understood why he was allowed to have visitors whenever he liked. His family gathered, ordered takeaway and sang to him in a language I didn't recognise. His dying happened slowly, without emergency, folded into the gentle routines of shift changes, morning visits from the doctor, the meals trolley, the afternoon flurry of visitors, the moment in the evening where the teacups were cleared away, the water jugs filled and the lights ceremonially turned off. I was bored and miserable and in pain – absolutely – but the utter ordinariness of what was happening to me and everyone else – a web of sickness and suffering, worry and care and work and love – seemed suddenly both unremarkable and beautiful: the stuff that life was made of.

On the very first walk that Clive and I took together he gave me a copy of a book he'd written. The book is called *Critical Care* and is partly an account of the community artist Vic McEwan's residency at Alder Hey Children's Hospital in Liverpool. Vic works with sound and the technologies that record and produce it, and his brief was to spend a number of days at the hospital, speaking with people and recording the various sounds of the building itself, then create a piece of work based on the art of his listening. Clive describes his own role in this project as the 'participant observer', there to watch Vic's interaction with the patients and staff and wonder about the meanings contained in the process of creation. *Critical Care* explores the place of the artist within healthcare settings and wonders more discursively about what 'care' means for an artist, for a patient, for someone who grieves a death and someone who observes at one remove the raw intimacy of someone else's grief.

Part of the story Clive tells is about a young woman called Elisha who they met on the oncology ward. They worked together to create a film that explores her experience in the hospital. Vic and Clive taught her to make cyanotypes and showed her how their recording equipment worked. She used it to record the sound of her own heartbeat. Then, after Elisha died, Clive's essay takes us out of the hospital, out of the city altogether, and we go with him and Vic to the far north of the Scottish Highlands, to a former fuel depot buried deep in the hills near Invergordon. There is an underground fuel chamber there and they have decided to take the recording of Elisha's heartbeat into that chamber and play it. This is a less simple task than it sounds. First, the long drive north, then the business of getting into the tank itself, which involves donning a suit of the type a crime scene investigator wears, lying down on a kind of stretcher and being pushed into the chamber itself through a narrow, ten-foot-long fuel duct. Even without Clive's photographs, the mental images I conjure of this – the darkness, the black stink of old fuel, the confined crawl into a bleak subterranean cathedral, both creepy and holy – are nightmarish. Clive describes the space as a 'great chambered cairn' and worked closely with Vic in the hollow dark, operating the equipment, testing the quality of sound, committing to fully witnessing what is happening.

The Parallel Path

Every place contains its own echo, but this fuel tank is where the recording of Elisha's heartbeat will reverberate audibly for the longest time on the entire planet: that's why Vic and Clive had chosen to come here. Reverberation, the medium of the artwork, is about the persistent continuation of a sound's vibrations long after it has been produced. It is about carrying on, about the difference between an event and the aftermath of it, about afterlife and presence, and it is always about the hope of a future listener. When the time comes to play the recording, Clive was the one who pressed the button. In his essay, he struggles to describe what he hears and its effect on him because the otherworldly texture of the sound is nearly overwhelming: 'dancing, shimmering invisible light, refracting and changing. Traces in time and space.' Clive's work calls my attention to the way listening involves a willingness to be transformed by what is heard: 'immersed in the moment, extended, distorted and alive'. I become amazed by this capacity to hear, to attend, to be changed by the world. This is what attending to the life of another does for us: we are distorted by it. Elisha's heartbeat, we find out later, was audible outside the chamber, right through the surrounding hills; the heavy landscape itself carried Elisha outwards and the sound of her heart became indivisible from the terrain that held it.

I've never heard the recording Elisha made of her own heartbeat, though I found myself imagining it often. I'd thought of it at the end of my first full day's walking in the summer when I'd arrived, elated, and puffed up with satisfaction, at Ennerdale Bridge. I'd been wearing a Fitbit and the gadget had been observing me through the day and, at the end of it, had collated all its data into a video. This video traced the route I'd taken: a beeline in orange rapidly slicing first northwards along the coast, then eastwards, up and down Dent Hill and towards Ennerdale Water, hours and hours shrunk into forty seconds. The day's facts and stats flashed over the screen; my average heart rate and steps per minute, my blood pressure, distance covered, elevation achieved, breaks taken. The music was jangly and tacky and I was thrilled with it. So much for solitude: I'd been alone the whole day and now I wanted someone to see what I'd done. I'd wandered around the room trying to get as strong a connection as I could so I could WhatsApp it to Clive.

'You have a good strong heart,' he'd typed.

I thought about what Clive knew about hearts and the continuing strength of them and about what he had heard and had carried on hearing inside that dark chamber at Invergordon. I thought about it especially during those weeks where I was tethered to various drips and catheters and drains, my body's functions observed and measured. I thought about the recording of Elisha's heartbeat, that circular ripple of sound captured inside a machine that had been tucked inside the earth itself. Each foot takes its turn in leaving the earth and returning to it, and so the heartbeat too contains its pauses and stops, the pattern of its sound reliant on the moments of its own silence; the song of a heartbeat or footfall always a conversation between itself and its undoing. At the project's end, Elisha's mother is presented with the box that holds the contraption that plays her daughter's heart's ongoing sound, and Clive watched her hear her daughter, 'who has animated the hills, the rock and the trees, the sheep that scatter at the very sound, like something deep in the earth has awoken'. In the neuro ward, I thought about that invitation that Clive had first made to me, so many months ago now. What might an artist have to say about death? It does not seem possible to answer Clive's question beyond pointing back to the way he helped Elisha's mother listen to her daughter's heartbeat.

I knew to expect it, but the change in my hearing was still shocking: sounds come to me as if from underwater now, speech is a muffled bubbling and the habit of the nurses speaking in raised, sing-song voices started to make sense. One Sunday afternoon, a cheerful and shouty nurse did her paperwork in the ward and, as she wrote, told us all how little money the trust had available to budget for our meals, how scandalous it was, and how we should remember that when we voted. She was a bank nurse, normally at another hospital in the trust, and went on to tell us about the nurses at that hospital who were agitating to get access to better parking spaces after one of them had been attacked walking alone to her car through a dark street at night. There were people we could write to about this, she prompted, knowing that the sick and incapacitated are still capable of caring for others.

I wrapped my head in silk scarves when my family came to see me: the stitches curved from my temple in a big question mark shape around the back of my ear, which stuck out like an open car door because of the swelling. For a while, it looked like the lumbar drain wasn't resolving the problem and the doctors told me I might need to have another surgery to fit a shunt. For this surgery, I was put on nil-by-mouth for three days in a row, only to have the

Tethered, Again

possible surgery cancelled in the late afternoon and delayed by another day each time. I spent these days in horror at the prospect of another operation and willed my body to heal. Every morning, I was given steroids. The blisters on my feet from my long walk around Preston healed in record time. I puffed up, and for a while, my left eye was taped shut. My phone, adapted for deafness, lit up whenever one of my friends sent me a message: every day and night for a fortnight it twinkled through the hours.

In one of those almost novelistic coincidences that I'd find hard to believe unless I'd experienced it myself, the time I spent tethered to the lumbar drain in the neuro ward overlapped with some of the days of my Coast to Coast walk, taken a year previously. Daily, my phone fed me reminders of what I'd been up to the year before in the form of all those bedraggled selfies, wonky landscape photos and sound recordings for Clive. I'd taken photographs of some of his letters too, and, though I couldn't focus well enough to read them, I squinted at their blurry shapes and remembered. My walk, which I'd designed as a break from the labour of care, turned out to be a path that led me deeper into understanding my own need for it. Clive's letters had become a series of anticipatory guides, a Charles Atlas-style correspondence course in the art of being cared for, and strange maps for the confined territory I found myself in, tethered again, this time to the bed. I waited to get better. I had learned to be soft enough now to let myself be changed by this experience.

Changed, but not cured: some things won't be fixed. Not deafness, which is not a diminishment but an expansion, another experience I haven't had before. Not stubbornness or an addiction to getting my own way, an instinctive refusal to be helped, a tendency to say something doesn't hurt when it does: all of that is still with me. I just have some other things now too.

Finally the problem resolved itself. I evaded another surgery (or my body evaded it for me), the tube in my spine was removed and I was allowed up.

The first time the physiotherapist came to assess my walking, she wore a plastic apron and a visor and slotted a sick bowl into place on the top of the walker.

'You can expect to have vertigo,' she said, and I, too seasick to shake my head, told her that I definitely wouldn't be vomiting *thankyouverymuch*, then, as I took my first steps, I did.

'Never mind,' she said.

There was all kinds of physio ahead so I could learn to balance again but this first walk I did down the hospital corridor while holding on to the walker reminded me of kinhin. Every step was slow and deliberate and getting somewhere was not the point. I had thought kinhin was designed to be a training in self-control and close direction of the attention. The way I would stumble and wobble as I tried to walk would frustrate me. Now I understood the practice to be a reminder that walking is, when you slow it down and really pay attention to what you're up to, really about falling. Every step is a lurch and topple forwards, a process of catching yourself on the following foot and trying again.

Sickness and wobbling aside, I managed better at these first steps than anyone expected. On the second day, I didn't need the walker.

Tethered, Again

'Walking up and down the stairs is good,' the physio advised me from behind her visor, 'and over rough ground, but make sure you have someone to hold on to.'

This made me smile. I don't know if there was some greater wisdom in my body that led me out on to the fells and over the rough ground the summer before, telling me I needed to learn how to walk, how to fall, how to manage when I lost my bearings, how to pick my way slowly along uneven ground. I don't know if my body – already knowing about the passenger in my skull – was seeking not a cure, but a way to care for itself. But I like to think such things are possible.

I was desperate to get out of the ward and see the rest of the building and put the world of the neuro ward into some kind of context, but I was advised to wait until I had a visitor who would take me down to the café in the main hospital atrium in a wheelchair. I nodded, then put on my slippers and headed out on my own, on foot, shuffling along with my hand against the wall. I bought two big packets of crisps and went outside to the smokers' benches, where I sat and ate them, not hearing the sounds of the traffic and breathing in cigarette smoke and exhaust fumes. It was early evening. There were some spindly saplings planted around the edge of the car park, and cars circled, looking for spaces as visiting hours began. It took me a long time to get back to my bed, to enjoy the headache I'd given myself, to throw up the crisps into a bowl. The nurse was right – of course she was – I *should* have asked someone to wheel me down. But this is what I am like and I will never be cured of that.

* * *

The Parallel Path

In the days after my surgery a doctor had inspected the stitches in my head and told me, 'We will treat you here, but you'll recover at home,' making that old and necessary distinction between cure and care. But finally released again and at home, I was reminded of the other meaning of the word 'treat'. I was still not able to let my friends see me cry over what had happened to me and I still refused to sit on the stool in the shower. I tried to convince my head of department I would be back to teach my classes as usual in the autumn. But the pleasures of care had become delicious and I, greedy for the voluptuous, bespoke delights of them, started to make my requests.

Those words I had found inside me back at Shap – *I want* – started to pour out of me without inhibition. I want tea in the blue cup and I want full-fat milk. I want ginger biscuits with chocolate on. I want all the flowers arranged so I can see them from the sofa. I want to be driven to Morecambe to go to the world food aisle in Morrisons and buy Turkish delight. I want my friend to print out my knitting patterns at A3 size so I can start a new tank top. I want rose-scented hand cream. Every day the postman came, and Duncan brought the cards up with a breakfast tray. A postcard of Helvellyn arrived: something to look forward to. My friend asked me what she could bring, and I sent her to the shop in town to bring me back a poke bowl. Another friend drove two hours to bring me a box of violet creams, just because I wanted them. Duncan took three months off work and shovelled food into me, trying to keep up with my steroid-enhanced appetite. Every day a friend came, and every day I sat up eagerly, like a child, to see what treats they had brought me.

Now and again, I felt a faint shadow of worry: *what if I get addicted to this? What if I am being too greedy? What if I am a burden?* There was pain and fear, frustration and self-pity too – I was still myself, which meant not always a good patient. But the difficulties of the experience blew through me like bad weather moving through a house with all the doors and windows flung open. What stayed with me and what I remember now when I think about that time is the pleasure of being taken care of, and the way I saw it made my friends happy when I asked them to treat me and showed them how thrilled I was to receive my treats. My need for care hurt nobody: nothing is injured by my wanting except the last shell of some old ideas about toughness, about independence, about being impervious to the world and the rough gifts it lavishly, gratuitously offered. *I want* became a compass – a guide, not a rule – a way of finding what is good for me and making myself available to be found.

While I am recovering Clive comes with Marks and Spencer's salted caramel teacakes and a drawing he made of his favourite old tree in Littledale. I make him look at my enormous scar and feel the dent in the side of my head and complain that my ear wasn't put back on straight and my glasses are sitting crooked. We laugh like ghouls. The months pass. Clive regularly makes the drive backwards and forwards to Blackpool to have his treatments and get his 'numbers' checked. For now, the clinical trial has him in a kind of remission. Once he comes out of remission, he'll either move to more experimental treatments ('I'd love to have a bash at the real Mary Shelley stuff,' he said once, gleefully) or – depending on how he feels – on to palliative care. There's no telling the time it will take but for now, he is busy with living. Between the monthly hospital visits to be pumped full of immunoglobulin extracted from the blood donations of hundreds of anonymous others he wanders in Bowland or makes another trip to Ross-on-Wye to think about Dennis Potter, or drives sixteen hours over two days to climb a French alp, have a picnic at the Castle of Vultures with his partner and get a suntan, or has his children visit for the weekend, or flies to Japan, deep-diving into a new culture, or comes out with me to eat teacakes on Morecambe seafront, or lies sick in bed with Covid, too breathless to speak but speaking anyway, about a film he thinks I'd like to see.

The following summer, I will go back and do Helvellyn and Striding Edge. My balance is about as good as my map reading, but I manage, parts of it on my hands and knees. My daughter will leave home and go back to the city where she began, and the river of her grief flows onwards. One foot in front of the other, even if the path takes us in circles. On a good long walk, there are whole moments where, without denial or delusion, nor with any extraordinary degree of bravery or saintliness, it is possible to be at rest in motion, to stay perpetually in the middle of things, to be both dependent and relied-upon, to find friendliness and neighbourliness in all circumstances and to stay available to – as the walker Nan Shepherd put it when she described her own porous heart's relationship with the world – the 'traffic of love'.

One day, Clive and I are at the Lancaster Castle café again, drinking coffee and people watching and talking about the book I am trying to write. We're thinking about his letters and the other story, the one he might tell about what it was like to write and send them to me. He might make a film.

'Did you not know I was trying to care for you?' he said, when we talk about the things he wanted to show me and tell me.

'I didn't,' I said, laughing at myself – that gruff, armoured little being stomping her way across the entire country in her big new boots, 'but I do now.'

Acknowledgements

Immeasurable thanks are due to Clive Parkinson who provided the title and all the other most important parts of this book. Thanks, too, to Federico Andornino, Holly Knox, Louise Court, Tamsin Shelton and the whole team at Sceptre, and to my agent, Anthony Goff. The writing of this book was interrupted by illness and evolved into a story I did not expect to tell: your careful and patient support has been invaluable. Thank you, too, to Carole Welch for early and wise encouragement. Thank you to Eleanor Birne who provided a home-from-home and a quiet sanctuary in Cambridge while I tiptoed through the final part of my recovery: a return to my writing. Thank you to my friends Louisa B., Tristan Burke, Jo Carruthers, Adam Farrer, Charlie Gere, Hilary Hinds, Elizabeth Oldfield, Kellee Rich, Imogen Tyler, Beth Underdown and Emma Wayland: our conversations have changed me. Thank you to my colleagues and students at the Department of English Literature and Creative Writing at Lancaster University. Big institutions are not always fertile places to thrive, and the compassionate and creative support of our department is a rare and precious thing and has become another kind of home to me. Finally, to my closest family. No parent, child or partner really *wants*

Acknowledgements

a memoirist in the house and the endeavour to tell my little part of a shared story and offer to the world a tender glimpse of a life lived together is a risky one: I am grateful.

Notes and References

All quotations from Wainwright's account of the walk are from *A Coast to Coast Walk: Readers Edition* (first published by the *Westmorland Gazette*, 1973, reprinted by Frances Lincoln, 2017). For biographical information, see Wainwright's own *Memoirs of a Fellwanderer* (Michael Joseph, 1993) and *Ex-Fellwanderer: A Thanksgiving* (*Westmorland Gazette*, 1987). The documentary I refer to is *A. Wainwright's Coast to Coast Walk* presented by Eric Robson, produced by BBC North East, Carlisle and first broadcast on the BBC in 1989, subsequently distributed by Striding Edge Productions.

For the actual walk, I used *A Coast to Coast Walk: Revised Walker's Edition* and *Coast to Coast Path: St Bees to Robin Hood's Bay* by Henry Stedman and Stuart Butler (Trailblazer Publications, ninth edition amended reprint 2021) – the remark about the Vale of Mowbray as a 'tepid agricultural tract' comes from this book.

Preambles

The Wicker Man, dir. Robin Hardy (1973)
Walter Benjamin, Rolf Tiedemann, Howard Eiland and Kevin Mclaughlin, *The Arcades Project* (Harvard University Press, 1999)

Notes and References

Frédéric Gros, *A Philosophy of Walking* (Verso, 2015)
Virginia Woolf, 'Street Haunting: A London Adventure' (first published 1927, later collected in Virginia Woolf, *Selected Essays*, ed. David Bradshaw (Oxford, 2008))

DAY THREE: *Alone at Last*

An Interview with Dennis Potter, a *Without Walls* special, LWT for Channel 4, transmitted 5 April 1994, dir. Tom Poole
A. G. Bradley, 'The Demon Dog of Ennerdale', *The English Review* (June 1926)
Hunter Davies, *Wainwright: The Biography* (Penguin, 2002)
William Hazlitt, 'On Going a Journey' (first published 1822, later collected as 'I like to Go By Myself' in *Beneath My Feet: Writers on Walking*, ed. Duncan Minshull (Notting Hill Editions, 2018))
Geoff Nicholson, *The Lost Art of Walking: The History, Science, Philosophy, Theory and Practice of Pedestrianism* (Harbour Books, 2011)
Henry David Thoreau, 'On Walking', *Atlantic Monthly*, Volume IX, Number LVI, June 1862
Alfred Wainwright, *Memoirs of a Fellwanderer* (Michael Joseph, 1993)
Alfred Wainwright, *A Pennine Companion: The Story of a Long Walk in 1938* (first published in 1986 reprinted by Francis Lincoln, 2004)

Notes and References

DAY FOUR: *Friends in High Places*

Nan Shepherd, *The Living Mountain* (first published 1977, reprinted by Canongate, 2011)

DAY FIVE: *Walking and Mourning*

The names of the boys that Clive refers to in his letter have been changed.

Erling Kagge, *Walking: One Step at a Time* (Penguin Random House, 2019)

DAY SEVEN: *A Girl from the North Country*

Marina Benjamin, *A Little Give: The Unsung, Unseen, Undone Work of Women* (Scribe, 2023)
Florence Nightingale, *Notes on Nursing: What It Is and What It Is Not* (first published 1858, reprinted by Barnes and Noble, 2003)

DAY EIGHT: *Brown, Blue, Black*

Bartholomew Ryan, 'Manifesto for Maintenance: A Conversation with Mierle Laderman Ukeles', *Art in America*, 18 March 2009
Rebecca Solnit, *A Field Guide to Getting Lost* (Canongate, 2005)
Henry David Thoreau, *Walden, or, A Life in the Woods* (first published 1854, reprinted by Yale University Press, 2004)

Notes and References

DAY NINE: *On Walking Well*

Clive Parkinson, 'Present-Tense' in Steven Gartside and Clive Parkinson, *Mortality: Death and the Imagination* (The Holden Gallery, 2013)

DAY TEN: *To Accompany a River*

Ellen Samuels, 'Six Ways of Looking at Crip Time', *Disability Studies Quarterly*, Volume 37, Number 3, Summer 2017

DAY ELEVEN: *The Green and the Grey*

Edge of Darkness; Director's Notes
K. E. Adolph, et al., 'How do you learn to walk? Thousands of steps and dozens of falls per day', *Psychological Science*, Volume 23, Issue 11, 2012
Chris Lloyd, 'Willance's Leap: The Dramatic Story Behind the Monument on Richmond's Whitcliffe Scar', *Darlington and Stockton Times*, 21 November 2020

DAY TWELVE: *A Marathon with the Almost-Dead*

Susan Silk and Barry Goldman, 'How not to say the wrong thing', *Los Angeles Times*, 7 April 2013

DAY THIRTEEN: *Every Home a Hospital*

I have changed some key details about the conversation with the fellow walker I dramatised in this chapter in order to preserve her privacy.

Notes and References

Richard Blakeborough, *Wit, Character, Folklore and Customs of the North Riding of Yorkshire* (first published 1898, revised 1911, republished E. P. Publishing, 1978)
Mel Grant, 'Befriending Heavy Breathers', The Wellcome Collection
Damion Searles, ed., *Henry David Thoreau: The Journal 1837–1861* (New York Review Books, 2009)
Chad Varah, *Before I Die Again: The Autobiography of the Founder of the Samaritans* (Constable, 1992)
Virginia Woolf, 'On Being Ill' (first published 1925, republished Paris Press, 2002)

DAYS FOURTEEN AND FIFTEEN:
The World's Greatest Moaner

For a more detailed account of walking, spiritual journeying and the history of early Quaker travel, see Hilary Hinds, *George Fox and Early Quaker Culture* (Manchester University Press, 2013), which I have drawn on for the discussion of George Fox's walking in this chapter.

For more on the Morecambe Time and Tide Bell, see timeandtidebell.org.

Werner Herzog, *Of Walking in Ice* (Vintage, 2014)
Mike Kendon, 'Unprecedented Extreme Heatwave, July 2022', report published by the Met Office National Climate Information Centre, September 2022. All other factual and statistical information about this weather event in this chapter is taken from this report.

Notes and References

Nella Last, *Nella Last's War: The Second World War Diaries of Housewife, 48*, ed. Richard Broad and Suzie Fleming (Profile, 2006)
Noreen Masud, *A Flat Place* (Hamish Hamilton, 2023)
Rebecca Solnit, *Wanderlust: A History of Walking* (Granta, 2001)

Walking Widdershins

Marion Shoard, 'Edgelands' in Jennifer Jenkins, ed., *Remaking the Landscape: The Changing Face of Britain* (Profile, 2002)

Tethered, Again

Clive Parkinson, *Critical Care* (Cad Factory, 2017)
Nan Shepherd, *The Living Mountain* (first published 1977, reprinted by Canongate, 2011)